A B[...]
A PR[...]

MW00791341

Enter Sydney O[...]
day-by-day predictions for every aspect of your life. With
expert readings and forecasts, you can chart a course to
romance, adventure, good health, or career opportunities
while gaining valuable insight into yourself and others. Offering a daily outlook for 18 full months, this fascinating
guide shows you:

- The important dates in your life
- What to expect from an astrological reading
- How the stars can help you stay healthy and fit
  And more!

Let this expert's sound advice guide you through a year of
heavenly possibilities—for today and for every day of 2005!

SYDNEY OMARR'S® DAY-BY-DAY
ASTROLOGICAL GUIDE FOR

ARIES—March 21–April 19
TAURUS—April 20–May 20
GEMINI—May 21–June 20
CANCER—June 21–July 22
LEO—July 23–August 22
VIRGO—August 23–September 22
LIBRA—September 23–October 22
SCORPIO—October 23–November 21
SAGITTARIUS—November 22–December 21
CAPRICORN—December 22–January 19
AQUARIUS—January 20–February 18
PISCES—February 19–March 20

IN 2005

SYDNEY OMARR'S®

DAY-BY-DAY ASTROLOGICAL GUIDE FOR

VIRGO

AUGUST 23–SEPTEMBER 22

2005

By Trish MacGregor
with Carol Tonsing

A SIGNET BOOK

SIGNET
Published by New American Library, a division of
Penguin Group (USA) Inc., 375 Hudson Street,
New York, New York 10014, U.S.A.
Penguin Books Ltd, 80 Strand,
London WC2R 0RL, England
Penguin Books Australia Ltd, 250 Camberwell Road,
Camberwell, Victoria 3124, Australia
Penguin Books Canada Ltd, 10 Alcorn Avenue,
Toronto, Ontario, Canada M4V 3B2
Penguin Books (NZ), cnr Airborne and Rosedale Roads,
Albany, Auckland 1310, New Zealand

Penguin Books Ltd, Registered Offices:
80 Strand, London WC2R 0RL, England

First published by Signet, an imprint of New American Library,
a division of Penguin Group (USA) Inc.

First Printing, June 2004
10 9 8 7 6 5 4 3 2 1

PUBLISHER'S NOTE
While the author has made every effort to provide accurate telephone numbers
and Internet addresses at the time of publication, neither the publisher nor the
author assumes any responsibility for errors, or for changes that occur after
publication.

BOOKS ARE AVAILABLE AT QUANTITY DISCOUNTS WHEN USED TO PROMOTE PROD-
UCTS OR SERVICES. FOR INFORMATION PLEASE WRITE TO PREMIUM MARKETING DIVI-
SION, PENGUIN GROUP (USA) INC., 375 HUDSON STREET, NEW YORK, NEW YORK 10014.

CONTENTS

INTRODUCTION

The Inside Scoop for 2005

In the remote Jordanian desert, a camel train weaves through a long, narrow canyon of sheer rock. It suddenly emerges into a wonderland of magnificent temples and tombs carved in rose-red cliffs: the lost city of Petra. This fabulously wealthy cultural and financial center of the ancient world controlled Middle Eastern trading routes for three hundred years, from roughly 200 B.C. to A.D. 100. Then the civilization disappeared after a devastating earthquake about A.D. 400, leaving the ghostly rock temples as enigmatic sentinels.

Petra has captured the imagination of adventurous travelers for centuries, as archaeologists slowly uncover the remaining pieces of its civilization. What interests us as astrologers is that the citizens of Petra turned to the stars for guidance.

One of the most important relics found there is a stone zodiac wheel, with most of the symbols we use today, supported aloft by the winged figure of Victory. The zodiac wheel was broken in half, with each part displayed in distant museums and only recently reunited. In the center of the zodiac is the beautiful Petran goddess of fortune, Tyche, a protective goddess who was a major deity of the period, linking our destiny to the stars.

Would astrology have survived if it had been mere guesswork or fortune-telling, if there was not something to it? Remarkably, in these modern times, we are still turning to one of the oldest forms of guidance, one that has been around so long that its longevity is proof that millions received the help they needed.

What continues to fascinate us is that astrology can

give such specific, practical information. Clearly this is one reason why this ancient combination of art and science, based on interpreting moments in time, has always had devoted followers among the elite of the world, kings, dictators, tycoons, and politicians since long before even the temples of Petra were carved.

In 2005, one thousand years after the height of Petra's glory, that ancient civilization is a perfect symbol for this year, when we have come through a dark passage of transition and, hopefully, will re-create a world of peace and harmony. Jupiter, our planet of fortune, will be traveling through Libra, the sign most associated with diplomacy, justice, elegance, beauty, balance, the color pink, artistic life, and quality goods. In our culture at large, Jupiter should bring a welcome emphasis on beauty, elegance, and style.

We will look through the ancient lens of astrology to predict the latest fashion trends, the dieting advice that will help you look and feel your best, and the timing that will help you make wise decisions. For those who want to know more about astrology, the basics are presented in a user-friendly way. And you'll find plenty of information about your own sun sign's potential for success. We give you the best astrology sites on the Internet, the organizations where you can meet and learn from the world's best astrologers, the resources for the tools you'll need—many of them free!

You can bring the ancient wisdom of astrology into your life every day with astonishingly accurate day-by-day forecasts for the next eighteen months. Let this book become your astrological partner and companion.

Here's wishing you a year of beauty, harmony, balance, and good fortune!

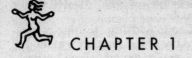

CHAPTER 1

This Year's Big Trends and What They Mean

Astrologers judge the trends of a year by the slow-moving planets, from Jupiter through Pluto. A change in sign indicates a new cycle, with a new emphasis. The farthest planets (Uranus, Neptune, and Pluto), which stay in a sign for at least seven years, cause a very significant change in the atmosphere when they change signs. Shifts in Jupiter and Saturn are more obvious in current events and daily lives. Jupiter changes every year, bringing a fortunate emphasis to its new sign. Saturn's two-year cycle is a reality check, bringing tests of maturity, discipline, and responsibility.

Saturn Moves into Leo—Elder Awareness

Saturn, the planet of limitation, testing, and restriction, has been transiting the sign of Cancer since June 2003, which has special significance for Americans, because the United States is a Cancer country, born on July 4, 1776. Therefore, this country has been experiencing the restrictive and disciplinary influence of Saturn, which we can see on a large scale in the conservative political trends. This year we should experience the rewards of a maturity that has been tested. Cancer areas under Saturn's influence have been patriotism, the homeland, the food supply, motherhood, dairy products, hotels, restaurants,

3

boating, cruise ships, waterways and water-related industries, the tides, and the moon.

Saturn will move into Leo in mid-July, shifting emphasis to Leo-related areas. Many of the fun things in life fall under the banner of Leo: entertainment, show business, children, play, recreation, self-expression, love affairs, performing, talent, the creative arts, and recognition by others. Since Saturn tends to put a damper on fun, we might expect some restrictions on the entertainment business. Responsibility in assuming the burdens of raising and educating children will be stressed. Love affairs and flirtations may involve older people, as Saturn rules the elderly and aging.

The subject of aging in general is associated with Saturn, and the Leo archetype in this area is the aging film star determined to hold on to youth. In this cycle, maturing baby boomers may assert themselves and demand more awareness from the media. We will see more older people on television and in films, more entertainment tailored to an aging population. Since Leo is also associated with speculation and gambling—in fact all games—expect more stringent regulation and controversy around big-time casinos and sports.

Saturn in Leo demands hard work in creative ventures, responsibility when interacting with others. You can't get away with casual love affairs and being high-handed, arrogant, or divalike in any way. Leos will have to earn their applause. This could put a damper on the blatant celebrity-worshipping culture that has arisen over the past few decades. No longer will it be enough to be famous for being famous. The emphasis will be on true values rather than on the trappings of success. Flashy lifestyles, "bling bling" jewelry, and showing off will be out.

This trend will be accentuated over the summer and fall, with a very long transit of Mars, the planet of action, through the steadfast and stubborn sign of Taurus from the end of July through mid-February of 2006. During that period, Mars will square off with Saturn, as these two planets jockey for power. Mars in Taurus is associated with down-to-earth values, moneymaking, and sensuality. Adding to the drama in late fall, Jupiter (luck) also moves into the fixed sign of Scorpio, and when the Scorpion, the Bull, and the Lion interact, there could be a Mexican standoff with dramatic international face-offs taking place.

Jupiter in Libra and Scorpio

When Jupiter enters a sign, the fields associated with that sign are the ones that currently arouse excitement and enthusiasm, usually providing excellent opportunities for expansion, fame, and fortune.

For most of the year, Jupiter will remain in Libra, a sign of diplomacy, balance, justice, artistic taste and sensibility, and marriage and relationships. This is good news for the fashion and jewelry industries; it signals a return to elegance in manners and style. The arts should also benefit. Libra is the marriage sign, so expect an emphasis on elegant formal weddings, as commitment becomes in. Expect new forms of marriage, such as same-sex marriage and legal agreements involving marital rights.

Jupiter will expand the Libra areas of lawyers and the law, and may increase the number of lawsuits and courtroom dramas. The countries of China, Argentina, Austria, Burma, and Tibet will be blessed with beneficent Libra vibrations.

In October, Jupiter moves to Scorpio, which creates a much more intense atmosphere, especially as it interacts with Mars in Taurus and Saturn in Leo. Scorpio is associated with all things sexual, waste disposal, underground areas, police and detective work, the meat trade, and leather in fashion. Expect one of the most sex-oriented years ever in mass market culture. Since Scorpio is associated with science and research, Jupiter could bring positive breakthroughs in medicine and surgery, perhaps a cure for sexually transmitted diseases.

Those born under Libra and Scorpio should have many opportunities during the year. However, the key is to keep your feet on the ground. The flip side of Jupiter is that there are no limits. You can expand off the planet under a Jupiter transit, which is why the planet is often called the Gateway to Heaven. If something is going to burst (such as an artery) or overextend or go over the top in some way, it could happen under a supposedly lucky Jupiter transit—so beware.

Those born under Aries and Taurus may find their best opportunities working with partners this year, as Jupiter will be transiting their seventh house of relationships.

Continuing Trends

Uranus and Neptune continue to do a kind of astrological dance called a mutual reception. This is a supportive relationship where Uranus is in Pisces, the sign ruled by Neptune, while Neptune is in Aquarius, the sign ruled by Uranus. When this seven-year dance is over, it is very likely that we will be living under very different political and social circumstances.

Uranus in Pisces

Uranus, known as the Great Awakener, tends to cause both upheaval and innovation in the sign it transits. During previous episodes of Uranus in Pisces, great religions and spiritual movements have come into being, most recently Mormonism and Christian Fundamentalism. In its most positive mode, Pisces promotes imagination and creativity, the art of illusion in theater and film, the inspiration of great artists. A water sign, Pisces is naturally associated with all things liquid—oceans, oil, alcohol—and with those creatures that live in the water—fish, the fishing industry, fish habitats, and fish farming. Currently there is a great debate going on about overfishing, contamination of fish and fish farming. The underdog, the enslaved, and the disenfranchised should also benefit from Uranus in Pisces.

Pisces is associated with the prenatal phase of life, which is related to regenerative medicine. The controversy over embryonic stem cell research should continue to be debated. Petroleum issues, both in the oil-producing countries and offshore oil drilling, will come to a head. Uranus in Pisces suggests that development of new hydroelectric sources may provide the power we need to continue our current power-thirsty lifestyle.

As in previous eras, there should continue to be a flourishing of the arts. We are seeing many new artistic forms developing now, such as computer-created actors and special effects. The sky's the limit on this influence.

Those who have problems with Uranus are those who resist change, so the key is to embrace the future.

Neptune in Aquarius

Neptune is a planet of imagination and creativity, but also of deception and illusion. Neptune is associated with hospitals, which have been the subject of much controversy. On the positive side, hospitals are acquiring cutting-edge technology. The atmosphere of many hospitals is already changing from the intimidating and sterile environment of the past to that of a health-promoting spa. Alternative therapies such as massage, diet counseling, and aromatherapy are becoming commonplace, which expresses this Neptune trend. New procedures in plastic surgery, also a Neptune glamour field, and anti-aging therapies are restoring the illusion of youth.

However, issues involving the expense and quality of health care and the evolving relationship between doctors, drug companies, and HMOs reflect a darker side of this trend.

Pluto in Sagittarius

The slow-moving planet Pluto is our guide to life-changing, long-term trends. In Sagittarius until 2008, Pluto has been emphasizing everything associated with this sign to prepare us philosophically and spiritually for things to come. Perhaps the most pervasive sign of Pluto in Sagittarius over the past few years has been globalization in all its forms. We are re-forming boundaries, creating new forms of travel, and interacting with exotic cultures and religions as never before.

In true Sagittarius fashion, Pluto will shift our emphasis away from acquiring wealth to a quest for the meaning of it all, as upward strivers discover that money and power are not enough and religious extremists assert themselves. Sagittarius is the sign of linking everything together; therefore, the trend will be to find ways to interconnect on a spiritual, philosophical, and intellectual level.

The spiritual emphasis of Pluto in Sagittarius has already filtered down to our home lives. Home altars and private sanctuaries are becoming a part of our personal environment.

Pluto in Sagittarius has expanded the experience of religion into other areas of our lives. For example, vast church complexes that combine religious activities with sports centers, health clubs, malls, and theme parks are now being built. Look for an expansion in religious education and religious book publishing as well.

Sagittarius is known for love of animals, especially horses. Horse racing has become popular again, and America has never been more pet happy. Look for extremes related to animal welfare—such as vegetarianism, which will become even more popular and widespread as a lifestyle. As habitats are destroyed, the care, feeding, and control of wild animals will become a large issue, especially when deer, bears, and coyotes invade our backyard.

The Sagittarius love of the outdoors combined with

Pluto's power has already promoted extreme sports, especially those that require strong legs, like rock climbing, trekking, or snowboarding. Rugged, sporty all-terrain vehicles continue to be popular. Expect the trend toward more adventurous travel as well as fitness or sports-oriented vacations to accelerate. Exotic hiking trips to unexplored territories, mountain-climbing expeditions, spa vacations, and sports-associated resorts are part of this trend.

Publishing, which is associated with Sagittarius, has been transformed by global conglomerates and the Internet. It is fascinating that the online bookstore Amazon.com took the Sagittarius-influenced name of the fierce female tribe of archer warriors. There should continue to be more inspirational books, aimed at those who are interested in spirituality outside of traditional religions.

CHAPTER 2

Red-Letter Days in 2005: How to Find and Use Them

You've surely observed that some days jobs get done effortlessly, people respond to you favorably, and perhaps you have some extra sex appeal. On other days, people are moody, you can't seem to make any headway, and projects stall. Astrology offers many explanations why this might happen. For instance, when mischievous Mercury creates havoc with communications, it's time to back up your vital computer files, read between the lines of contracts, and be extra patient with coworkers. When Venus passes through your sign, you've got extra sex appeal, time for a new outfit or hairstyle, and the urge to ask someone you'd like to know better to dinner. Venus timing can also help you charm clients with a stunning sales pitch or make an offer they won't refuse.

Here are some tips for finding your own personal red-letter days. In this chapter, you will learn how to find your best times as well as which times to avoid. You will also learn how to read the moods of the moon and make them work for you. Use the information and tables in this chapter and in chapter 4 on the planets, and also use the moon sign listings in your daily forecasts.

Here are the happenings to note on your agenda:

- Dates of your sun sign (high-energy period)
- The month previous to your sun sign (low-energy period)
- Dates of planets in your sign this year

- Full and new moons (Pay special attention when these fall in your sun sign!)
- Eclipses
- Moon in your sun sign every month, as well as moon in the opposite sign (listed in daily forecast)
- Mercury retrogrades
- Other retrograde periods

Your Red-Letter Month: The Month of Your Sign

You should feel a new surge of vitality as the powerful sun enters your sign. This is the time when predominant energies are most favorable to you. So go for it! Start new projects, make your big moves (especially when the new moon is in your sign, doubling your charisma). You'll get the recognition you deserve now, when everyone is attuned to your sun sign. Look in the tables in this book to see if others planets will also be passing through your sun sign at this time. Venus (love, beauty), Mars (energy, drive), and Mercury (communication, mental sharpness) reinforce the sun and give an extra boost to your life in the areas they affect. Venus will rev up your social and love life, making you seem especially attractive. Mars amplifies your energy and drive. Mercury fuels your brainpower and helps you communicate. Jupiter signals an especially lucky period of expansion.

There are two downtimes related to the sun. During the month before your birthday period, when you are winding up your annual cycle, you could be feeling especially vulnerable and depleted. So at that time get extra rest, watch your diet, and take it easy. Don't overstress yourself. Use this time to gear up for a big "push" when the sun enters your sign.

Another downtime is when the sun is in a sign opposite your sun sign (six months from your birthday). That's when the prevailing energies are very different from yours. You may feel at odds with the world. You'll have to work harder for recognition because people are not on your wavelength. However, this could be a good time to work on a team, in cooperation with others, or behind the scenes.

Plan Your Day by the Moon

The moon is a powerful tool to divine the mood of the moment. You can work with the moon in two ways. Plan by the *sign* the moon is in; plan by the *phase* of the moon. The sign will tell you the kind of activities that suit the moon's mood. The phase will tell you the best time to start or finish a certain activity.

Working with the phases of the moon is as easy as looking up at the night sky. During the new moon, when both the sun and moon are in the same sign, begin new ventures—especially activities that are favored by that sign. Then you'll utilize the powerful energies pulling you in the same direction. You'll be focused outward, toward action, and in a doing mode. Postpone breaking off, terminating, deliberating, or reflecting—activities that require introspection and passive work. These are better suited to a later moon phase.

Get your project under way during the first quarter. Then go public at the full moon, a time of high intensity, when feelings come out into the open. This is your time to shine—to express yourself. Be aware, however, that because pressures are being released, other people will also be letting off steam. Since confrontations are possible, take advantage of this time either to air grievances or to avoid arguments. Traditionally, astrologers often advise against surgery at this time, which could produce heavier bleeding.

About three days after the full moon comes the disseminating phase, a time when the energy of the cycle begins to wind down. From the last quarter of the moon to the next new moon, it's a time to cut off unproductive relationships, do serious thinking, and focus on inward-directed activities.

You'll feel some new and full moons more strongly than others, especially those new moons that fall in your sun sign and full moons in your opposite sign. Because that full moon happens at your low-energy time of year, it is likely to be an especially stressful time in a relationship, when any hidden problems or unexpressed emotions could surface.

Full and New Moons in 2005

All dates are calculated for eastern standard time and eastern daylight time.

New Moon—January 10 in Cancer
Full Moon—January 25 in Leo

New Moon—February 8 in Aquarius
Full Moon—February 23 in Virgo

New Moon—March 10 in Pisces
Full Moon—March 25 in Libra

New Moon—April 8 in Aries (solar eclipse)
Full Moon—April 24 in Scorpio (lunar eclipse)

New Moon—May 8 in Taurus
Full Moon—May 23 in Sagittarius

New Moon—June 6 in Gemini
Full Moon—June 21 in Capricorn

New Moon—July 6 in Cancer
Full Moon—July 21 in Capricorn

New Moon—August 4 in Leo
Full Moon—August 19 in Aquarius

New Moon—September 3 in Virgo
Full Moon—September 17 in Pisces

New Moon—October 3 in Libra (solar eclipse)
Full Moon—October 17 in Aries (lunar eclipse)

New Moon—November 1 in Scorpio
Full Moon—November 15 in Taurus

New Moon—December 1 in Sagittarius
Full Moon—December 15 in Gemini
New Moon—December 30 in Capricorn

How To Time by the Moon Sign

To forecast the daily emotional "weather," to determine
your monthly high and low days, or to synchronize your
activities with the cycles of the moon, take note of the
moon sign under your daily forecast at the end of the book.
Here are some of the activities favored and the moods you
are likely to encounter under each moon sign.

Moon in Aries: Get Moving!

The new moon in Aries is an ideal time to start new
projects. Everyone is pushy, raring to go, rather impatient, and short-tempered. Leave details and follow-up
for later. Competitive sports or martial arts are great
ways to let off steam. Quiet types could use some assertiveness, but it's a great day for dynamos. Be careful not
to step on too many toes.

Moon in Taurus: Lay the Foundations for Success

Do solid, methodical tasks like follow-through or backup
work. Make investments, buy real estate, do appraisals,

do some hard bargaining. Attend to your property. Get out in the country or spend some time in your garden. Enjoy creature comforts, music, a good dinner, sensual lovemaking. Forget starting a diet—this is a day when you'll feel self-indulgent.

Moon in Gemini: Communicate

Talk means action today. Telephone, write letters, fax! Make new contacts, stay in touch with steady customers. You can juggle lots of tasks today. It's a great time for mental activity of any kind. Don't try to pin people down—they, too, are feeling restless. Keep it light. Flirtations and socializing are good. Watch gossip—and don't give away secrets.

Moon in Cancer: Pay Attention to Loved Ones

This is a moody, sensitive, emotional time. People respond to personal attention, to mothering. Stay at home, have a family dinner, call your mother. Nostalgia, memories, and psychic powers are heightened. You'll want to hang on to people and things (don't clean out your closets now). You could have shrewd insights into what others really need and want. Pay attention to dreams, intuition, and gut reactions.

Moon in Leo: Be Confident

Everybody is in a much more confident, warm, generous mood. It's a good day to ask for a raise, show what you can do, dress like a star. People will respond to flattery, enjoy a bit of drama and theater. You may be extravagant, treat yourself royally, and show off a bit—but don't break the bank! Be careful you don't promise more than you can deliver.

Moon in Virgo: Be Practical

Do practical down-to-earth chores. Review your budget, make repairs, be an efficiency expert. Not a day to ask for a raise. Tend to personal care and maintenance. Have a health checkup, go on a diet, buy vitamins or health food. Make your home spotless. Take care of details and piled-up chores. Reorganize your work and life so they run more smoothly and efficiently. Save money. Be prepared for others to be in a critical, faultfinding mood.

Moon in Libra: Be Diplomatic

Attend to legal matters. Negotiate contracts. Arbitrate. Do things with your favorite partner. Socialize. Be romantic. Buy a special gift, a beautiful object. Decorate yourself or your surroundings. Buy new clothes. Throw a party. Have an elegant, romantic evening. Smooth over any ruffled feathers. Avoid confrontations. Stick to civilized discussions.

Moon in Scorpio: Solve Problems

This is a day to do things with passion. You'll have excellent concentration and focus. Try not to get too intense emotionally. Avoid sharp exchanges with loved ones. Others may tend to go to extremes, get jealous, overreact. Great for troubleshooting, problem solving, research, scientific work—and making love. Pay attention to those psychic vibes.

Moon in Sagittarius: Sell and Motivate

A great time for travel, philosophical discussions, setting long-range career goals. Work out, do sports, buy athletic equipment. Others will be feeling upbeat, exuberant, and adventurous. Risk taking is favored. You may feel like taking a gamble, betting on the horses, visiting a local casino, buying a lottery ticket. Teaching, writing, and spiritual activities also get the green light. Relax outdoors. Take care of animals.

Moon in Capricorn: Get Organized

You can accomplish a lot now, so get on the ball! Attend to business. Issues concerning your basic responsibilities, duties, family, and elderly parents could crop up. You'll be expected to deliver on promises. Weed out the deadwood from your life. Get a dental checkup. Not a good day for gambling or taking risks.

Moon in Aquarius: Join the Group

A great day for doing things with groups—clubs, meetings, outings, politics, parties. Campaign for your candidate. Work for a worthy cause. Deal with larger issues that affect humanity—the environment and metaphysical questions. Buy a computer or electronic gadget. Watch TV. Wear something outrageous. Try something you've never done before. Present an original idea. Don't stick to a rigid schedule—go with the flow. Take a class in meditation, mind control, yoga.

Moon in Pisces: Be Creative

This can be a very creative day, so let your imagination work overtime. Film, theater, music, ballet could inspire you. Spend some time alone, resting and reflecting, reading or writing poetry. Daydreams can also be profitable. Help those less fortunate. Lend a listening ear to someone who may be feeling blue. Don't overindulge in self-pity or escapism, however. People are especially vulnerable to substance abuse now. Turn your thoughts to romance and someone special.

Prepare Ahead of Time for Eclipses

One of the most amazing phenomena, which many of us take for granted, is the spatial relationship between the sun and moon. How many of us have ever noticed or marveled that, relative to our viewpoint here on earth, both the largest source of energy (the sun) and the smallest (the moon) appear to be almost exactly the same size? Or wondered what would happen if the moon's orbit became closer to earth or farther away?

This fascinating relationship is most evident to us at the time of the solar eclipse, when the moon is directly aligned with the sun and so nearly covers it that scientists use the moment of eclipse to study solar flares. The darkening of the sun has been used in history and mythology to indicate dire happenings ahead. In some parts of the world, people hide in their homes during the darkening of the sun. When the two most powerful forces in astrology—the sun and moon—are lined up, we're sure to feel the effects both in world events and in our personal lives. Both solar and lunar eclipses are times when our natural rhythms are changed, depending on where the eclipse falls in your horoscope. If the eclipse falls on or close to your birthday, you're going to have important changes in your life, perhaps a turning point.

Lunar Eclipses

Lunar eclipse: A momentary "turnoff" that could help us turn our lives around.

A lunar eclipse happens during a full moon when the earth moves exactly between the sun and moon, breaking their natural monthly opposition. Normally, the earth is not on a level plane; otherwise, eclipses would occur every month. During a lunar eclipse, the earth "short-circuits" the connection between the sun and moon. The effect on us can be either confusion or clarity. Our subconscious lunar energies, which normally respond to the rhythmic cycle of opposing sun and moon, are momentarily turned off. This could cause a bewildering disorientation that intensifies our insecurities. On the other hand, this moment of clarity might give us insights that could help change destructive emotional patterns such as addictions.

Solar Eclipses

Solar eclipse: Deep feelings come to the surface.

The solar eclipse occurs during the new moon. This time, the moon blocks the sun's energies as it passes exactly between the sun and the earth. In astrological interpretation, the moon darkens the objective, conscious force, represented by the sun, allowing subconscious lunar forces, which activate our deepest emotions, to dominate. Emotional truths can be revealed or emotions can run wild, as our solar objectivity is cut off. If your sign is affected, you may find yourself beginning a period of work on a deep inner level. And you may have psychic experiences or deep feelings that come to the surface.

You'll start feeling the energies of an upcoming eclipse a few days after the previous new or full moon. The energy continues to intensify until the actual eclipse, then disperses for three or four days. So plan ahead at least a week or more before an eclipse, then allow several days afterward for the natural rhythms to return. Try not to make major moves during this period. (It's not a great time to get married, change jobs, or buy a home, for instance.)

Eclipses in 2005

There are four eclipses this year.

New Moon and Solar Eclipse—April 8 in Aries
Full Moon and Lunar Eclipse—April 24 in Scorpio
New Moon and Solar Eclipse—October 3 in Libra
Full Moon and Lunar Eclipse—October 17 in Aries

Retrogrades: When the Planets Seem to Backstep

All the planets, except for the sun and moon, have times when they appear to move backward—or retrograde—as it seems from our point of view on earth. At these times, planets do not work as they normally do. So it's best to "take a break" from that planet's energies in our life and to do some work on an inner level.

Mercury Retrograde: The Key Is in "Re"

Mercury goes retrograde most often, and its effects can be especially irritating. When it reaches a short distance ahead of the sun several times a year, it seems to move backward from our point of view. Astrologers often compare retrograde motion to the optical illusion that occurs when we ride on a train that passes another train traveling at a different speed—the second train appears to be moving in reverse.

What this means to you is that the Mercury-ruled areas of your life—analytical thought processes, communications, scheduling—are subject to all kinds of confusion. Be prepared. Communications equipment can break down. Schedules may be changed on short notice. People are late for appointments or don't show up at all. Traffic is terrible. Major purchases malfunction, don't work out, or get delivered in the wrong color. Letters don't arrive or are delivered to the wrong address. Employees will make errors that have to be corrected later. Contracts don't work out or must be renegotiated.

Since most of us can't put our lives on "hold" during Mercury retrogrades, we should learn to tame the trickster and make it work for us. The key is in the prefix *re-*. This is the time to go back over things in your life, *re*flect on what you've done during the previous months. Now you can get deeper insights, spot errors you've missed. So take time to *re*view and *re*evaluate what has happened. *Re*st and *re*ward yourself—it's a good time to take a vacation, especially if you *re*visit a favorite place. *Re*organize your work and finish up projects that are backed up. Clean out your desk and closets. Throw away what you can't *re*cycle. If you must sign contracts or agreements, do so with a contingency clause that lets you *re*evaluate the terms later.

Postpone major purchases or commitments for the time being. Don't get married (unless you're *re*marrying the same person). Try not to *re*ly on other people keeping appointments, contracts, or agreements to the letter; have several alternatives. Double-check and *re*ad between the lines. Don't buy anything connected with communications or transportation (if you must, be sure to cover yourself).

Mercury retrograding through your sun sign will intensify its effect on your life.

If Mercury was retrograde when you were born, you may be one of the lucky people who don't suffer the frustrations of this period. If so, your mind probably works in a very intuitive, insightful way.

The sign in which Mercury is retrograding can give you an idea of what's in store—as well as the sun signs that will be especially challenged.

Mercury Retrogrades in 2005

Mercury has three retrograde periods this year.
  March 19 to April 12 in Aries
  July 22 to August 15 in Leo
  November 14 to December 3 from Sagittarius to Scorpio

Venus Retrograde: Relationships Are Affected

Retrograding Venus can cause your relationships to take a backward step, or it can make you extravagant and impractical. Shopping till you drop and buying what you cannot afford are problems at this time. It's *not* a good time to redecorate—you'll hate the color of the walls later. Postpone getting a new hairstyle. Try not to fall in love either. But if you wish to make amends in an already troubled relationship, make peaceful overtures at this time.

Venus Retrogrades in 2005

For most of the year, Venus is behaving. However, Venus turns retrograde in Aquarius on December 24, 2005, until February 3, 2006 (back to Capricorn).

Use the Go Power of Mars

Mars shows how and when to get where you want to go. Timing your moves with Mars on your side can give you a big push. On the other hand, pushing Mars the wrong way can guarantee that you'll run into frustrations in every corner. Your best times to forge ahead are during the weeks when Mars is traveling through your sun sign or your Mars sign (look these up at the end of chapter 4 on the planets). Also consider times when Mars is in a compatible sign (fire with air signs, or earth with water signs). You'll be sure to have planetary power on your side.

Hold your fire when Mars retrogrades in Taurus in 2005, especially if you are a Taurus. Let someone else run with the ball, especially if it's the opposing team. You may feel you're not accomplishing much, but that's the right idea. Slow down and work off any frustrations at the gym. It's also best to postpone buying mechanical devices, which are Mars-ruled, and to take extra care handling sharp objects.

During a Mars retrograde, be sure to use the appropriate protective gear when playing sports or exercising. This year, be careful to protect the Taurus-ruled neck area. This is not the time for daredevil moves or neck-twisting yoga positions.

Mars Retrogrades in 2005

The Mars retrograde period lasts from October 1 to December 9 (in Taurus).

When Other Planets Retrograde

The slower-moving planets stay retrograde for months at a time (Jupiter, Saturn, Neptune, Uranus, and Pluto).

When Saturn is retrograde, it's an uphill battle with self-discipline. You may not be in the mood for work. You may feel more like hanging out at the beach than getting things done.

Neptune retrograde promotes a dreamy escapism from reality, when you may feel you're in a fog (Pisces will feel this, especially).

Uranus retrograde may mean setbacks in areas where there have been sudden changes, when you may be forced to regroup or reevaluate the situation.

Pluto retrograde is a time to work on establishing proportion and balance in areas where there have been recent dramatic transformations.

When the planets move forward again, there's a shift in the atmosphere. Activities connected with each planet start moving ahead, plans that were stalled get rolling. Make a special note of those days on your calendar and proceed accordingly.

Other Retrogrades in 2005

The five slower-moving planets all go retrograde in 2005. Jupiter retrogrades from February 1 to June 5 in Libra. Saturn retrogrades from November 8, 2004, to March 21,

2005, in Cancer, then turns retrograde again on November 22 in Leo, for the duration of the year.

Uranus retrogrades from June 14 to November 15 in Pisces.

Neptune retrogrades from May 19 to October 26 in Aquarius.

Pluto retrogrades from March 26 to September 2 in Sagittarius.

CHAPTER 3

Astrology Made Easy

Would you like to know more about astrology but feel a bit daunted by the terminology? Here's a fast user-friendly introduction to a subject that has many layers. With the information in this chapter, you'll soon be off and running. You'll learn the most important basic principles, such as what a sign is and what each section of an astrology chart means—a good starting point to understanding astrology's map of the cosmos.

The Signs and the Stars: Is There a Difference?

One of the most confusing terms for beginners is the one most often encountered: the signs. What is a sign exactly? Signs are actually a type of celestial real estate, located on the zodiac, an imaginary 360-degree belt circling the earth. This belt is divided into twelve equal 30-degree segments, and these portions are the signs.

There's often confusion about the difference between the signs and the constellations of the zodiac. Constellations are patterns of stars that originally marked the twelve segments, like signposts. Though a sign is named after the constellation that once marked the same area, the constellations are no longer in the same place relative to the earth as they were centuries ago. Over hundreds of years, the earth's orbit has shifted; so from our point of view here on earth the constellations moved. However, the signs remain in place. Most Western astrologers use the divisions of the zodiac. However, there are some methods of astrology that do still use the constellations instead of the signs.

Most people think of themselves in terms of their sun sign. A sun sign refers to the sign the sun is orbiting through at a given moment from our point of view here on earth. (Of course, it is the earth that is really orbiting, not the sun. It only seems so to us as we watch the sky.)

For instance "I'm an Aries" means that the sun was passing through Aries when that person was born. However, there are nine other planets (plus asteroids, fixed stars, and sensitive points) that also form our total astrological personality, and some or many of these will be located in other signs. No one is completely "Aries," with all his astrological components in one sign! (Please note that, in astrology, the sun and moon are usually referred to as planets, though of course they're not.) As mentioned before, the sun signs are areas on the zodiac. They do not do anything (planets are the doers). However, they are associated with many things, depending on their locations.

Why Is a Sign Defined a Certain Way?

What makes Aries the sign of go-getters, Taurus savvy with money, Gemini talk a blue streak, and Sagittarius footloose? Definitions of the signs are not accidental. They are derived from different combinations of four concepts: a sign's *element, quality* (*modality,* or the way it operates), *polarity*, and *place (order)* in the zodiac lineup.

Take the element of fire: it's hot, passionate. Then add the active cardinal mode. Give it a jolt of positive energy, and place it first in line. And doesn't that sound like the active, me-first, driving, hotheaded, energetic Aries?

Then take the element of earth: it's practical, sensual,

where things grow. Add the fixed, stable mode. Give it energy that reacts to its surroundings, that settles in. Put it after Aries. Now you've got a good idea of how sensual, earthy Taurus operates.

Another way to grasp the idea is to pretend you're doing a magical puzzle based on the numbers that can divide into twelve (the number of signs): 4, 3, and 2. There are four "building blocks" or elements, three ways a sign operates (qualities), and two polarities. These alternate in turn around the zodiac, with a different combination coming up for each sign.

The Four Elements

First, consider the four elements that describe the physical concept of the sign. Is it *fiery* (dynamic), *earthy* (practical), *airy* (mental), *watery* (emotional)? There are three zodiac signs of each of the four elements: *fire* (Aries, Leo, Sagittarius); *earth* (Taurus, Virgo, Capricorn); *air* (Gemini, Libra, Aquarius); *water* (Cancer, Scorpio, Pisces). These are the same elements that make up our planet: earth, air, fire, and water. But astrology uses the elements as *symbols* that link our body and psyche to the rhythms of the planets.

Fire signs spread warmth and enthusiasm. They are able to fire up or motivate others. They have hot tempers. These are people who make ideas catch fire and spring into existence. Earth signs are the builders of the zodiac who follow through after the initiative of fire signs to make things happen. These people are solid, practical realists who enjoy material things and sensual pleasures. They are interested in ideas that can be used to achieve concrete results. Air signs are mental people, great communicators. Following the consolidating earth signs, they'll reach out to inspire others through the use of words, social contacts, discussion, and debate. Water signs complete each four-sign series adding the ingredients of emotion, compassion, and imagination. Water sign people are nonverbal communicators who attune themselves to their surroundings and react through the medium of feelings.

The Three Qualities

The second consideration when defining a sign is how it will operate. Will it take the initiative, or move slowly and deliberately, or adapt easily? It's quality (or modality) will tell. There are three qualities and four signs of each quality: cardinal, fixed, and mutable.

Cardinal signs are the start-up signs that begin each season (Aries, Cancer, Libra, Capricorn). These people love to be active, involved in projects. They are usually on the fast track to success, impatient to get things under way. *Fixed signs* (Taurus, Leo, Scorpio, Aquarius) move steadily, always in control. They happen in the middle of a season, after the initial character of the season is established. Fixed signs are naturally more centered. They tend to move more deliberately, do things more slowly but thoroughly. They govern parts of your horoscope where you take root and integrate your experiences. *Mutable signs* (Gemini, Virgo, Sagittarius, Pisces) embody the principle of distribution. These are the signs that break up the cycle, then prepare the way for a change by distributing the energy to the next group. Mutables are flexible, adaptable, communicative. They can move in many directions easily, darting around obstacles.

The Two Polarities

In addition to an element and a quality, each sign has a polarity, either a positive or a negative electrical charge that generates energy around the zodiac, like a giant battery. Polarity refers to opposites, which you could also define as masculine/feminine, yin/yang, active/reactive. Alternating around the zodiac, the six fire and air signs are positive, active, masculine, and yang in polarity. These signs are open, expanding outward. The six earth and water signs are reactive, negative, and yin in polarity.

They are nurturing and receptive, which allows the energy to develop and take shape. All positive energy would be like a car without brakes. All negative energy would be like a stalled vehicle, going nowhere. Both polarities are needed in balanced proportion.

The Order of the Signs: Their Place

Finally we must consider the order of the signs—that is the place each sign occupies in the zodiac. This consideration is vital to the balance of the zodiac and the transmission of energy throughout the zodiac. Each sign is quite different from its neighbors on either side. Yet each seems to grow out of its predecessor like links in a chain. And each transmits a synthesis of energy gathered along the chain to the following sign—beginning with the fiery, active, positive, cardinal sign of Aries and ending with the watery, mutable, reactive Pisces.

The table shows how the signs shape up according to the four characteristics discussed.

How the Signs Add Up

Sign	Element	Quality	Polarity	Place
Aries	fire	cardinal	masculine	first
Taurus	earth	fixed	feminine	second
Gemini	air	mutable	masculine	third
Cancer	water	cardinal	feminine	fourth
Leo	fire	fixed	masculine	fifth
Virgo	earth	mutable	feminine	sixth
Libra	air	cardinal	masculine	seventh

Sign	Element	Quality	Polarity	Place
Scorpio	water	fixed	feminine	eighth
Sagittarius	fire	mutable	masculine	ninth
Capricorn	earth	cardinal	feminine	tenth
Aquarius	air	fixed	masculine	eleventh
Pisces	water	mutable	feminine	twelfth

The Houses and the Horoscope Chart

A horoscope chart is a map of the heavens at a given moment in time. It looks somewhat like a wheel divided with twelve spokes. In between each of the "spokes" is a section called a *house*.

Each house deals with a different area of life and is influenced by a special sign and a planet. In addition, the house is governed by the sign passing over the spoke (or cusp of the house) at that particular moment. For example, the first house is naturally associated with Aries and Mars. However, if Capricorn was the sign passing over the house cusp at the time the chart was cast, that house would have a Capricorn influence as well.

The houses start at the left center spoke (the number 9 position if you were reading a clock) and are read *counterclockwise* around the chart.

Astrologers look at the houses to tell in what area of a subject's life an event is happening or about to happen in the subject's career, finances, health, or other area designated by the house.

The First House: Home of Aries and Mars

The sign passing over the first house at the time of your birth is known as your *ascendant,* or *rising sign.* The first house is the house of "firsts"—the first impression you

30

make, how you initiate matters, the image you choose to project. This is where you advertise yourself, where you project your personality. Planets that fall here will intensify the way you come across to others. Often the first house will project an entirely different type of personality than the sun sign. For instance, a Capricorn with Leo in the first house will come across as much more flamboyant than the average Capricorn.

The Second House: Home of Taurus and Venus

This house is where you experience the material world— what you value. Here are your attitudes about money, possessions, finances, whatever belongs to you, and what you own, as well as your earning and spending capacity. On a deeper level, this house reveals your sense of self-worth, the inner values that draw wealth in various forms.

The Third House: Home of Gemini and Mercury

This house describes how you communicate with others, how you reach out to others nearby, and how you interact with the immediate environment. It shows how your thinking process works and the way you express your thoughts. Are you articulate or tongue-tied? Can you think on your feet? This house also shows your first relationships, your experiences with brothers and sisters, and how you deal with people close to you such as your neighbors or pals. It's where you take short trips, write letters, or use the telephone. It shows how your mind works in terms of left-brain logical and analytical functions.

The Fourth House: Home of Cancer and the Moon

The fourth house shows the foundation of life, the psychological underpinnings. At the bottom of the chart, this house shows how you are nurtured and made to feel secure—your roots! It shows your early home environment and the circumstances at the end of your life (your final "home") as well as the place you call home now. Astrologers look here for information about the parental nurturers in your life.

The Fifth House: Home of Leo and the Sun

The fifth house is where the creative potential develops. Here you express yourself and procreate in the sense that children are outgrowths of your creative ability. But this house most represents your inner childlike self who delights in play. If your inner security has been established by the time you reach this house, you are now free to have fun, romance, and love affairs and to give of yourself. This is also the place astrologers look for playful love affairs, flirtations, and brief romantic encounters (rather than long-term commitments).

The Sixth House: Home of Virgo and Mercury

The sixth house has been called the "repair and maintenance" department. This house shows how you take care of your body and organize yourself to perform efficiently in the world. Here is where you get things done, where you look after others, and fulfill service duties such as taking care of pets. Here is what you do to survive on a day-to-day basis. The sixth house demands order in your life; otherwise there would be chaos. This house is your "job" (as opposed to your career, which is the domain of the tenth house), your diet, and your health and fitness regimens.

The Seventh House: Home of Libra and Venus

This house shows your attitude toward partners and those with whom you enter commitments, contracts, or agreements. Here is the way you relate to others, as well as your close, intimate, one-on-one relationships (including open enemies—those you "face off" with). Open hostilities, lawsuits, divorces, and marriages happen here. If the first house represents the "I," the seventh or opposite house is the "not-I"—the complementary partner you attract by the way you come across. If you are having trouble with partnerships, consider what you are attracting by the energies of your first and seventh house.

The Eighth House: Home of Scorpio and Pluto (also Mars)

The eighth house refers to how you merge with something or someone, and how you handle power and control. This is one of the most mysterious and powerful houses, where your energy transforms itself from "I" to "we." As you give up power and control by uniting with something or someone, two kinds of energies merge and become something greater, leading to a regeneration of the self on a higher level. Here are your attitudes toward sex, shared resources, taxes (what you share with the government). Because this house involves what belongs to others, you face issues of control and power struggles, or undergo a deep psychological transformation as you bond with another. Here you transcend yourself with dreams, drugs, and occult or psychic experiences that reflect the collective unconscious.

The Ninth House: Home of Sagittarius and Jupiter

The ninth house shows your search for wisdom and higher knowledge—your belief system. As the third house represents the "lower mind," its opposite on the wheel, the ninth house, is the "higher mind"—the abstract, intuitive, spiritual mind that asks "big" questions like "Why are we here?" After the third house has explored what was close at hand, the ninth stretches out to broaden you mentally with higher education and travel. Here you stretch spiritually with religious activity. Since you are concerned with how everything is related, you tend to push boundaries, take risks. Here is where you express your ideas in a book or thesis, where you pontificate, philosophize, or preach.

The Tenth House: Home of Capricorn and Saturn

The tenth house is associated with your public life and high-profile activities. Located directly overhead at the "high noon" position on the horoscope wheel, this is the most "visible" house in the chart, the one where the world sees you. It deals with your career (but not your routine "job") and your reputation. Here is where you go public, take on responsibilities (as opposed to the fourth house, where you stay home). This will affect the career you choose and your "public relations." This house is also associated with your father figure or the main authority figure in your life.

The Eleventh House: Home of Aquarius and Uranus

The eleventh house is where you extend yourself to a group, a goal, or a belief system. This house is where you define what you really want, the kinds of friends you have, your political affiliations, and the kind of groups you identify with as an equal. Here is where you become concerned with "what other people think" or where you rebel against social conventions. Here is where you could become a socially conscious humanitarian or a partygoing social butterfly. It's where you look to others to stimulate you and discover your kinship to the rest of humanity. The sign on this house can help you understand what you gain and lose from friendships.

The Twelfth House: Home of Pisces and Neptune

The twelfth house is where the boundaries between yourself and others become blurred, and you become selfless. Old-fashioned astrologers used to put a rather negative spin on this house, calling it the "house of self-undoing." When we "undo ourselves," we surrender control, boundaries, limits, and rules. But instead of being self-undoing, the twelfth house can be a place of great creativity and talent. It is the place where you can tap into the collective unconscious, where your imagination is limitless.

In your trip around the zodiac, you've gone from the "I" of self-assertion in the first house to the final house symbolizing the dissolution that happens before rebirth. It's where accumulated experiences are processed in the unconscious.

Spiritually oriented astrologers look to this house for evidence of past lives and karma. Places where we go for solitude or to do spiritual or reparatory work such as retreats, religious institutions, and hospitals belong to the twelfth house. Here is also where we withdraw from society voluntarily or involuntarily, put to prison because of antisocial activity. Selfless giving through charitable acts is part of this house, as is helpless receiving or dependence on charity.

In your daily life, the twelfth house reveals your deepest intimacies, your best-kept secrets, especially those you hide from yourself and keep repressed deep in the unconscious. It is where we surrender a sense of a separate self to a deep feeling of wholeness, such as selfless service in religion or any activity that involves merging with the greater whole. Many sports stars have important planets in the twelfth house that enable them to lay in the "zone," finding an inner, almost mystical, strength that transcends their limits.

Who's Home in Your Houses?

Houses are stronger or weaker depending on how many planets are inhabiting them. If there are many planets in a given house, it follows that the activities of that house will be especially important in your life. If the planet that rules the house is also located there, this also adds power to the house.

In the next chapter we will visit the planets.

CHAPTER 4

Your Planetary Team

Although you already know your sun sign, did you know that astrology gives you not one but ten ways to get to know yourself and others? If you've been sticking with sun sign, you've been missing out on nine other planetary forces that act like a team to define your personality. And they are terrific sources of information. If you want to know what turns someone on, consult their Venus. How about mastering a fear? Look up Saturn. Having a power struggle? Pluto might shed some light.

Think of the other planets as your own special task force that can be put to work for you, supplying you with tips you can use in every area of your life to help you focus your goals, define your objectives, handle other people, and get what you want. The sign and the house where each planet is located in your horoscope represents how and where its force will operate. And like a real-life team, some planets will support each other and others may work at cross-purposes, creating the dynamics and tension that make each person interesting.

The keyword for a planet's influence is: location, location, location! (For a moment, think of your horoscope as real estate.) Prime property is close to your rising sign or at the top of your chart. If two or more planets are grouped together in one sign, they usually operate together, playing off each other, rather than expressing their energy singularly. But a loner, a planet that stands far away from the others, is usually outstanding and often calls the shots.

Each planet has two signs where it is especially at home. These are called its *dignities*. The most favorable place for a planet is in the sign or signs it rules; the next-best place is in a sign where it is *exalted*, or especially harmonious. On the other hand, there are places in the horoscope where a planet has to work harder to play its role. These places are called the planets *detriment* and *fall*. The sign opposite a planet's rulership, which embodies the opposite area of life, is its detriment. The sign opposite its exaltation is its fall. Though these terms may suggest unfortunate circumstances for the planet, that is not always true. In fact, a planet that is debilitated can actually be more complete because it must stretch itself to meet the challenges of living in a more difficult sign. Like world leaders who've had to struggle for greatness, this planet may actually develop great strength and character.

Here's a list of the best places for each planet to be. Note that, as new planets were discovered, they replaced the traditional rulers of signs which best complemented their energies.

ARIES—Mars

TAURUS—Venus, in its most sensual form

GEMINI—Mercury, in its communicative role

CANCER—the moon

LEO—the sun

VIRGO—also Mercury, this time in its more critical capacity

LIBRA—also Venus, in its more aesthetic, judgmental form

SCORPIO—Pluto, replacing Mars, the sign's original ruler

SAGITTARIUS—Jupiter

CAPRICORN—Saturn

AQUARIUS—Uranus, replacing Saturn, its original ruler

PISCES—Neptune, replacing Jupiter, its original ruler

A person who has many planets in exalted signs is lucky indeed, for here is where the planet can accomplish the most and be its most influential and creative.

SUN—exalted in Aries, where its energy creates action

MOON—exalted in Taurus, where instincts and reactions operate on a highly creative level

MERCURY—exalted in Aquarius, where it can reach analytical heights

VENUS—exalted in Pisces, a sign whose sensitivity encourages love and creativity

MARS—exalted in Capricorn, a sign that puts energy to work productively

JUPITER—exalted in Cancer, where it encourages nurturing and growth

SATURN—at home in Libra, where it steadies the scales of justice and promotes balanced, responsible judgment

URANUS—powerful in Scorpio, where it promotes transformation

NEPTUNE—especially favored in Cancer, where it gains the security to transcend to a higher state

PLUTO—exalted in Pisces, where it dissolves the old cycle to make way for transition to the new

The Sun Is Always Captain of the Team

Because the sun shows your basic will and ego, it's always the strongest personality in your chart. Treat it with respect, as the captain of your team. It takes center stage even when sharing turf with other planets. This is why sun sign astrology works for so many people. If nothing else, sun sign mates have this key team player in common.

The sun rules the sign of Leo, gaining strength through the pride, dignity, and confidence of this fixed, fiery personality. It is exalted in "me-first" Aries. In its detriment, Aquarius, the sun ego is strengthened through group participation and social consciousness rather than through self-centeredness. Note how many Aquarius people are involved in politics, social work, public life, and follow the demands of their sun sign to be spokesperson for a group. In its fall, Libra, the sun needs the strength of a partner—an "other"—to enhance balance and self-expression.

Like your sun sign, each of the other nine planets' personalities is colored by the sign it is passing through at the time. For example, Mercury, the planet that rules the way you communicate, will express itself in a dynamic, headstrong Aries way if it is passing through the sign of Aries when you were born. You would communicate in a much different way if it is passing through the slower, more patient sign of Taurus. And so on through the list.

Here's a rundown of the planets and how they behave in every sign.

The Moon Expresses Your Inner Feelings

The moon can teach you about the inner side of yourself, your needs and secrets, as well as those of others. It is your most personal planet—the receptive, reflective, female, nurturing side of you. And it reflects who you were nurtured by—the "mother" or mother figure in your chart. In a man's chart, the moon position also describes his female, receptive, emotional side as well as the woman in his life who will have the deepest effect. (Venus reveals the kind of woman who attracts him physically.)

The sign the moon was passing through at your birth reflects your instinctive emotional nature, what appeals to you subconsciously. Since accurate moon tables are too extensive for this book, check through these descriptions to find the moon sign that feels most familiar. Or, better yet, have your chart calculated by a computer service to get your accurate moon placement.

The moon rules maternal Cancer and is exalted in Taurus—both comforting, home-loving signs where the natural emotional energies of the moon are easily and productively expressed. But when the moon is in the opposite signs—in its Capricorn detriment and its Scorpio fall—it leaves the comfortable nest and deals with emotional issues of power and achievement in the outside world. Those of you with the moon in these signs will find your emotional role more challenging in life.

Moon in Aries

You are an idealistic, impetuous person who falls in and out of love easily. This moon placement makes you both independent and ardent. You love a challenge, but could cool once your quarry is captured. You should cultivate patience and tolerance. Otherwise, you might gravitate toward those who treat you rough, just for the sake of challenge and excitement.

Moon in Taurus

You are a sentimental soul who is very fond of the good life. You gravitate toward solid, secure relationships. You like displays of affection and creature comforts—all the tangible trappings of a cozy, safe, calm atmosphere. You are sensual and steady emotionally, but very stubborn and determined. You can't be pushed and tend to dislike changes. You should make an effort to broaden your horizons and to take a risk sometimes.

Moon in Gemini

You crave mental stimulation and variety in life, which you usually get through an ever-varied social life or the excitement of flirtation, or multiple professional involvements—or all of these. You may marry more than once and have a rather chaotic emotional life due to your difficulty with commitment and settling down. Be sure to

41

find a partner who is as outgoing as you are. You will have to learn at some point to focus your energies because you tend to be somewhat fragmented—to do two things at once, to have two homes, even to have two lovers. If you can find a creative way to express your many-faceted nature, you'll be ahead of the game.

Moon in Cancer

This is the most powerful lunar position. It is sure to make a deep imprint on your character. Your needs are very much associated with your reaction to the needs of others. You are very sensitive and self-protective, though some of you may mask this with a hard shell. This placement also gives an excellent memory, keen intuition, and an uncanny ability to perceive the needs of others. All of the lunar phases will affect you, especially full moons and eclipses, so you would do well to mark them on your calendar. Because you're happiest at home, you may work at home or turn your office into a second home where you can nurture and comfort people. (You may tend to "mother the world.") With natural psychic and intuitive ability, you might be drawn to occult work in some way. Or you may get professionally involved with providing food and shelter to others.

Moon in Leo

This warm, passionate moon takes everything to heart. You are attracted to all that is noble, generous, and aristocratic in life (and may be a bit of a snob). You have an innate ability to take command emotionally, but you do need strong support, loyalty, and loud applause from those you love. You are possessive of your loved ones and your turf, and will roar if anyone threatens to take over your territory.

Moon in Virgo

You are rather cool until you decide if others measure up. But once someone or something meets your ideal standards, you hold up your end of the arrangement perfectly. You may, in fact, drive yourself too hard to attain some notion of perfection. Try to be a bit easier on yourself and others. Don't always act the censor! You love to be the teacher. You are drawn to situations where you can change others for the better, but sometimes you must learn to accept others for what they are. Enjoy what you have!

Moon in Libra

As a partnership-oriented moon, you may find it difficult to be alone or to do things alone. After you have learned emotional balance by leaning on yourself first, you can have excellent relationships. It is best for you to avoid extremes, which set your scales swinging and can make your love life precarious. You thrive in a rather conservative, traditional, romantic relationship where you receive attention and flattery—but not possessiveness—from your partner. You'll be your most charming in an elegant, harmonious atmosphere.

Moon in Scorpio

This is a moon that enjoys and responds to intense, passionate feelings. You may go to extremes and have a very dramatic emotional life, full of ardor, suspicion, jealousy, and obsession. It would be much healthier to channel your need for power and control into meaningful work. This is a good position for anyone in the fields of medicine, police work, research, the occult, psychoanalysis, or intuitive work, because life-and-death situations don't faze you. However, you do take personal disappointments very hard.

Moon in Sagittarius

You take life's ups and downs with good humor and the proverbial grain of salt. You'll love 'em and leave 'em, taking off on a great adventure at a moment's notice. "Born free" could be your slogan. Attracted by the exotic, you have wanderlust mentally and physically. You may be too much in search of new mental and spiritual stimulation to ever settle down.

Moon in Capricorn

Are you ever accused of being too cool and calculating? You have an earthy side, but you take prestige and position very seriously. Your strong drive to succeed extends to your romantic life where you will be devoted to improving your lifestyle and rising to the top. A structured situation where you can advance methodically makes you feel wonderfully secure. You may be attracted to someone older or very much younger or from a different social world. It may be difficult to look at the lighter side of emotional relationships. Though this moon is placed in the sign of its detriment, the good news is that you tend to be very dutiful and responsible to those you care for.

Moon in Aquarius

You are a people collector with many friends of all backgrounds. You are happiest surrounded by people and may feel uneasy when left alone. Though you usually stay friends with lovers, intense emotions and demanding one-on-one relationships turn you off. You don't like anything to be too rigid or scheduled. Though tolerant and understanding, you can be emotionally unpredictable and may opt for an unconventional love life. With plenty of space, you will be able to sustain relationships with liberal, freedom-loving types.

Moon in Pisces

You are very responsive and empathic to others, especially if they have problems or are the underdog. (Be on guard against attracting too many people with sob stories!) You'll be happiest if you can express your creative imagination in the arts or in the spiritual or healing professions. Because you may tend to escape in fantasies or overreact to the moods of others, you need an emotional anchor to help you keep a firm foothold in reality. Steer clear of too much escapism (especially in alcohol) or reclusiveness. Places near water soothe your moods. Working in a field that gives you emotional variety will also help you be productive.

The Personal Planets: Mercury, Venus, and Mars

These planets work in your immediate personal life.

Mercury affects how you communicate and how your mental processes work. Are you a quick study who grasps information rapidly? Or do you learn more slowly and thoroughly? How is your concentration? Can you express yourself easily? Are you a good writer? All these questions can be answered by your Mercury placement.

Venus shows what you react to. What turns you on? What appeals to your aesthetically? Are you charming to others? Are you attractive to look at? Your taste, your refinement, your sense of balance and proportion are all Venus-ruled.

Mars is your outgoing energy, your drive and ambition. Do you reach out for new adventures? Are you assertive? Are you motivated? Self-confident? Hot-tempered? How you channel your energy and drive is revealed by your Mars placement.

Mercury Shows How Your Mind Works

Mercury is the strategist on your team. It shows how a person thinks and speaks, how logically the mind works. Since it stays close to the sun, read the description for Mercury in your sun sign, then the sign preceding and following it. Then decide which reflects the way you think.

Mercury in Aries

Your mind is very active and assertive. You never hesitate to say what you think, never shy away from a battle. In fact, you may relish a verbal confrontation. Tact is not your strong point, so you may have to learn not to trip over your tongue.

Mercury in Taurus

Though you may be a slow learner, you have good concentration and mental stamina. You want to make your ideas really happen. You'll attack a problem methodically and consider every angle thoroughly, never jumping to conclusions. You'll stick with a subject until you master it.

Mercury in Gemini

You are a wonderful communicator with great facility for expressing yourself both verbally and in writing. You love gathering all kinds of information. You probably finish other people's sentences, and express yourself with eloquent hand gestures. You can talk to anybody anytime . . . and probably have phone and e-mail bills to prove it. You read anything from sci-fi to Shakespeare, and might need an extra room just for your book collection. Though you learn fast, you may lack focus and discipline. Watch a tendency to jump from subject to subject.

Mercury in Cancer

You rely on intuition more than logic. Your mental processes are usually colored by your emotions, so you may seem shy or hesitant to voice your opinions. However, this placement gives you the advantage of great imagination and empathy in the way you communicate with others.

Mercury in Leo

You are enthusiastic and very dramatic in the way you express yourself. You like to hold the attention of groups, and could be a great public speaker. Your mind thinks big, so you prefer to deal with the overall picture rather than with the details.

Mercury in Virgo

This is one of the best places for Mercury. It should give you critical ability, attention to details, and thorough analysis. Your mind focuses on the practical side of things. This type of thinking is very well suited to being a teacher or editor.

Mercury in Libra

You're either a born diplomat who smoothes over ruffled feathers or a talented debater. Many lawyers have this placement. However, since you're forever weighing the pros and cons of a situation, you may vacillate when making decisions.

Mercury in Scorpio

This is an investigative mind that stops at nothing to get the answers. You may have a sarcastic, stinging wit or a gift for the cutting remark. There's always a grain of truth to your verbal sallies, thanks to your penetrating insight.

Mercury in Sagittarius

You are a supersalesman with a tendency to expound. Though you are very broad-minded, you can be dogmatic when it comes to telling others what's good for them. You won't hesitate to tell the truth as you see it, so watch a tendency toward tactlessness. On the plus side, you have a great sense of humor. This position of Mercury is often considered by astrologers to be at a disadvantage because Sagittarius opposes Gemini, the sign Mercury rules, and squares off with Virgo, another Mercury-ruled sign. What often happens is that Mercury in Sagittarius oversteps its bounds and loses sight of the facts in a situation. Do a reality check before making promises you may not be able to deliver.

Mercury in Capricorn

This placement endows good mental discipline. You have a love of learning and a very orderly approach to your subjects. You will patiently plod through the facts and figures until you have mastered the tasks. You grasp structured situations easily, but may be short on creativity.

Mercury in Aquarius

An independent, original thinker, you'll have more cutting-edge ideas than the average person. You will be quick to check out any unusual opportunities. Your opinions are so well-researched and grounded that once your mind is made up, it is difficult to change.

Mercury in Pisces

You have the psychic and intuitive mind of a natural poet. Learn to make use of your creative imagination. You may think in terms of helping others, but check a tendency to be vague and forgetful of details.

Venus Is the Popularity Planet

Venus tells how you relate to others and to your environment. It shows where you receive pleasure, what you love to do. Find your Venus placement from the charts at the end of this chapter (pages 80–87) by looking for the year of your birth in the left-hand column. Then follow the line of that year across the page until you reach the time period of your birthday. The sign heading that column will be your Venus. If you were born on a day when Venus was changing signs, check the signs preceding or following that day to determine if that sign feels more like your Venus nature.

Venus in Aries

You can't stand to be bored, confined, or ordered around. But a good challenge, maybe even a rousing row, turns you on. Confess—don't you pick a fight now and then just to get someone stirred up? You're attracted by the chase, not the catch, which could cause some problems in your love life if the object of your affection becomes too attainable. You like to wear red, and you can spot a trend before anyone else.

Venus in Taurus

All your senses work in high gear. You love to be surrounded by glorious tastes, smells, textures, sounds, and visuals. Austerity is not for you! Neither is being rushed. You like time to enjoy your pleasures. Soothing surroundings with plenty of creature comforts are your cup of tea. You like to feel secure in your nest, with no sudden jolts or surprises. You like familiar objects—in fact, you may hate to let anything or anyone go.

Venus in Gemini

You are a lively, sparkling personality who thrives in a situation that affords a constant variety and a frequent change of scenery. A varied social life is important to you, with plenty of stimulation and a chance to engage in some light flirtation. Commitment may be difficult, because playing the field is so much fun.

Venus in Cancer

An atmosphere where you feel protected, coddled, and mothered is best for you. You love to be surrounded by children in a cozy, homelike situation. You are attracted to those who are tender and nurturing, who make you feel secure and well provided for. You may be quite secretive about your emotional life, or attracted to clandestine relationships.

Venus in Leo

First-class attention in large doses turns you on, and so does the glitter of real gold and the flash of mirrors. You like to feel like a star at all times, surrounded by your admiring audience. The side effect is that you may be attracted to flatterers and tinsel, while the real gold requires some digging.

Venus in Virgo

Everything neatly in its place? On the surface, you are attracted to an atmosphere where everything is in perfect order, but underneath are some basic, earthy urges. You are attracted to those who appeal to your need to teach, to be of service, or to play out a Pygmalion fantasy. You are at your best when you are busy doing something useful.

Venus in Libra

Elegance and harmony are your key words. You can't abide an atmosphere of contention. Your taste tends toward the classic, with light harmonies of color—nothing clashing, trendy, or outrageous. You love doing things with a partner, and should be careful to pick one who is decisive but patient enough to let you weigh the pros and cons. And steer clear of argumentative types!

Venus in Scorpio

Hidden mysteries intrigue you. In fact, anything that is too open and aboveboard is a bit of a bore. You surely have a stack of whodunits by the bed, along with an erotic magazine or two. You like to solve puzzles, and may also be fascinated with the occult, crime, or scientific research. Intense, all-or-nothing situations add spice to your life, and you love to ferret out the secrets of others. But you could get burned by your flair for living dangerously. The color black, spicy food, dark wood furniture, and heady perfume all get you in the right mood.

Venus in Sagittarius

If you are not actually a world traveler, your surroundings are sure to reflect your love of faraway places. You like a casual outdoor atmosphere and a dog or two to pet. There should be plenty of room for athletic equipment and suitcases. You're attracted to kindred souls who love to travel and who share your freedom-loving philosophy of life. Athletics and spiritual or New Age pursuits could be other interests.

Venus in Capricorn

No fly-by-night relationships for you! You want substance in life, and you are attracted to whatever will help you get where you are going. Status objects turn you on. And so do those who have a serious, responsible, businesslike approach as well as those who remind you of a beloved parent. It is characteristic of this placement to be attracted to someone of a different generation. Antiques, traditional clothing, and dignified behavior are becoming to you.

Venus in Aquarius

This Venus wants to make friends, to be "cool." You like to be in a group, particularly one pushing a worthy cause. You feel quite at home surrounded by people, and could even court fame. Yet all the while you remain detached from any intense commitment. Original ideas and unpredictable people fascinate you. You don't like everything to be planned out in advance, preferring spontaneity and delightful surprises.

Venus in Pisces

This Venus loves to give of yourself, and you find plenty of takers. Stray animals and people appeal to your heart and your pocketbook, but be careful to look at their motives realistically once in a while. You are extremely vulnerable to sob stories of all kinds. Fantasy, the arts (especially film, dance, and theater), and psychic or spiritual activities also speak to you.

Mars Scores the Goals

Mars is the mover and shaker in your life. It shows how you pursue your goals, whether you have energy to burn or proceed in a slow, steady pace. It will also show how you get angry. Do you explode or do a slow burn or hold everything inside, then get revenge later?

To find your Mars, turn to the charts on pages 88–96. Then find your birth year in the left-hand column and trace the line across horizontally until you come to the column headed by the month of your birth. There you will find an abbreviation of your Mars sign. If the description of your Mars sign doesn't ring true, read the description of the sign preceding and following it. You may have been born on a day when Mars was changing signs, in which case your Mars might be in the adjacent sign.

Mars in Aries

In the sign it rules, Mars shows its brilliant fiery nature. You have an explosive temper and can be quite impatient. On the other hand, you have tremendous courage, energy, and drive. You'll let nothing stand in your way as you race to be first! Obstacles are met head-on and broken through by force. However, those that require patience and persistence can have you exploding in rage. You're a great starter, but not necessarily around for the finish.

Mars in Taurus

Slow, steady, concentrated energy gives you staying power to last until the finish line. You have great stamina, and you never give up. Your tactic is to wear away obstacles with your persistence. Often you come out a winner because you've had the patience to hang in there. When angered, you do a slow burn.

Mars in Gemini

You can't sit still for long. This Mars craves variety. You often have two or more things going on at once—it's all an amusing game to you. Your life can get very complicated, but that only adds spice and stimulation. What drives you into a nervous, hyper state? Boredom, sameness, routine, and confinement. You can do wonderful things with your hands, and you have a way with words.

Mars in Cancer

You rarely attack head-on. Instead, you'll keep things to yourself, make plans in secret, and always cover your actions. This might be interpreted by some as manipulative, but you are only being self-protective. You get furious when anyone knows too much about you. But you do like to know all about others. Your mothering and feeding instincts can be put to good use if you work in the food, hotel, or child-care businesses. You may have to overcome your fragile sense of security, which prompts you not to take risks and to get physically upset when criticized. Don't take things so personally!

Mars in Leo

You have a very dominant personality that takes center stage. Modesty is not one of your traits, nor is taking a backseat. You prefer giving the orders, and have been known to make a dramatic scene if they are not obeyed. Properly used, this Mars confers leadership ability, endurance, and courage.

Mars in Virgo

You are the faultfinder of the zodiac. You notice every detail. Mistakes of any kind make you very nervous. You may worry, even if everything is going smoothly. You may not express your anger directly, but you sure can nag. You have definite likes and dislikes, and you are sure you can do the job better than anyone else. You are certainly more industrious and detail-oriented than other signs. Your Mars energy is often most positively expressed in some kind of teaching role.

Mars in Libra

This Mars will have a passion for beauty, justice, and art. Generally, you will avoid confrontations at all costs. You prefer to spend your energy finding diplomatic solutions or weighing pros and cons. Your other techniques are passive aggression or exercising your well-known charm to get people to do what you want.

Mars in Scorpio

This is a powerful placement, so intense that it demands careful channeling into worthwhile activities. Otherwise, you could become obsessed with your sexuality or might use your need for power and control to manipulate others. You are strong-willed, shrewd, and very private about your affairs, and you'll usually have a secret agenda behind your actions. Your great stamina, focus, and discipline would be excellent assets for careers in the military or medical fields, especially research or surgery. When angry, you don't get mad—you get even!

Mars in Sagittarius

This expansive Mars often propels people into sales, travel, athletics, or philosophy. Your energies function well when you are on the move. You have a hot temper, and are inclined to say what you think before you consider the consequences. You shoot for high goals—and talk endlessly about them—but you may be weak on groundwork. This Mars needs a solid foundation. Watch a tendency to take unnecessary risks.

Mars in Capricorn

This is an ambitious Mars with an excellent sense of timing. You have an eye for those who can be of use to you, and you may dismiss people ruthlessly when you're angry. But you drive yourself hard and deliver full value. This is a good placement for an executive. You'll aim for status and a high material position in life, and you'll keep climbing despite the odds. A great Mars to have!

Mars in Aquarius

This is the most rebellious Mars. You seem to have a drive to assert yourself against the status quo. You may enjoy provoking people, shocking them out of traditional views. Or this placement could express itself in an offbeat sex life. Somehow you often find yourself in unconventional situations. You enjoy being a leader of an active group, which pursues forward-looking studies, politics, or goals.

Mars in Pisces

This Mars is a good actor who knows just how to appeal to the sympathies of others. You create and project wonderful fantasies, or you use your sensitive antennae to crusade for those less fortunate. You get what you want through creating a veil of illusion and glamour. This is a good Mars for someone in the creative and imaginative fields—a dancer, performer, photographer, actor. Many famous film stars have this placement. Watch a tendency to manipulate by making others feel sorry for you.

Jupiter Brings the Lucky Breaks

The last-minute touchdown, that slot-machine windfall, that bonanza that seemed like a fluke: all are blessed by Jupiter, the planet of luck. You don't earn what Jupiter gives—it is bestowed. Under Jupiter's influence, anything seems possible, which is why this is often called the planet of optimism.

When Jupiter is aspecting your chart, you'll travel, expand your mind with higher education, publish to share your knowledge. On the other hand, Jupiter doesn't discriminate or apply discipline. The flip side of Jupiter is the tendency to overdo everything, want more of everything. It's not easy to concentrate or focus when there's fun to be had. Therefore, if not kept in check, Jupiter could result in some unfortunate overspending, weight gain, laziness, or carelessness.

Be sure to look up your Jupiter in the tables in this book. When the current position of Jupiter is favorable, you may get that lucky break. This is a great time to try new things, take risks, travel, or get more education. Opportunities seem to open up easily, so take advantage of them.

Once a year, Jupiter changes signs. That means you are due for an expansive time every twelve years, when Jupiter travels through your sun sign. You'll also have "up" periods every four years, when Jupiter is in the same element as your sun sign.

Jupiter in Aries

You are the soul of enthusiasm and optimism. Your luckiest times are when you are getting started on an exciting project or selling an idea that you really believe in. You may have to watch a tendency to be arrogant with those who do not share your enthusiasm. You follow your impulses, often ignoring budget or other commonsense limitations. To produce real, solid benefits, you'll need patience and follow-through wherever this Jupiter falls in your horoscope.

Jupiter in Taurus

You'll spend on beautiful material things, especially those that come from nature—items made of rare woods, natural fabrics, or precious gems, for instance. You can't have too much comfort or too many sensual pleasures. Watch a tendency to overindulge in good food, or to overpamper yourself with nothing but the best. Spartan living is not for you! You may be especially lucky in matters of real estate.

Jupiter in Gemini

You are the great talker of the zodiac, and you may be a great writer, too. But restlessness could be your weak point. You jump around, talk too much, and could be a jack-of-all-trades. Keeping a secret is especially difficult, so you'll also have to watch a tendency to spill the beans. Since you love to be at the center of a beehive of activity, you'll have a vibrant social life. Your best opportunities will come through your talent for language—speaking, writing, communicating, and selling.

Jupiter in Cancer

You are luckiest in situations where you can find emotional closeness or deal with basic security needs such as food, nurturing, or shelter. You may be a great collector. Or you may simply love to accumulate things—you are the one who stashes things away for a rainy day. You probably have a very good memory and love children. In fact, you may have many children to care for. The food, hotel, child-care, and shipping businesses hold good opportunities for you.

Jupiter in Leo

You are a natural showman who loves to live in a larger-than-life way. Yours is a personality full of color that always finds its way into the limelight. You can't have too much attention or applause. Showbiz is a natural place for you, and so is any area where you can play to a crowd. Exercising your flair for drama, your natural playfulness, and your romantic nature brings you good fortune. But watch a tendency to be overly extravagant or to monopolize center stage.

Jupiter in Virgo

You actually love those minute details others find boring. To you, they make all the difference between the perfect and the ordinary. You are the fine craftsman who spots every flaw. You expand your awareness by finding the most efficient methods and by being of service to others. Many of you will be drawn to medical or teaching fields. You'll also have luck in publishing, crafts, nutrition, and service professions. Watch out for a tendency to overwork.

Jupiter in Libra

This is an other-directed Jupiter that develops best with a partner. The stimulation of others helps you grow. You are also most comfortable in harmonious, beautiful situations, and you work well with artistic people. You have a great sense of fair play and an ability to evaluate the pros and cons of a situation. You usually prefer to play the role of diplomat rather than adversary.

Jupiter in Scorpio

You love the feeling of power and control, of taking things to their limit. You can't resist a mystery. Your shrewd, penetrating mind sees right through to the heart of most situations and people. You have luck in work that provides for solutions to matters of life and death. You may be drawn to undercover work, behind-the-scenes intrigue, psychotherapy, the occult, and sex-related ventures. Your challenge will be to develop a sense of moderation and tolerance for other beliefs. This Jupiter can be fanatical. You may have luck in handling other people's money—insurance, taxes, and inheritance can bring you a windfall.

Jupiter in Sagittarius

Independent, outgoing, and idealistic, you'll shoot for the stars. This Jupiter compels you to travel far and wide, both physically and mentally, via higher education. You may have luck while traveling in an exotic place. You also have luck with outdoor ventures, exercise, and animals, particularly horses. Since you tend to be very open about your opinions, watch a tendency to be tactless and to exaggerate. Instead, use your wonderful sense of humor to make your point.

Jupiter in Capricorn

Jupiter is much more restrained in Capricorn, the sign of rules and authority. Here, Jupiter can make you overwork and heighten any ambition or sense of duty you may have. You'll expand in areas that advance your position, putting you farther up the social or corporate ladder. You are lucky working within the establishment in a very structured situation where you can show off your ability to organize and reap rewards for your hard work.

Jupiter in Aquarius

This is another freedom-loving Jupiter, with great tolerance and originality. You are at your best when you are working for a humanitarian cause and in the company of many supporters. This is a good Jupiter for a political career. You'll relate to all kinds of people on all social levels. You have an abundance of original ideas, but you are best off away from routine and any situation that imposes rigid rules. You need mental stimulation!

Jupiter in Pisces

You are a giver whose feelings and pocketbook are easily touched by others, so choose your companions with care. You could be the original sucker for a hard-luck story. Better find a worthy hospital or a charity that will appreciate your selfless support. You have a great creative imagination. You may attract good fortune in fields related to oil, perfume, pharmaceuticals, petroleum, dance, footwear, and alcohol. But beware of overindulgence in alcohol—focus on a creative outlet instead.

Saturn Is the Demanding Coach

Jupiter speeds you up with *lucky breaks,* then along comes Saturn to slow you down with the *disciplinary brakes.* Saturn has unfairly been called a malefic planet, one of the bad guys of the zodiac. On the contrary, Saturn is one of our best friends, the kind who tells you what you need to hear even if it's not good news. Under a Saturn transit, we grow up, take responsibility for our lives, and emerge from whatever test this planet has in store as far wiser, more capable, and mature human beings. It is when we are under pressure that we grow stronger.

When Saturn hits a critical point in your horoscope, you can count on an experience that will make you slow up, pull back, and reexamine your life. It is a call to eliminate what is not working and to shape up. By the end of its twenty-eight-year trip around the zodiac, Saturn will have tested you in all areas of your life. The major tests happen in seven-year cycles, when Saturn passes over the *angles* of your chart—your rising sign, midheaven, descendant, and nadir. This is when the real life-changing experiences happen. But you are also in for a testing period whenever Saturn passes a *planet* in your chart or stresses that planet from a distance. Therefore, it is useful to check your planetary positions with the timetable of Saturn to prepare in advance, or at least to brace yourself.

When Saturn returns to its location at the time of your birth, at approximately age twenty-eight, you'll have your first Saturn return. At this time, a person usually takes stock or settles down to find his or her mission in life and assumes full adult duties and responsibilities.

Another way Saturn helps us is to reveal the karmic lessons from previous lives and to give us the chance to overcome them. So look at Saturn's challenges as much-needed opportunities for self-improvement. Under a Jupiter influence, you'll have more fun. But Saturn gives you solid, long-lasting results.

Look up your natal Saturn in the tables in this book for clues on where you need work.

Saturn in Aries

Saturn here puts the brakes on Aries natural drive and enthusiasm. There is often an angry side to this placement. You don't let anyone push you around, and you know what's best for yourself. Following orders is not your strong point, and neither is diplomacy. You tend to be quick to go on the offensive in relationships, attacking first, before anyone attacks you. Because no one quite lives up to your standards, you often wind up doing everything yourself. You'll have to learn to cooperate and tone down self-centeredness. Both Pat Buchanan and Saddam Hussein have this Saturn.

Saturn in Taurus

A big issue is getting control of the cash flow. There will be lean periods that can be frightening, but you have the patience and endurance to stick them out and the methodical drive to prosper in the end. Learn to take a philosophical attitude, like Ben Franklin who also had this placement and who said, "A penny saved is a penny earned."

Saturn in Gemini

You are a serious student of life, but you may have difficulty communicating or sharing your knowledge. You may be shy, speak slowly, or have fears about communicating, like Eleanor Roosevelt. You dwell in the realms of science, theory, or abstract analysis—even when you are dealing with the emotions, like Sigmund Freud who also had this placement.

Saturn in Cancer

Your tests come with establishing a secure emotional base. In doing so, you may have to deal with some very basic fears centering on your early home environment. Most of your Saturn tests will have emotional roots in those early childhood experiences. You may have difficulty remaining objective in terms of what you try to achieve. So it will be especially important for you to deal with negative feelings such as guilt, paranoia, jealousy, resentment, and suspicion. Galileo and Michelangelo also navigated these murky waters.

Saturn in Leo

This is an authoritarian Saturn—a strict, demanding parent who may deny the pleasure principle in your zeal to see that rules are followed. Though you may feel guilty about taking the spotlight, you are very ambitious and loyal. You have to watch a tendency toward rigidity, also toward overwork and holding back affection. Joseph Kennedy and Billy Graham share this placement.

Saturn in Virgo

This is a cautious, exacting Saturn. You are intensely hard on yourself. Most of all, you give yourself the roughest time with your constant worries about every little detail, often making yourself sick. You may have difficulties setting priorities and getting the job done. Your tests will come in learning tolerance and understanding of others. Charles de Gaulle, Mae West, and Nathaniel Hawthorne had this meticulous Saturn.

Saturn in Libra

Saturn is exalted here, which makes this planet an ally. You may choose very serious, older partners in life, perhaps stemming from a fear of dependency. You need to learn to stand solidly on your own before you commit to another. You are extremely cautious as you deliberate every involvement—with good reason. It is best that you find an occupation that makes good use of your sense of duty and honor. Steer clear of fly-by-night situations. Both Khrushchev and Mao Tse-tung had this placement.

Saturn in Scorpio

You have great staying power. This Saturn tests you in situations involving the control of others. You may feel drawn to some kind of intrigue or undercover work, like J. Edgar Hoover. Or there may be an air of mystery surrounding your life and death, like Marilyn Monroe and Robert Kennedy who both had this placement. There are lessons to be learned from your sexual involvements. Often sex is used for manipulation or is somehow out of the ordinary. The Roman emperor Caligula and the transvestite Christine Jorgensen are extreme cases.

Saturn in Sagittarius

Your challenges and lessons will come from tests of your spiritual and philosophical values, as happened to Martin Luther King and Gandhi. You are high-minded and sincere with this reflective, moral placement. Uncompromising in your ethical standards, you could become a benevolent despot.

Saturn in Capricorn

With the help of Saturn at maximum strength, your judgment will improve with age. And like Spencer Tracy's screen image, you'll be the gray-haired hero with a strong sense of responsibility. You advance in life slowly but steadily, always with a strong hand at the helm and an eye for the advantageous situation. Like Pat Robertson, you're likely to stand for conservative values. Negatively, you may be a loner, prone to periods of melancholy.

Saturn in Aquarius

Your tests come from relationships with groups. Do you care too much about what others think? Do you feel like an outsider, like Greta Garbo? You may fear being different from others and therefore slight your own unique, forward-looking gifts. Or like Lord Byron and Howard Hughes, you may take the opposite tack and rebel in the extreme. You can apply discipline to accomplish great humanitarian goals, as Albert Schweitzer did.

Saturn in Pisces

Your fear of the unknown and the irrational may lead you to the safety and protection of an institution. You may go on the run like Jesse James, who had this placement, to avoid looking too deeply inside. Or you might go in the opposite, more positive direction and develop a disciplined psychoanalytic approach, which puts you more in control of your feelings. Some of you will take refuge in work with hospitals, charities, or religious institutions. Queen Victoria, who had this placement, symbolized an era when institutions of all kinds were sustained. Discipline applied to artistic work, especially poetry and dance, or to spiritual work, such as yoga or meditation, might be helpful.

How Uranus, Neptune, and Pluto Influence a Whole Generation

These three planets remain in signs such a long time that a whole generation bears the imprint of the sign. Mass movements, great sweeping changes, fads that characterize a generation, even the issues of the conflicts and wars of the time are influenced by these "outer three" planets. When one of these distant planets changes signs, there is a definite shift in the atmosphere, the feeling of the end of an era.

Since these planets are so far away from the sun—too distant to be seen by the naked eye—they pick up signals from the universe at large. These planetary receivers literally link the sun with distant energies, and then perform a similar function in your horoscope by linking your central character with intuitive, spiritual, transformative forces from the cosmos. Each planet has a special domain, and will reflect this in the area of your chart where it falls.

Uranus: The Great Awakener

There is nothing ordinary about this quirky green planet that seems to be traveling on its side, surrounded by a swarm of moons. Is it any wonder that astrologers assigned it to Aquarius, the most eccentric and gregarious sign? Uranus seems to wend its way around the sun, marching to its own tune.

Significantly, Uranus follows Saturn, the planet of limitations and structures. Often we get caught up in the structures we have created to give ourselves a sense of security. However, if we lose contact with our spiritual roots, then Uranus is likely to jolt us out of our comfortable rut and wake us up.

Uranus energy is electrical, happening in sudden flashes. It is not influenced by karma or past events, nor does it regard tradition, sex, or sentiment. The Uranus key words are surprise and awakening. Suddenly, there's that flash of inspiration, that bright idea, that totally new approach to revolutionize whatever scheme you were undertaking. A Uranus event takes you by surprise; it happens from out of the blue, for better or for worse. The Uranus place in your life is where you awaken and become your own person, leaving the structures of Saturn behind. And it is probably the most unconventional place in your chart.

Look up the sign of Uranus at the time of your birth and see where you follow your own tune.

Uranus in Aries

Birth Dates:
  March 31, 1927–November 4, 1927
  January 13, 1928–June 6, 1934
  October 10, 1934–March 28, 1935

Your generation is original, creative, pioneering. It developed the computer, the airplane, and the cyclotron. You let nothing hold you back from exploring the unknown, and you have a powerful mixture of fire and electricity behind you. Women of your generation were among the first to be liberated. You were the unforgettable style setters. You have a surprise in store for everyone. Like Yoko Ono, Grace Kelly, and Jacqueline Onassis, your life may be jolted by sudden and violent changes.

Uranus in Taurus

Birth Dates:
  June 6, 1934–October 10, 1934
  March 28, 1935–August 7, 1941
  October 5, 1941–May 15, 1942

The great territorial shake of World War II began during your generation. You are independent, probably self-employed or would like to be. You have original ideas about making money, and you brace yourself for sudden changes of fortune. This Uranus can cause shake-ups, particularly in finances, but it can also make you a born entrepreneur.

Uranus in Gemini

Birth Dates:
    August 7, 1941–October 5, 1941
    May 15, 1942–August 30, 1948
    November 12, 1948–June 10, 1949

You were the first children to be influenced by television. Now, in your adult years, your generation stocks up on answering machines, cell phones, computers, and fax machines—any new way you can communicate. You have an inquiring mind, but your interests may be rather short-lived. This Uranus can be easily fragmented if there is no structure and focus.

Uranus in Cancer

Birth Dates:
    August 30, 1948–November 12, 1948
    June 10, 1949–August 24, 1955
    January 28, 1956–June 10, 1956

This generation came at a time when divorce was becoming commonplace, so your home image is unconventional. You may have an unusual relationship with your parents; you may have come from a broken home or an unconventional one. You'll have unorthodox ideas about parenting, intimacy, food, and shelter. You may also be interested in dreams, psychic phenomena, and memory work.

Uranus in Leo

Birth Dates:
   August 24, 1955–January 28, 1956
   June 10, 1956–November 1, 1961
   January 10, 1962–August 10, 1962

This generation understood how to use electronic media. Many of your group are now leaders in the high-tech industries, and you also understand how to use the new media to promote yourself. Like Isadora Duncan, you may have a very eccentric kind of charisma and a life that is sparked by unusual love affairs. Your children, too, may have traits that are out of the ordinary. Where this planet falls in your chart, you'll have a love of freedom, be a bit of an egomaniac, and show the full force of your personality in a unique way, like tennis great Martina Navratilova.

Uranus in Virgo

Birth Dates:
   November 1, 1961–January 10, 1962
   August 10, 1962–September 28, 1968
   May 20, 1969–June 24, 1969

You'll have highly individual work methods. Many of you will be finding newer, more practical ways to use computers. Like Einstein, who had this placement, you'll break the rules brilliantly. Your generation came at a time of student rebellions, the civil rights movement, and the general acceptance of health foods. Chances are, you're concerned about pollution and cleaning up the environment. You may also be involved with nontraditional healing methods. Heavyweight champ Mike Tyson has this placement.

Uranus in Libra

Birth Dates:
   September 28, 1968–May 20, 1969

June 24, 1969–November 21, 1974
May 1, 1975–September 8, 1975

Your generation will be always changing partners. Born during the era of women's liberation, you may have come from a broken home and have no clear image of what a marriage entails. There will be many sudden splits and experiments before you settle down. Your generation will be much involved in legal and political reforms and in changing artistic and fashion looks.

Uranus in Scorpio

Birth Dates:
   November 21, 1974–May 1, 1975
   September 8, 1975–February 17, 1981
   March 20, 1981–November 16, 1981

Interest in transformation, meditation, and life after death signaled the beginning of New Age consciousness. Your generation recognizes no boundaries, no limits, and no external controls. You'll have new attitudes toward death and dying, psychic phenomena, and the occult. Like Mae West and Casanova, you'll shock 'em sexually, too.

Uranus in Sagittarius

Birth Dates:
   February 17, 1981–March 20, 1981
   November 16, 1981–February 15, 1988
   May 27, 1988–December 2, 1988

Could this generation be the first to travel in outer space? An earlier generation with this placement included Charles Lindbergh and a time when the first zeppelins and the Wright Brothers were conquering the skies. Uranus here forecasts great discoveries, mind expansion, and long-distance travel. Like Galileo and

Martin Luther, those born in these years will generate new theories about the cosmos and mankind's relation to it.

Uranus in Capricorn

Birth Dates:
  December 20, 1904–January 30, 1912
  September 4, 1912–November 12, 1912
  February 15, 1988–May 27, 1988
  December 2, 1988–April 1, 1995
  June 9, 1995–January 12, 1996

This generation, now growing up, will challenge traditions with the help of electronic gadgets. In these years, we got organized with the help of technology put to practical use. The Internet was born following the great economic boom of the 1990s. Great leaders, who were movers and shakers of history, like Julius Caesar and Henry VIII, were born under this placement.

Uranus in Aquarius

Birth Dates:
  January 30, 1912–September 4, 1912
  November 12, 1912–April 1, 1919
  August 16, 1919–January 22, 1920
  April 1, 1995–June 9, 1995
  January 12, 1996–March 10, 2003
  September 15, 2003–December 30, 2003

The last generation with this placement produced great innovative minds such as Leonard Bernstein and Orson Welles. The next will become another radical breakthrough generation, much concerned with global issues that involve all humanity. Already this is a time of high-tech experimentation on every level, when home computers are becoming as ubiquitous as television. It is also a time of globalization, of surprise attacks (9/11), and of

71

"wake-up" calls, as underdeveloped countries demand attention.

Uranus in Pisces

Birth Dates:
    April 1, 1919–August 16, 1919
    January 22, 1920–March 31, 1927
    November 4, 1927–January 12, 1928
    March 10, 2003–September 15, 2003
    December 20, 2003–May 28, 2010

Uranus is ushering in a new generation that will surely spark innovations and creativity in the arts as well as in the sciences. In the past century, Uranus in Pisces focused attention on the rise of such electronic entertainment as radio and the cinema as well as the secretiveness of Prohibition. This produced a generation of idealists exemplified by Judy Garland's theme, "Somewhere Over the Rainbow." Uranus in Pisces hints at stealth activities, at hospital and prison reform, at high-tech drugs and medical experiments.

Neptune Takes You Beyond Reality

Neptune is often called the planet of dissolution. It is the "dissolver" of reality. It is often maligned as the planet of illusions, drugs, and alcohol where you escape the real world. Under Neptune's influence, you see what you want to see. But Neptune also encourages you to create, to let your imagination run free. Neptune embodies the energy of glamour, subtlety, mystery, and mysticism. It governs anything that takes you beyond the mundane world, including out-of-body experiences.

Neptune acts to break through and transcend your ordinary perceptions to take you to another level of reality where you experience either confusion or ecstasy. Neptune's force can pull you off course, but only if you allow this to happen. Those who use Neptune wisely can translate their daydreams into poetry, theater, design, or inspired moves in the business world, avoiding the tricky "con artist" side of this planet.

Find your Neptune listed below.

Neptune in Cancer

Birth Dates:
  July 19, 1901–December 25, 1901
  May 21, 1902–September 23, 1914
  December 14, 1914–July 19, 1915
  March 19, 1916–May 2, 1916

Dreams of the homeland, idealistic patriotism, and glamorization of the nurturing assets of women characterized this time. You who were born here have unusual psychic ability and deep insights into basic needs of others.

Neptune in Leo

Birth Dates:
  September 23, 1914–December 14, 1914
  July 19, 1915–March 19, 1916
  May 2, 1916–September 21, 1928
  February 19, 1929–July 24, 1929

Neptune in Leo brought us the glamour and high living of the 1920s and the big spenders of that time. The Neptune temptations of gambling, seduction, theater, and lavish entertaining distracted from the realities of the age. Those born in that generation also made great advances in the arts.

Neptune in Virgo

Birth Dates:
  September 21, 1928–February 19, 1929
  July 24, 1929–October 3, 1942
  April 17, 1943–August 2, 1943

Neptune in Virgo encompassed the 1930s, the Great Depression, and the beginning of World War II, when a new order was born. There was a time of facing "what doesn't work." Many were unemployed and found solace at the movies, watching the great Virgo star Greta Garbo or the escapist dance films of Busby Berkeley. New public services were born. Those with Neptune in Virgo later spread the gospel of health and fitness. This generation's devotion to spending hours at the office inspired the term *workaholic*.

Neptune in Libra

Birth Dates:
    October 3, 1942–April 17, 1943
    August 2, 1943–December 24, 1955
    March 12, 1956–October 19, 1956
    June 15, 1957–August 6, 1957

This was the time of World War II and the postwar period, when the world regained balance and returned to relative stability. Neptune in Libra was the romantic generation who would later be concerned with relating. As this generation matured, there was a new trend toward marriage and commitment. Racial and sexual equality became important issues, as they redesigned traditional roles to suit modern times.

Neptune in Scorpio

Birth Dates:
    December 24, 1955–March 12, 1956
    October 19, 1956–June 15, 1957
    August 6, 1957–January 4, 1970
    May 3, 1970–November 6, 1970

Neptune in Scorpio brought in a generation that would become interested in transformative power. Born in an era that glamorized sex, drugs, rock and roll, and Eastern religion, they matured in a more sobering time of AIDS, cocaine abuse, and New Age spirituality. As they evolve, they will become active in healing the planet from the results of the abuse of power.

Neptune in Sagittarius

Birth Dates:
 January 4, 1970–May 3, 1970
 November 6, 1970–January 19, 1984
 June 23, 1984–November 21, 1984

Neptune in Sagittarius was the time when space and astronaut travel became a reality. The Neptune influence glamorized new approaches to mysticism, religion, and mind expansion. This generation will take a new approach to spiritual life, with emphasis on visions, mysticism, and clairvoyance.

Neptune in Capricorn

Birth Dates:
 January 19, 1984–June 23, 1984
 November 21, 1984–January 29, 1998

Neptune in Capricorn brought a time when delusions about material power were glamorized in the mid-1980s and 1990s. There was a boom in the stock market, and the Internet era spawned young tycoons who later lost it all. It was also a time when the psychic and occult worlds spawned a new category of business enterprise, and sold services on television.

Neptune in Aquarius

Birth Dates:
 January 29, 1998–April 4, 2111

This should continue to be a time of breakthroughs. Here the creative influence of Neptune reaches a universal audience. This is a time of dissolving barriers, of globalization—when we truly become one world.

Pluto: The Power Planet

Pluto is a mysterious little planet with a strange elliptical orbit that occasionally runs inside the orbit of its neighbor Neptune. Because of its eccentric path, the length of time Pluto stays in any given sign can vary from thirteen to thirty-two years. It covered only seven signs in the last century. Though it is a tiny planet, its influence is great. When Pluto zaps a strategic point in your horoscope, your life changes dramatically.

This little planet is the power behind the scenes. It affects you at deep levels of consciousness, causing events to come to the surface that will transform you and your generation. Nothing escapes, or is sacred, with this probing planet. Its purpose is to wipe out the past so something new can happen. The Pluto place in your horoscope is where you have invisible power (Mars governs the visible power)—where you can transform, heal, and affect the unconscious needs of the masses. Pluto tells lots about how your generation projects power, what makes it seem "cool" to others. And when Pluto changes signs, there's a whole new concept of what's "cool."

Pluto in Gemini

Birth Dates:
  Late 1800s–May 26, 1914

This was a time of mass suggestion and breakthroughs in communications, a time when many brilliant writers such as Ernest Hemingway and F. Scott Fitzgerald were born. Henry Miller, D. H. Lawrence, and James Joyce scandalized society by using explicit sexual images and language in their literature. "Muckraking" journalists exposed corruption. Pluto-ruled Scorpio President Theodore Roosevelt said, "Speak softly, but carry a big stick." This generation had an intense need to communicate and made major breakthroughs in knowledge. A compulsive restlessness and a thirst for a variety of experiences characterized many of this generation.

Pluto in Cancer

Birth Dates:
  May 26, 1914–June 14, 1939

Dictators and mass media arose to wield emotional power over the masses. Women's rights was a popular issue. Deep sentimental feelings, acquisitiveness, and possessiveness characterized these times and people. Most of the great stars of the Hollywood era that embodied the American image were born during this period: Grace Kelly, Esther Williams, Frank Sinatra, Lana Turner, to name a few.

Pluto in Leo

Birth Dates:
  June 14, 1939–August 19, 1957

The performing arts played on the emotions of the masses. Mick Jagger, John Lennon, and rock and roll were born at this time. So were "baby boomers" like Bill and Hillary Clinton. Those born here tend to be self-centered, powerful, and boisterous. This generation does its own thing, for better or for worse.

Pluto in Virgo

Birth Dates:
  August 19, 1957–October 5, 1971
  April 17, 1972–July 30, 1972

This is the "yuppie" generation that sparked a mass movement toward fitness, health, and career. It is a much more sober, serious, driven generation than the fun-loving Pluto in Leo. During this time, machines were invented to process detail work efficiently. Inventions took a practical turn with answering machines, fax machines, car phones, and home office equipment—all making the workplace far more efficient.

Pluto in Libra

Birth Dates:
  October 5, 1971–April 17, 1972
  July 30, 1972–November 5, 1983
  May 18, 1984–August 27, 1984

A mellower generation, people born at this time are concerned with partnerships, working together, and finding diplomatic solutions to problems. Marriage is important to this generation, and they will redefine it by combining traditional values with equal partnership. This was a time of women's liberation, gay rights, ERA, and legal battles over abortion, all of which transformed our ideas about relationships.

Pluto in Scorpio

Birth Dates:
  November 5, 1983–May 18, 1984
  August 27, 1984–January 17, 1995

Pluto was in the sign it rules for a comparatively short period of time. In 1989, it was at its perihelion, or closest point to the sun and earth. We have all felt the transforming power somewhere in our lives. This was a time of record achievements, destructive sexually transmitted diseases, nuclear power controversies, and explosive political issues. Pluto destroys in order to create new understanding—the phoenix rising from the ashes—which should be some consolation for those of you who felt Pluto's force before 1995. Sexual shockers were par for the course during these intense years when black clothing, transvestites, body piercing, tattoos, and sexually explicit advertising pushed the boundaries of good taste.

Pluto in Sagittarius

Birth Dates:
  January 17, 1995–April 20, 1995
  November 10, 1995–January 27, 2008

During our current Pluto transit, we are being pushed to expand our horizons, to find deeper spiritual meaning in life. Pluto's opposition with Saturn in 2001 brought an enormous conflict between traditional societies and the forces of change. It signals a time when religious convictions will exert more power in our political life as well.

Since Sagittarius is the sign that rules travel, there's a good possibility that Pluto, the planet of extremes, will make space travel a reality for some of us. Already, we are seeing wealthy adventurers paying for the privilege of travel on space shuttles. Discovery of life-forms on other planets could transform our ideas about where we came from.

New dimensions in electronic publishing, concern with animal rights and the environment, and an increasing emphasis on extreme forms of religion are other signs of these times. Look for charismatic religious leaders to arise now. We'll also be developing far-reaching philosophies designed to elevate our lives with a new sense of purpose.

VENUS SIGNS 1901-2005

	Aries	Taurus	Gemini	Cancer	Leo	Virgo
1901	3/29-4/22	4/22-5/17	5/17-6/10	6/10-7/5	7/5-7/29	7/29-8/23
1902	5/7-6/3	6/3-6/30	6/30-7/25	7/25-8/19	8/19-9/13	9/13-10/7
1903	2/28-3/24	3/24-4/18	4/18-5/13	5/13-6/9	6/9-7/7	7/7-8/17
						9/6-11/8
1904	3/13-5/7	5/7-6/1	6/1-6/25	6/25-7/19	7/19-8/13	8/13-9/6
1905	2/3-3/6	3/6-4/9	7/8-8/6	8/6-9/1	9/1-9/27	9/27-10/21
	4/9-5/28	5/28-7/8				
1906	3/1-4/7	4/7-5/2	5/2-5/26	5/26-6/20	6/20-7/16	7/16-8/11
1907	4/27-5/22	5/22-6/16	6/16-7/11	7/11-8/4	8/4-8/29	8/29-9/22
1908	2/14-3/10	3/10-4/5	4/5-5/5	5/5-9/8	9/8-10/8	10/8-11/3
1909	3/29-4/22	4/22-5/16	5/16-6/10	6/10-7/4	7/4-7/29	7/29-8/23
1910	5/7-6/3	6/4-6/29	6/30-7/24	7/25-8/18	8/19-9/12	9/13-10/6
1911	2/28-3/23	3/24-4/17	4/18-5/12	5/13-6/8	6/9-7/7	7/8-11/8
1912	4/13-5/6	5/7-5/31	6/1-6/24	6/24-7/18	7/19-8/12	8/13-9/5
1913	2/3-3/6	3/7-5/1	7/8-8/5	8/6-8/31	9/1-9/26	9/27-10/20
	5/2-5/30	5/31-7/7				
1914	3/14-4/6	4/7-5/1	5/2-5/25	5/26-6/19	6/20-7/15	7/16-8/10
1915	4/27-5/21	5/22-6/15	6/16-7/10	7/11-8/3	8/4-8/28	8/29-9/21
1916	2/14-3/9	3/10-4/5	4/6-5/5	5/6-9/8	9/9-10/7	10/8-11/2
1917	3/29-4/21	4/22-5/15	5/16-6/9	6/10-7/3	7/4-7/28	7/29-8/21
1918	5/7-6/2	6/3-6/28	6/29-7/24	7/25-8/18	8/19-9/11	9/12-10/5
1919	2/27-3/22	3/23-4/16	4/17-5/12	5/13-6/7	6/8-7/7	7/8-11/8
1920	4/12-5/6	5/7-5/30	5/31-6/23	6/24-7/18	7/19-8/11	8/12-9/4
1921	2/3-3/6	3/7-4/25	7/8-8/5	8/6-8/31	9/1-9/25	9/26-10/20
	4/26-6/1	6/2-7/7				
1922	3/13-4/6	4/7-4/30	5/1-5/25	5/26-6/19	6/20-7/14	7/15-8/9
1923	4/27-5/21	5/22-6/14	6/15-7/9	7/10-8/3	8/4-8/27	8/28-9/20
1924	2/13-3/8	3/9-4/4	4/5-5/5	5/6-9/8	9/9-10/7	10/8-11/12
1925	3/28-4/20	4/21-5/15	5/16-6/8	6/9-7/3	7/4-7/27	7/28-8/21

Libra	Scorpio	Sagittarius	Capricorn	Aquarius	Pisces
8/23-9/17	9/17-10/12	10/12-1/16	1/16-2/9	2/9-3/5	3/5-3/29
			11/7-12/5	12/5-1/11	
10/7-10/31	10/31-11/24	11/24-12/18	12/18-1/11	2/6-4/4	1/11-2/6
					4/4-5/7
8/17-9/6	12/9-1/5			1/11-2/4	2/4-2/28
11/8-12/9					
9/6-9/30	9/30-10/25	1/5-1/30	1/30-2/24	2/24-3/19	3/19-4/13
		10/25-11/18	11/18-12/13	12/13-1/7	
10/21-11/14	11/14-12/8	12/8-1/1/06			1/7-2/3
8/11-9/7	9/7-10/9	10/9-12/15	1/1-1/25	1/25-2/18	2/18-3/14
	12/15-12/25	12/25-2/6			
9/22-10/16	10/16-11/9	11/9-12/3	2/6-3/6	3/6-4/2	4/2-4/27
			12/3-12/27	12/27-1/20	
11/3-11/28	11/28-12/22	12/22-1/15			1/20-2/4
8/23-9/17	9/17-10/12	10/12-11/17	1/15-2/9	2/9-3/5	3/5-3/29
			11/17-12/5	12/5-1/15	
10/7-10/30	10/31-11/23	11/24-12/17	12/18-12/31	1/1-1/15	1/16-1/28
				1/29-4/4	4/5-5/6
11/19-12/8	12/9-12/31		1/1-1/10	1/11-2/2	2/3-2/27
9/6-9/30	1/1-1/4	1/5-1/29	1/30-2/23	2/24-3/18	3/19-4/12
	10/1-10/24	10/25-11/17	11/18-12/12	12/13-12/31	
10/21-11/13	11/14-12/7	12/8-12/31		1/1-1/6	1/7-2/2
8/11-9/6	9/7-10/9	10/10-12/5	1/1-1/24	1/25-2/17	2/18-3/13
	12/6-12/30	12/31			
9/22-10/15	10/16-11/8	1/1-2/6	2/7-3/6	3/7-4/1	4/2-4/26
		11/9-12/2	12/3-12/26	12/27-12/31	
11/3-11/27	11/28-12/21	12/22-12/31		1/1-1/19	1/20-2/13
8/22-9/16	9/17-10/11	1/1-1/14	1/15-2/7	2/8-3/4	3/5-3/28
		10/12-11/6	11/7-12/5	12/6-12/31	
10/6-10/29	10/30-11/22	11/23-12/16	12/17-12/31	1/1-4/5	4/6-5/6
11/9-12/8	12/9-12/31		1/1-1/9	1/10-2/2	2/3-2/26
9/5-9/30	1/1-1/3	1/4-1/28	1/29-2/22	2/23-3/18	3/19-4/11
	9/31-10/23	10/24-11/17	11/18-12/11	12/12-12/31	
10/21-11/13	11/14-12/7	12/8-12/31		1/1-1/6	1/7-2/2
8/10-9/6	9/7-10/10	10/11-11/28	1/1-1/24	1/25-2/16	2/17-3/12
	11/29-12/31				
9/21-10/14	1/1	1/2-2/6	2/7-3/5	3/6-3/31	4/1-4/26
	10/15-11/7	11/8-12/1	12/2-12/25	12/26-12/31	
11/13-11/26	11/27-12/21	12/22-12/31		1/1-1/19	1/20-2/12
8/22-9/15	9/16-10/11	1/1-1/14	1/15-2/7	2/8-3/3	3/4-3/27
		10/12-11/6	11/7-12/5	12/6-12/31	

VENUS SIGNS 1901-2005

	Aries	Taurus	Gemini	Cancer	Leo	Virgo
1926	5/7-6/2	6/3-6/28	6/29-7/23	7/24-8/17	8/18-9/11	9/12-10/5
1927	2/27-3/22	3/23-4/16	4/17-5/11	5/12-6/7	6/8-7/7	7/8-11/9
1928	4/12-5/5	5/6-5/29	5/30-6/23	6/24-7/17	7/18-8/11	8/12-9/4
1929	2/3-3/7	3/8-4/19	7/8-8/4	8/5-8/30	8/31-9/25	9/26-10/19
	4/20-6/2	6/3-7/7				
1930	3/13-4/5	4/6-4/30	5/1-5/24	5/25-6/18	6/19-7/14	7/15-8/9
1931	4/26-5/20	5/21-6/13	6/14-7/8	7/9-8/2	8/3-8/26	8/27-9/19
1932	2/12-3/8	3/9-4/3	4/4-5/5	5/6-7/12	9/9-10/6	10/7-11/1
			7/13-7/27	7/28-9/8		
1933	3/27-4/19	4/20-5/28	5/29-6/8	6/9-7/2	7/3-7/26	7/27-8/20
1934	5/6-6/1	6/2-6/27	6/28-7/22	7/23-8/16	8/17-9/10	9/11-10/4
1935	2/26-3/21	3/22-4/15	4/16-5/10	5/11-6/6	6/7-7/6	7/7-11/8
1936	4/11-5/4	5/5-5/28	5/29-6/22	6/23-7/16	7/17-8/10	8/11-9/4
1937	2/2-3/8	3/9-4/13	7/7-8/3	8/4-8/29	8/30-9/24	9/25-10/18
	4/14-6/3	6/4-7/6				
1938	3/12-4/4	4/5-4/28	4/29-5/23	5/24-6/18	6/19-7/13	7/14-8/8
1939	4/25-5/19	5/20-6/13	6/14-7/8	7/9-8/1	8/2-8/25	8/26-9/19
1940	2/12-3/7	3/8-4/3	4/4-5/5	5/6-7/4	9/9-10/5	10/6-10/31
			7/5-7/31	8/1-9/8		
1941	3/27-4/19	4/20-5/13	5/14-6/6	6/7-7/1	7/2-7/26	7/27-8/20
1942	5/6-6/1	6/2-6/26	6/27-7/22	7/23-8/16	8/17-9/9	9/10-10/3
1943	2/25-3/20	3/21-4/14	4/15-5/10	5/11-6/6	6/7-7/6	7/7-11/8
1944	4/10-5/3	5/4-5/28	5/29-6/21	6/22-7/16	7/17-8/9	8/10-9/2
1945	2/2-3/10	3/11-4/6	7/7-8/3	8/4-8/29	8/30-9/23	9/24-10/18
	4/7-6/3	6/4-7/6				
1946	3/11-4/4	4/5-4/28	4/29-5/23	5/24-6/17	6/18-7/12	7/13-8/8
1947	4/25-5/19	5/20-6/12	6/13-7/7	7/8-8/1	8/2-8/25	8/26-9/18
1948	2/11-3/7	3/8-4/3	4/4-5/6	5/7-6/28	9/8-10/5	10/6-10/31
			6/29-8/2	8/3-9/7		
1949	3/26-4/19	4/20-5/13	5/14-6/6	6/7-6/30	7/1-7/25	7/26-8/19
1950	5/5-5/31	6/1-6/26	6/27-7/21	7/22-8/15	8/16-9/9	9/10-10/3
1951	2/25-3/21	3/22-4/15	4/16-5/10	5/11-6/6	6/7-7/7	7/8-11/9

Libra	Scorpio	Sagittarius	Capricorn	Aquarius	Pisces
10/6-10/29	10/30-11/22	11/23-12/16	12/17-12/31	1/1-4/5	4/6-5/6
11/10-12/8	12/9-12/31	1/1-1/7	1/8	1/9-2/1	2/2-2/26
9/5-9/28	1/1-1/3	1/4-1/28	1/29-2/22	2/23-3/17	3/18-4/11
	9/29-10/23	10/24-11/16	11/17-12/11	12/12-12/31	
10/20-11/12	11/13-12/6	12/7-12/30	12/31	1/1-1/5	1/6-2/2
8/10-9/6	9/7-10/11	10/12-11/21	1/1-1/23	1/24-2/16	2/17-3/12
	11/22-12/31				
9/20-10/13	1/1-1/3	1/4-2/6	2/7-3/4	3/5-3/31	4/1-4/25
	10/14-11/6	11/7-11/30	12/1-12/24	12/25-12/31	
11/2-11/25	11/26-12/20	12/21-12/31		1/1-1/18	1/19-2/11
8/21-9/14	9/15-10/10	1/1-1/13	1/14-2/6	2/7-3/2	3/3-3/26
		10/11-11/5	11/6-12/4	12/5-12/31	
10/5-10/28	10/29-11/21	11/22-12/15	12/16-12/31	1/1-4/5	4/6-5/5
11/9-12/7	12/8-12/31		1/1-1/7	1/8-1/31	2/1-2/25
9/5-9/27	1/1-1/2	1/3-1/27	1/28-2/21	2/22-3/16	3/17-4/10
	9/28-10/22	10/23-11/15	11/16-12/10	12/11-12/31	
10/19-11/11	11/12-12/5	12/6-12/29	12/30-12/31	1/1-1/5	1/6-2/1
8/9-9/6	9/7-10/13	10/14-11/14	1/1-1/22	1/23-2/15	2/16-3/11
	11/15-12/31				
9/20-10/13	1/1-1/3	1/4-2/5	2/6-3/4	3/5-3/30	3/31-4/24
	10/14-11/6	11/7-11/30	12/1-12/24	12/25-12/31	
11/1-11/25	11/26-12/19	12/20-12/31		1/1-1/18	1/19-2/11
8/21-9/14	9/15-10/9	1/1-1/12	1/13-2/5	2/6-3/1	3/2-3/26
		10/10-11/5	11/6-12/4	12/5-12/31	
10/4-10/27	10/28-11/20	11/21-12/14	12/15-12/31	1/1-4/5	4/6-5/5
11/9-12/7	12/8-12/31		1/1-1/7	1/8-1/31	2/1-2/24
9/3-9/27	1/1-1/2	1/3-1/27	1/28-2/20	2/21-3/16	3/17-4/9
	9/28-10/21	10/22-11/15	11/16-12/10	12/11-12/31	
10/19-11/11	11/12-12/5	12/6-12/29	12/30-12/31	1/1-1/4	1/5-2/1
8/9-9/6	9/7-10/15	10/16-11/7	1/1-1/21	1/22-2/14	2/15-3/10
	11/8-12/31				
9/19-10/12	1/1-1/4	1/5-2/5	2/6-3/4	3/5-3/29	3/30-4/24
	10/13-11/5	11/6-11/29	11/30-12/23	12/24-12/31	
11/1-11/25	11/26-12/19	12/20-12/31		1/1-1/17	1/18-2/10
8/20-9/14	9/15-10/9	1/1-1/12	1/13-2/5	2/6-3/1	3/2-3/25
		10/10-11/5	11/6-12/5	12/6-12/31	
10/4-10/27	10/28-11/20	11/21-12/13	12/14-12/31	1/1-4/5	4/6-5/4
11/10-12/7	12/8-12/31		1/1-1/7	1/8-1/31	2/1-2/24

VENUS SIGNS 1901–2005

	Aries	Taurus	Gemini	Cancer	Leo	Virgo
1952	4/10-5/4	5/5-5/28	5/29-6/21	6/22-7/16	7/17-8/9	8/10-9/3
1953	2/2-3/3	3/4-3/31	7/8-8/3	8/4-8/29	8/30-9/24	9/25-10/18
	4/1-6/5	6/6-7/7				
1954	3/12-4/4	4/5-4/28	4/29-5/23	5/24-6/17	6/18-7/13	7/14-8/8
1955	4/25-5/19	5/20-6/13	6/14-7/7	7/8-8/1	8/2-8/25	8/26-9/18
1956	2/12-3/7	3/8-4/4	4/5-6/7	5/8-6/23	9/9-10/5	10/6-10/31
			6/24-8/4	8/5-9/8		
1957	3/26-4/19	4/20-5/13	5/14-6/6	6/7-7/1	7/2-7/26	7/27-8/19
1958	5/6-5/31	6/1-6/26	6/27-7/22	7/23-8/15	8/16-9/9	9/10-10/3
1959	2/25-3/20	3/21-4/14	4/15-5/10	5/11-6/6	9/21-9/24	7/9-9/20 9/25-11/9
1960	4/10-5/3	5/4-5/28	5/29-6/21	6/22-7/15	7/16-8/9	8/10-9/2
1961	2/3-6/5	6/6-7/7	7/8-8/3	8/4-8/29	8/30-9/23	9/24-10/17
1962	3/11-4/3	4/4-4/28	4/29-5/22	5/23-6/17	6/18-7/12	7/13-8/8
1963	4/24-5/18	5/19-6/12	6/13-7/7	7/8-7/31	8/1-8/25	8/26-9/18
1964	2/11-3/7	3/8-4/4	4/5-5/9	5/10-6/17	9/9-10/5	10/6-10/31
			6/18-8/5	8/6-9/8		
1965	3/26-4/18	4/19-5/12	5/13-6/6	6/7-6/30	7/1-7/25	7/26-8/19
1966	5/6-6/31	6/1-6/26	6/27-7/21	7/22-8/15	8/16-9/8	9/9-10/2
1967	2/24-3/20	3/21-4/14	4/15-5/10	5/11-6/6	6/7-7/8	7/9-9/9
					9/10-10/1	10/2-11/9
1968	4/9-5/3	5/4-5/27	5/28-6/20	6/21-7/15	7/16-8/8	8/9-9/2
1969	2/3-6/6	6/7-7/6	7/7-8/3	8/4-8/28	8/29-9/22	9/23-10/17
1970	3/11-4/3	4/4-4/27	4/28-5/22	5/23-6/16	6/17-7/12	7/13-8/8
1971	4/24-5/18	5/19-6/12	6/13-7/6	7/7-7/31	8/1-8/24	8/25-9/17
1972	2/11-3/7	3/8-4/3	4/4-5/10	5/11-6/11		
			6/12-8/6	8/7-9/8	9/9-10/5	10/6-10/30
1973	3/25-4/18	4/18-5/12	5/13-6/5	6/6-6/29	7/1-7/25	7/26-8/19
1974	5/5-5/31	6/1-6/25	6/26-7/21	7/22-8/14	8/15-9/8	9/9-10/2
1975	2/24-3/20	3/21-4/13	4/14-5/9	5/10-6/6	6/7-7/9	7/10-9/2
					9/3-10/4	10/5-11/9

84

Libra	Scorpio	Sagittarius	Capricorn	Aquarius	Pisces
9/4-9/27	1/1-1/2	1/3-1/27	1/28-2/20	2/21-3/16	3/17-4/9
	9/28-10/21	10/22-11/15	11/16-12/10	12/11-12/31	
10/19-11/11	11/12-12/5	12/6-12/29	12/30-12/31	1/1-1/5	1/6-2/1
8/9-9/6	9/7-10/22	10/23-10/27	1/1-1/22	1/23-2/15	2/16-3/11
	10/28-12/31				
9/19-10/13	1/1-1/6	1/7-2/5	2/6-3/4	3/5-3/30	3/31-4/24
	10/14-11/5	11/6-11/30	12/1-12/24	12/25-12/31	
11/1-11/25	11/26-12/19	12/20-12/31		1/1-1/17	1/18-2/11
8/20-9/14	9/15-10/9	1/1-1/12	1/13-2/5	2/6-3/1	3/2-3/25
		10/10-11/5	11/6-12/6	12/7-12/31	
10/4-10/27	10/28-11/20	11/21-12/14	12/15-12/31	1/1-4/6	4/7-5/5
11/10-12/7	12/8-12/31		1/1-1/7	1/8-1/31	2/1-2/24
9/3-9/26	1/1-1/2	1/3-1/27	1/28-2/20	2/21-3/15	3/16-4/9
	9/27-10/21	10/22-11/15	11/16-12/10	12/11-12/31	
10/18-11/11	11/12-12/4	12/5-12/28	12/29-12/31	1/1-1/5	1/6-2/2
8/9-9/6	9/7-12/31		1/1-1/21	1/22-2/14	2/15-3/10
9/19-10/12	1/1-1/6	1/7-2/5	2/6-3/4	3/5-3/29	3/30-4/23
	10/13-11/5	11/6-11/29	11/30-12/23	12/24-12/31	
11/1-11/24	11/25-12/19	12/20-12/31		1/1-1/16	1/17-2/10
8/20-9/13	9/14-10/9	1/1-1/12	1/13-2/5	2/6-3/1	3/2-3/25
		10/10-11/5	11/6-12/7	12/8-12/31	
10/3-10/26	10/27-11/19	11/20-12/13	2/7-2/25	1/1-2/6	4/7-5/5
			12/14-12/31	2/26-4/6	
11/10-12/7	12/8-12/31		1/1-1/6	1/7-1/30	1/31-2/23
9/3-9/26	1/1	1/2-1/26	1/27-2/20	2/21-3/15	3/16-4/8
	9/27-10/21	10/22-11/14	11/15-12/9	12/10-12/31	
10/18-11/10	11/11-12/4	12/5-12/28	12/29-12/31	1/1-1/4	1/5-2/2
8/9-9/7	9/8-12/31		1/1-1/21	1/22-2/14	2/15-3/10
9/18-10/11	1/1-1/7	1/8-2/5	2/6-3/4	3/5-3/29	3/30-4/23
	10/12-11/5	11/6-11/29	11/30-12/23	12/24-12/31	
	11/25-12/18	12/19-12/31		1/1-1/16	1/17-2/10
10/31-11/24					
8/20-9/13	9/14-10/8	1/1-1/12	1/13-2/4	2/5-2/28	3/1-3/24
		10/9-11/5	11/6-12/7	12/8-12/31	
			1/30-2/28	1/1-1/29	
10/3-10/26	10/27-11/19	11/20-12/13	12/14-12/31	3/1-4/6	4/7-5/4
11/10-12/7	12/8-12/31		1/1-1/6	1/7-1/30	1/31-2/23

VENUS SIGNS 1901-2005

	Aries	Taurus	Gemini	Cancer	Leo	Virgo
1976	4/8-5/2	5/2-5/27	5/27-6/20	6/20-7/14	7/14-8/8	8/8-9/1
1977	2/2-6/6	6/6-7/6	7/6-8/2	8/2-8/28	8/28-9/22	9/22-10/17
1978	3/9-4/2	4/2-4/27	4/27-5/22	5/22-6/16	6/16-7/12	7/12-8/6
1979	4/23-5/18	5/18-6/11	6/11-7/6	7/6-7/30	7/30-8/24	8/24-9/17
1980	2/9-3/6	3/6-4/3	4/3-5/12	5/12-6/5	9/7-10/4	10/4-10/30
			6/5-8/6	8/6-9/7		
1981	3/24-4/17	4/17-5/11	5/11-6/5	6/5-6/29	6/29-7/24	7/24-8/18
1982	5/4-5/30	5/30-6/25	6/25-7/20	7/20-8/14	8/14-9/7	9/7-10/2
1983	2/22-3/19	3/19-4/13	4/13-5/9	5/9-6/6	6/6-7/10	7/10-8/27
					8/27-10/5	10/5-11/9
1984	4/7-5/2	5/2-5/26	5/26-6/20	6/20-7/14	7/14-8/7	8/7-9/1
1985	2/2-6/6	6/7-7/6	7/6-8/2	8/2-8/28	8/28-9/22	9/22-10/16
1986	3/9-4/2	4/2-4/26	4/26-5/21	5/21-6/15	6/15-7/11	7/11-8/7
1987	4/22-5/17	5/17-6/11	6/11-7/5	7/5-7/30	7/30-8/23	8/23-9/16
1988	2/9-3/6	3/6-4/3	4/3-5/17	5/17-5/27	9/7-10/4	10/4-10/29
			5/27-8/6	8/28-9/22	9/22-10/16	
1989	3/23-4/16	4/16-5/11	5/11-6/4	6/4-6/29	6/29-7/24	7/24-8/18
1990	5/4-5/30	5/30-6/25	6/25-7/20	7/20-8/13	8/13-9/7	9/7-10/1
1991	2/22-3/18	3/18-4/13	4/13-5/9	5/9-6/6	6/6-7/11	7/11-8/21
					8/21-10/6	10/6-11/9
1992	4/7-5/1	5/1-5/26	5/26-6/19	6/19-7/13	7/13-8/7	8/7-8/31
1993	2/2-6/6	6/6-7/6	7/6-8/1	8/1-8/27	8/27-9/21	9/21-10/16
1994	3/8-4/1	4/1-4/26	4/26-5/21	5/21-6/15	6/15-7/11	7/11-8/7
1995	4/22-5/16	5/16-6/10	6/10-7/5	7/5-7/29	7/29-8/23	8/23-9/16
1996	2/9-3/6	3/6-4/3	4/3-8/7	8/7-9/7	9/7-10/4	10/4-10/29
1997	3/23-4/16	4/16-5/10	5/10-6/4	6/4-6/28	6/28-7/23	7/23-8/17
1998	5/3-5/29	5/29-6/24	6/24-7/19	7/19-8/13	8/13-9/6	9/6-9/30
1999	2/21-3/18	3/18-4/12	4/12-5/8	5/8-6/5	6/5-7/12	7/12-8/15
					8/15-10/7	10/7-11/9
2000	4/6-5/1	5/1-5/25	5/25-6/13	6/13-7/13	7/13-8/6	8/6-8/31
2001	2/2-6/6	6/6-7/5	7/5-8/1	8/1-8/26	8/26-9/20	9/20-10/15
2002	3/7-4/1	4/1-4/25	4/25-5/20	5/20-6/14	6/14-7/10	7/10-8/7
2003	4/21-5/16	5/16-6/9	6/9-7/4	7/4-7/29	7/29-8/22	8/22-9/15
2004	2/8-3/5	3/5-4/3	4/3-8/7	8/7-9/6	9/6-10/3	10/3-10/28
2005	3/22-4/15	4/15-5/10	5/10-6/3	6/3-6/28	6/28-7/23	7/23-8/17

Libra	Scorpio	Sagittarius	Capricorn	Aquarius	Pisces
9/1-9/26	9/26-10/20	1/1-1/26	1/26-2/19	2/19-3/15	3/15-4/8
10/17-11/10	11/10-12/4	12/4-12/27	12/27-1/20/78		1/4-2/2
8/6-9/7	9/7-1/7			1/20-2/13	2/13-3/9
9/17-10/11	10/11-11/4	1/7-2/5	2/5-3/3	3/3-3/29	3/29-4/23
		11/4-11/28	11/28-12/22	12/22-1/16/80	
10/30-11/24	11/24-12/18	12/18-1/11/81			1/16-2/9
8/18-9/12	9/12-10/9	10/9-11/5	1/11-2/4	2/4-2/28	2/28-3/24
			11/5-12/8	12/8-1/23/82	
10/2-10/26	10/26-11/18	11/18-12/12	1/23-3/2	3/2-4/6	4/6-5/4
			12/12-1/5/83		
11/9-12/6	12/6-1/1/84			1/5-1/29	1/29-2/22
9/1-9/25	9/25-10/20	1/1-1/25	1/25-2/19	2/19-3/14	3/14-4/7
		10/20-11/13	11/13-12/9	12/10-1/4	
10/16-11/9	11/9-12/3	12/3-12/27	12/28-1/19		1/4-2/2
8/7-9/7	9/7-1/7			1/20-2/13	2/13-3/9
9/16-10/10	10/10-11/3	1/7-2/5	2/5-3/3	3/3-3/28	3/28-4/22
		11/3-11/28	11/28-12/22	12/22-1/15	
10/29-11/23	11/23-12/17	12/17-1/10			1/15-2/9
8/18-9/12	9/12-10/8	10/8-11/5	1/10-2/3	2/3-2/27	2/27-3/23
			11/5-12/10	12/10-1/16/90	
10/1-10/25	10/25-11/18	11/18-12/12	1/16-3/3	3/3-4/6	4/6-5/4
			12/12-1/5		
11/9-12/6	12/6-12/31	12/31-1/25/92		1/5-1/29	1/29-2/22
8/31-9/25	9/25-10/19	10/19-11/13	1/25-2/18	2/18-3/13	3/13-4/7
			11/13-12/8	12/8-1/3/93	
10/16-11/9	11/9-12/2	12/2-12/26	12/26-1/19		1/3-2/2
8/7-9/7	9/7-1/7			1/19-2/12	2/12-3/8
9/16-10/10	10/10-11/13	1/7-2/4	2/4-3/2	3/2-3/28	3/28-4/22
		11/3-11/27	11/27-12/21	12/21-1/15	
10/29-11/23	11/23-12/17	12/17-1/10/97			1/15-2/9
8/17-9/12	9/12-10/8	10/8-11/5	1/10-2/3	2/3-2/27	2/27-3/23
			11/5-12/12	12/12-1/9	
9/30-10/24	10/24-11/17	11/17-12/11	1/9-3/4	3/4-4/6	4/6-5/3
11/9-12/5	12/5-12/31	12/31-1/24		1/4-1/28	1/28-2/21
8/31-9/24	9/24-10/19	10/19-11/13	1/24-2/18	2/18-3/12	3/13-4/6
			11/13-12/8	12/8	
10/15-11/8	11/8-12/2	12/2-12/26	12/26/01– 12 1/18/02	/8/00-1/3/01	1/3-2/2
8/7-9/7	9/7-1/7/03		12/26/01-1/18	1/18-2/11	2/11-3/7
9/15-10/9	10/9-11/2	1/7-2/4	2/4-3/2	3/2-3/27	3/27-4/21
		11/2-11/26	11/26-12/21	12/21-1/14/04	
10/28-11/22	11/22-12/16	12/16-1/9/05		1/1-1/14	1/14-2/8
8/17-9/11	9/11-10/8	10/8-11/15	1/9-2/2	2/2-2/26	2/26-3/22
			11/5-12/15	12/15-1/1/06	

How to Use the Mars, Jupiter, and Saturn Tables

Find the year of your birth on the left side of each column. The dates when the planet entered each sign are listed on the right side of each column. (Signs are abbreviated to three letters.) Your birthday should fall on or between each date listed, and your planetary placement should correspond to the earlier sign of that period.

MARS SIGNS 1901–2005

Year	Month	Day	Sign		Year	Month	Day	Sign
1901	MAR	1	Leo		1905	JAN	13	Scp
	MAY	11	Vir			AUG	21	Sag
	JUL	13	Lib			OCT	8	Cap
	AUG	31	Scp			NOV	18	Aqu
	OCT	14	Sag			DEC	27	Pic
	NOV	24	Cap		1906	FEB	4	Ari
1902	JAN	1	Aqu			MAR	17	Tau
	FEB	8	Pic			APR	28	Gem
	MAR	19	Ari			JUN	11	Can
	APR	27	Tau			JUL	27	Leo
	JUN	7	Gem			SEP	12	Vir
	JUL	20	Can			OCT	30	Lib
	SEP	4	Leo			DEC	17	Scp
	OCT	23	Vir		1907	FEB	5	Sag
	DEC	20	Lib			APR	1	Cap
1903	APR	19	Vir			OCT	13	Aqu
	MAY	30	Lib			NOV	29	Pic
	AUG	6	Scp		1908	JAN	11	Ari
	SEP	22	Sag			FEB	23	Tau
	NOV	3	Cap			APR	7	Gem
	DEC	12	Aqu			MAY	22	Can
1904	JAN	19	Pic			JUL	8	Leo
	FEB	27	Ari			AUG	24	Vir
	APR	6	Tau			OCT	10	Lib
	MAY	18	Gem			NOV	25	Scp
	JUN	30	Can		1909	JAN	10	Sag
	AUG	15	Leo			FEB	24	Cap
	OCT	1	Vir			APR	9	Aqu
	NOV	20	Lib			MAY	25	Pic

	JUL	21	Ari		AUG	19	Can
	SEP	26	Pic		OCT	7	Leo
	NOV	20	Ari	1916	MAY	28	Vir
1910	JAN	23	Tau		JUL	23	Lib
	MAR	14	Gem		SEP	8	Scp
	MAY	1	Can		OCT	22	Sag
	JUN	19	Leo		DEC	1	Cap
	AUG	6	Vir	1917	JAN	9	Aqu
	SEP	22	Lib		FEB	16	Pic
	NOV	6	Scp		MAR	26	Ari
	DEC	20	Sag		MAY	4	Tau
1911	JAN	31	Cap		JUN	14	Gem
	MAR	14	Aqu		JUL	28	Can
	APR	23	Pic		SEP	12	Leo
	JUN	2	Ari		NOV	2	Vir
	JUL	15	Tau	1918	JAN	11	Lib
	SEP	5	Gem		FEB	25	Vir
	NOV	30	Tau		JUN	23	Lib
1912	JAN	30	Gem		AUG	17	Scp
	APR	5	Can		OCT	1	Sag
	MAY	28	Leo		NOV	11	Cap
	JUL	17	Vir		DEC	20	Aqu
	SEP	2	Lib	1919	JAN	27	Pic
	OCT	18	Scp		MAR	6	Ari
	NOV	30	Sag		APR	15	Tau
1913	JAN	10	Cap		MAY	26	Gem
	FEB	19	Aqu		JUL	8	Can
	MAR	30	Pic		AUG	23	Leo
	MAY	8	Ari		OCT	10	Vir
	JUN	17	Tau		NOV	30	Lib
	JUL	29	Gem	1920	JAN	31	Scp
	SEP	15	Can		APR	23	Lib
1914	MAY	1	Leo		JUL	10	Scp
	JUN	26	Vir		SEP	4	Sag
	AUG	14	Lib		OCT	18	Cap
	SEP	29	Scp		NOV	27	Aqu
	NOV	11	Sag	1921	JAN	5	Pic
	DEC	22	Cap		FEB	13	Ari
1915	JAN	30	Aqu		MAR	25	Tau
	MAR	9	Pic		MAY	6	Gem
	APR	16	Ari		JUN	18	Can
	MAY	26	Tau		AUG	3	Leo
	JUL	6	Gem		SEP	19	Vir

	NOV	6	Lib	APR	7	Pic
	DEC	26	Scp	MAY	16	Ari
1922	FEB	18	Sag	JUN	26	Tau
	SEP	13	Cap	AUG	9	Gem
	OCT	30	Aqu	OCT	3	Can
	DEC	11	Pic	DEC	20	Gem
1923	JAN	21	Ari	1929 MAR	10	Can
	MAR	4	Tau	MAY	13	Leo
	APR	16	Gem	JUL	4	Vir
	MAY	30	Can	AUG	21	Lib
	JUL	16	Leo	OCT	6	Scp
	SEP	1	Vir	NOV	18	Sag
	OCT	18	Lib	DEC	29	Cap
	DEC	4	Scp	1930 FEB	6	Aqu
1924	JAN	19	Sag	MAR	17	Pic
	MAR	6	Cap	APR	24	Ari
	APR	24	Aqu	JUN	3	Tau
	JUN	24	Pic	JUL	14	Gem
	AUG	24	Aqu	AUG	28	Can
	OCT	19	Pic	OCT	20	Leo
	DEC	19	Ari	1931 FEB	16	Can
1925	FEB	5	Tau	MAR	30	Leo
	MAR	24	Gem	JUN	10	Vir
	MAY	9	Can	AUG	1	Lib
	JUN	26	Leo	SEP	17	Scp
	AUG	12	Vir	OCT	30	Sag
	SEP	28	Lib	DEC	10	Cap
	NOV	13	Scp	1932 JAN	18	Aqu
	DEC	28	Sag	FEB	25	Pic
1926	FEB	9	Cap	APR	3	Ari
	MAR	23	Aqu	MAY	12	Tau
	MAY	3	Pic	JUN	22	Gem
	JUN	15	Ari	AUG	4	Can
	AUG	1	Tau	SEP	20	Leo
1927	FEB	22	Gem	NOV	13	Vir
	APR	17	Can	1933 JUL	6	Lib
	JUN	6	Leo	AUG	26	Scp
	JUL	25	Vir	OCT	9	Sag
	SEP	10	Lib	NOV	19	Cap
	OCT	26	Scp	DEC	28	Aqu
	DEC	8	Sag	1934 FEB	4	Pic
1928	JAN	19	Cap	MAR	14	Ari
	FEB	28	Aqu	APR	22	Tau

	JUN	2	Gem		AUG	19	Vir
	JUL	15	Can		OCT	5	Lib
	AUG	30	Leo		NOV	20	Scp
	OCT	18	Vir	1941	JAN	4	Sag
	DEC	11	Lib		FEB	17	Cap
1935	JUL	29	Scp		APR	2	Aqu
	SEP	16	Sag		MAY	16	Pic
	OCT	28	Cap		JUL	2	Ari
	DEC	7	Aqu	1942	JAN	11	Tau
1936	JAN	14	Pic		MAR	7	Gem
	FEB	22	Ari		APR	26	Can
	APR	1	Tau		JUN	14	Leo
	MAY	13	Gem		AUG	1	Vir
	JUN	25	Can		SEP	17	Lib
	AUG	10	Leo		NOV	1	Scp
	SEP	26	Vir		DEC	15	Sag
	NOV	14	Lib	1943	JAN	26	Cap
1937	JAN	5	Scp		MAR	8	Aqu
	MAR	13	Sag		APR	17	Pic
	MAY	14	Scp		MAY	27	Ari
	AUG	8	Sag		JUL	7	Tau
	SEP	30	Cap		AUG	23	Gem
	NOV	11	Aqu	1944	MAR	28	Can
	DEC	21	Pic		MAY	22	Leo
1938	JAN	30	Ari		JUL	12	Vir
	MAR	12	Tau		AUG	29	Lib
	APR	23	Gem		OCT	13	Scp
	JUN	7	Can		NOV	25	Sag
	JUL	22	Leo	1945	JAN	5	Cap
	SEP	7	Vir		FEB	14	Aqu
	OCT	25	Lib		MAR	25	Pic
	DEC	11	Scp		MAY	2	Ari
1939	JAN	29	Sag		JUN	11	Tau
	MAR	21	Cap		JUL	23	Gem
	MAY	25	Aqu		SEP	7	Can
	JUL	21	Cap		NOV	11	Leo
	SEP	24	Aqu		DEC	26	Can
	NOV	19	Pic	1946	APR	22	Leo
1940	JAN	4	Ari		JUN	20	Vir
	FEB	17	Tau		AUG	9	Lib
	APR	1	Gem		SEP	24	Scp
	MAY	17	Can		NOV	6	Sag
	JUL	3	Leo		DEC	17	Cap

1947	JAN	25	Aqu		MAR	20	Tau
	MAR	4	Pic		MAY	1	Gem
	APR	11	Ari		JUN	14	Can
	MAY	21	Tau		JUL	29	Leo
	JUL	1	Gem		SEP	14	Vir
	AUG	13	Can		NOV	1	Lib
	OCT	1	Leo		DEC	20	Scp
	DEC	1	Vir	1954	FEB	9	Sag
1948	FEB	12	Leo		APR	12	Cap
	MAY	18	Vir		JUL	3	Sag
	JUL	17	Lib		AUG	24	Cap
	SEP	3	Scp		OCT	21	Aqu
	OCT	17	Sag		DEC	4	Pic
	NOV	26	Cap	1955	JAN	15	Ari
1949	JAN	4	Aqu		FEB	26	Tau
	FEB	11	Pic		APR	10	Gem
	MAR	21	Ari		MAY	26	Can
	APR	30	Tau		JUL	11	Leo
	JUN	10	Gem		AUG	27	Vir
	JUL	23	Can		OCT	13	Lib
	SEP	7	Leo		NOV	29	Scp
	OCT	27	Vir	1956	JAN	14	Sag
	DEC	26	Lib		FEB	28	Cap
1950	MAR	28	Vir		APR	14	Aqu
	JUN	11	Lib		JUN	3	Pic
	AUG	10	Scp		DEC	6	Ari
	SEP	25	Sag	1957	JAN	28	Tau
	NOV	6	Cap		MAR	17	Gem
	DEC	15	Aqu		MAY	4	Can
1951	JAN	22	Pic		JUN	21	Leo
	MAR	1	Ari		AUG	8	Vir
	APR	10	Tau		SEP	24	Lib
	MAY	21	Gem		NOV	8	Scp
	JUL	3	Can		DEC	23	Sag
	AUG	18	Leo	1958	FEB	3	Cap
	OCT	5	Vir		MAR	17	Aqu
	NOV	24	Lib		APR	27	Pic
1952	JAN	20	Scp		JUN	7	Ari
	AUG	27	Sag		JUL	21	Tau
	OCT	12	Cap		SEP	21	Gem
	NOV	21	Aqu		OCT	29	Tau
	DEC	30	Pic	1959	FEB	10	Gem
1953	FEB	8	Ari		APR	10	Can

	JUN	1	Leo		NOV	14	Cap
	JUL	20	Vir		DEC	23	Aqu
	SEP	5	Lib	1966	JAN	30	Pic
	OCT	21	Scp		MAR	9	Ari
	DEC	3	Sag		APR	17	Tau
1960	JAN	14	Cap		MAY	28	Gem
	FEB	23	Aqu		JUL	11	Can
	APR	2	Pic		AUG	25	Leo
	MAY	11	Ari		OCT	12	Vir
	JUN	20	Tau		DEC	4	Lib
	AUG	2	Gem	1967	FEB	12	Scp
	SEP	21	Can		MAR	31	Lib
1961	FEB	5	Gem		JUL	19	Scp
	FEB	7	Can		SEP	10	Sag
	MAY	6	Leo		OCT	23	Cap
	JUN	28	Vir		DEC	1	Aqu
	AUG	17	Lib	1968	JAN	9	Pic
	OCT	1	Scp		FEB	17	Ari
	NOV	13	Sag		MAR	27	Tau
	DEC	24	Cap		MAY	8	Gem
1962	FEB	1	Aqu		JUN	21	Can
	MAR	12	Pic		AUG	5	Leo
	APR	19	Ari		SEP	21	Vir
	MAY	28	Tau		NOV	9	Lib
	JUL	9	Gem		DEC	29	Scp
	AUG	22	Can	1969	FEB	25	Sag
	OCT	11	Leo		SEP	21	Cap
1963	JUN	3	Vir		NOV	4	Aqu
	JUL	27	Lib		DEC	15	Pic
	SEP	12	Scp	1970	JAN	24	Ari
	OCT	25	Sag		MAR	7	Tau
	DEC	5	Cap		APR	18	Gem
1964	JAN	13	Aqu		JUN	2	Can
	FEB	20	Pic		JUL	18	Leo
	MAR	29	Ari		SEP	3	Vir
	MAY	7	Tau		OCT	20	Lib
	JUN	17	Gem		DEC	6	Scp
	JUL	30	Can	1971	JAN	23	Sag
	SEP	15	Leo		MAR	12	Cap
	NOV	6	Vir		MAY	3	Aqu
1965	JUN	29	Lib		NOV	6	Pic
	AUG	20	Scp		DEC	26	Ari
	OCT	4	Sag	1972	FEB	10	Tau

	MAR	27	Gem	1978	JAN	26	Can
	MAY	12	Can		APR	10	Leo
	JUN	28	Leo		JUN	14	Vir
	AUG	15	Vir		AUG	4	Lib
	SEP	30	Lib		SEP	19	Scp
	NOV	15	Scp		NOV	2	Sag
	DEC	30	Sag		DEC	12	Cap
1973	FEB	12	Cap	1979	JAN	20	Aqu
	MAR	26	Aqu		FEB	27	Pic
	MAY	8	Pic		APR	7	Ari
	JUN	20	Ari		MAY	16	Tau
	AUG	12	Tau		JUN	26	Gem
	OCT	29	Ari		AUG	8	Can
	DEC	24	Tau		SEP	24	Leo
1974	FEB	27	Gem		NOV	19	Vir
	APR	20	Can	1980	MAR	11	Leo
	JUN	9	Leo		MAY	4	Vir
	JUL	27	Vir		JUL	10	Lib
	SEP	12	Lib		AUG	29	Scp
	OCT	28	Scp		OCT	12	Sag
	DEC	10	Sag		NOV	22	Cap
1975	JAN	21	Cap		DEC	30	Aqu
	MAR	3	Aqu	1981	FEB	6	Pic
	APR	11	Pic		MAR	17	Ari
	MAY	21	Ari		APR	25	Tau
	JUL	1	Tau		JUN	5	Gem
	AUG	14	Gem		JUL	18	Can
	OCT	17	Can		SEP	2	Leo
	NOV	25	Gem		OCT	21	Vir
1976	MAR	18	Can		DEC	16	Lib
	MAY	16	Leo	1982	AUG	3	Scp
	JUL	6	Vir		SEP	20	Sag
	AUG	24	Lib		OCT	31	Cap
	OCT	8	Scp		DEC	10	Aqu
	NOV	20	Sag	1983	JAN	17	Pic
1977	JAN	1	Cap		FEB	25	Ari
	FEB	9	Aqu		APR	5	Tau
	MAR	20	Pic		MAY	16	Gem
	APR	27	Ari		JUN	29	Can
	JUN	6	Tau		AUG	13	Leo
	JUL	17	Gem		SEP	30	Vir
	SEP	1	Can		NOV	18	Lib
	OCT	26	Leo	1984	JAN	11	Scp

	AUG	17	Sag		JUL	12	Tau
	OCT	5	Cap		AUG	31	Gem
	NOV	15	Aqu		DEC	14	Tau
	DEC	25	Pic	1991	JAN	21	Gem
1985	FEB	2	Ari		APR	3	Can
	MAR	15	Tau		MAY	26	Leo
	APR	26	Gem		JUL	15	Vir
	JUN	9	Can		SEP	1	Lib
	JUL	25	Leo		OCT	16	Scp
	SEP	10	Vir		NOV	29	Sag
	OCT	27	Lib	1992	JAN	9	Cap
	DEC	14	Scp		FEB	18	Aqu
1986	FEB	2	Sag		MAR	28	Pic
	MAR	28	Cap		MAY	5	Ari
	OCT	9	Aqu		JUN	14	Tau
	NOV	26	Pic		JUL	26	Gem
1987	JAN	8	Ari		SEP	12	Can
	FEB	20	Tau	1993	APR	27	Leo
	APR	5	Gem		JUN	23	Vir
	MAY	21	Can		AUG	12	Lib
	JUL	6	Leo		SEP	27	Scp
	AUG	22	Vir		NOV	9	Sag
	OCT	8	Lib		DEC	20	Cap
	NOV	24	Scp	1994	JAN	28	Aqu
1988	JAN	8	Sag		MAR	7	Pic
	FEB	22	Cap		APR	14	Ari
	APR	6	Aqu		MAY	23	Tau
	MAY	22	Pic		JUL	3	Gem
	JUL	13	Ari		AUG	16	Can
	OCT	23	Pic		OCT	4	Leo
	NOV	1	Ari		DEC	12	Vir
1989	JAN	19	Tau	1995	JAN	22	Leo
	MAR	11	Gem		MAY	25	Vir
	APR	29	Can		JUL	21	Lib
	JUN	16	Leo		SEP	7	Scp
	AUG	3	Vir		OCT	20	Sag
	SEP	19	Lib		NOV	30	Cap
	NOV	4	Scp	1996	JAN	8	Aqu
	DEC	18	Sag		FEB	15	Pic
1990	JAN	29	Cap		MAR	24	Ari
	MAR	11	Aqu		MAY	2	Tau
	APR	20	Pic		JUN	12	Gem
	MAY	31	Ari		JUL	25	Can

	SEP	9	Leo
	OCT	30	Vir
1997	JAN	3	Lib
	MAR	8	Vir
	JUN	19	Lib
	AUG	14	Scp
	SEP	28	Sag
	NOV	9	Cap
	DEC	18	Aqu
1998	JAN	25	Pic
	MAR	4	Ari
	APR	13	Tau
	MAY	24	Gem
	JUL	6	Can
	AUG	20	Leo
	OCT	7	Vir
	NOV	27	Lib
1999	JAN	26	Scp
	MAY	5	Lib
	JUL	5	Scp
	SEP	2	Sag
	OCT	17	Cap
	NOV	26	Aqu
2000	JAN	4	Pic
	FEB	12	Ari
	MAR	23	Tau
	MAY	3	Gem
	JUN	16	Can
	AUG	1	Leo
	SEP	17	Vir
	NOV	4	Lib
	DEC	23	Scp
2001	FEB	14	Sag
	SEP	8	Cap
	OCT	27	Aqu
	DEC	8	Pic
2002	JAN	18	Ari
	MAR	1	Tau
	APR	13	Gem
	MAY	28	Can
	JUL	13	Leo
	AUG	29	Vir
	OCT	15	Lib
	DEC	1	Scp
2003	JAN	17	Sag
	MAR	4	Cap
	APR	21	Aqu
	JUN	17	Pic
	DEC	16	Ari
2004	FEB	3	Tau
	MAR	21	Gem
	MAY	7	Can
	JUN	23	Leo
	AUG	10	Vir
	SEP	26	Lib
	NOV	11	Sep
	DEC	25	Sag
2005	FEB	6	Cap
	MAR	20	Aqu
	MAY	1	Pic
	JUN	12	Ari
	JUL	28	Tau

JUPITER SIGNS 1901–2005

1901	JAN	19	Cap
1902	FEB	6	Aqu
1903	FEB	20	Pic
1904	MAR	1	Ari
	AUG	8	Tau
	AUG	31	Ari
1905	MAR	7	Tau
	JUL	21	Gem
	DEC	4	Tau
1906	MAR	9	Gem
	JUL	30	Can
1907	AUG	18	Leo
1908	SEP	12	Vir
1909	OCT	11	Lib

1910	NOV	11	Scp	1943	JUN	30	Leo
1911	DEC	10	Sag	1944	JUL	26	Vir
1913	JAN	2	Cap	1945	AUG	25	Lib
1914	JAN	21	Aqu	1946	SEP	25	Scp
1915	FEB	4	Pic	1947	OCT	24	Sag
1916	FEB	12	Ari	1948	NOV	15	Cap
	JUN	26	Tau	1949	APR	12	Aqu
	OCT	26	Ari		JUN	27	Cap
1917	FEB	12	Tau		NOV	30	Aqu
	JUN	29	Gem	1950	APR	15	Pic
1918	JUL	13	Can		SEP	15	Aqu
1919	AUG	2	Leo		DEC	1	Pic
1920	AUG	27	Vir	1951	APR	21	Ari
1921	SEP	25	Lib	1952	APR	28	Tau
1922	OCT	26	Scp	1953	MAY	9	Gem
1923	NOV	24	Sag	1954	MAY	24	Can
1924	DEC	18	Cap	1955	JUN	13	Leo
1926	JAN	6	Aqu		NOV	17	Vir
1927	JAN	18	Pic	1956	JAN	18	Leo
	JUN	6	Ari		JUL	7	Vir
	SEP	11	Pic		DEC	13	Lib
1928	JAN	23	Ari	1957	FEB	19	Vir
	JUN	4	Tau		AUG	7	Lib
1929	JUN	12	Gem	1958	JAN	13	Scp
1930	JUN	26	Can		MAR	20	Lib
1931	JUL	17	Leo		SEP	7	Scp
1932	AUG	11	Vir	1959	FEB	10	Sag
1933	SEP	10	Lib		APR	24	Scp
1934	OCT	11	Scp		OCT	5	Sag
1935	NOV	9	Sag	1960	MAR	1	Cap
1936	DEC	2	Cap		JUN	10	Sag
1937	DEC	20	Aqu		OCT	26	Cap
1938	MAY	14	Pic	1961	MAR	15	Aqu
	JUL	30	Aqu		AUG	12	Cap
	DEC	29	Pic		NOV	4	Aqu
1939	MAY	11	Ari	1962	MAR	25	Pic
	OCT	30	Pic	1963	APR	4	Ari
	DEC	20	Ari	1964	APR	12	Tau
1940	MAY	16	Tau	1965	APR	22	Gem
1941	MAY	26	Gem		SEP	21	Can
1942	JUN	10	Can		NOV	17	Gem

1966	MAY	5	Can		SEP	29	Vir
	SEP	27	Leo	1980	OCT	27	Lib
1967	JAN	16	Can	1981	NOV	27	Scp
	MAY	23	Leo	1982	DEC	26	Sag
	OCT	19	Vir	1984	JAN	19	Cap
1968	FEB	27	Leo	1985	FEB	6	Aqu
	JUN	15	Vir	1986	FEB	20	Pic
	NOV	15	Lib	1987	MAR	2	Ari
1969	MAR	30	Vir	1988	MAR	8	Tau
	JUL	15	Lib		JUL	22	Gem
	DEC	16	Scp		NOV	30	Tau
1970	APR	30	Lib	1989	MAR	11	Gem
	AUG	15	Scp		JUL	30	Can
1971	JAN	14	Sag	1990	AUG	18	Leo
	JUN	5	Scp	1991	SEP	12	Vir
	SEP	11	Sag	1992	OCT	10	Lib
1972	FEB	6	Cap	1993	NOV	10	Scp
	JUL	24	Sag	1994	DEC	9	Sag
	SEP	25	Cap	1996	JAN	3	Cap
1973	FEB	23	Aqu	1997	JAN	21	Aqu
1974	MAR	8	Pic	1998	FEB	4	Pic
1975	MAR	18	Ari	1999	FEB	13	Ari
1976	MAR	26	Tau		JUN	28	Tau
	AUG	23	Gem		OCT	23	Ari
	OCT	16	Tau	2000	FEB	14	Tau
1977	APR	3	Gem		JUN	30	Gem
	AUG	20	Can	2001	JUL	14	Can
	DEC	30	Gem	2002	AUG	1	Leo
1978	APR	12	Can	2003	AUG	27	Vir
	SEP	5	Leo	2004	SEP	24	Lib
1979	FEB	28	Can	2005	OCT	26	Scp
	APR	20	Leo				

SATURN SIGNS 1903–2005

1903	JAN	19	Aqu	1910	MAY	17	Tau
1905	APR	13	Pic		DEC	14	Ari
	AUG	17	Aqu	1911	JAN	20	Tau
1906	JAN	8	Pic	1912	JUL	7	Gem
1908	MAR	19	Ari		NOV	30	Tau

Year	Month	Day	Sign		Year	Month	Day	Sign
1913	MAR	26	Gem		1962	JAN	3	Aqu
1914	AUG	24	Can		1964	MAR	24	Pic
	DEC	7	Gem			SEP	16	Aqu
1915	MAY	11	Can			DEC	16	Pic
1916	OCT	17	Leo		1967	MAR	3	Ari
	DEC	7	Can		1969	APR	29	Tau
1917	JUN	24	Leo		1971	JUN	18	Gem
1919	AUG	12	Vir		1972	JAN	10	Tau
1921	OCT	7	Lib			FEB	21	Gem
1923	DEC	20	Scp		1973	AUG	1	Can
1924	APR	6	Lib		1974	JAN	7	Gem
	SEP	13	Scp			APR	18	Can
1926	DEC	2	Sag		1975	SEP	17	Leo
1929	MAR	15	Cap		1976	JAN	14	Can
	MAY	5	Sag			JUN	5	Leo
	NOV	30	Cap		1977	NOV	17	Vir
1932	FEB	24	Aqu		1978	JAN	5	Leo
	AUG	13	Cap			JUL	26	Vir
	NOV	20	Aqu		1980	SEP	21	Lib
1935	FEB	14	Pic		1982	NOV	29	Scp
1937	APR	25	Ari		1983	MAY	6	Lib
	OCT	18	Pic			AUG	24	Scp
1938	JAN	14	Ari		1985	NOV	17	Sag
1939	JUL	6	Tau		1988	FEB	13	Cap
	SEP	22	Ari			JUN	10	Sag
1940	MAR	20	Tau			NOV	12	Cap
1942	MAY	8	Gem		1991	FEB	6	Aqu
1944	JUN	20	Can		1993	MAY	21	Pic
1946	AUG	2	Leo			JUN	30	Aqu
1948	SEP	19	Vir		1994	JAN	28	Pic
1949	APR	3	Leo		1996	APR	7	Ari
	MAY	29	Vir		1998	JUN	9	Tau
1950	NOV	20	Lib			OCT	25	Ari
1951	MAR	7	Vir		1999	MAR	1	Tau
	AUG	13	Lib		2000	AUG	10	Gem
1953	OCT	22	Scp			OCT	16	Tau
1956	JAN	12	Sag		2001	APR	21	Gem
	MAY	14	Scp		2003	JUN	3	Can
	OCT	10	Sag		2005	JUL	16	Leo
1959	JAN	5	Cap					

CHAPTER 5

Why You Should Know Your Rising Sign

What makes a horoscope truly yours is your rising sign, also called the ascendant. It determines the way your chart is set up and the location of planets within the chart.

The rising sign is the sign of the zodiac passing over the eastern horizon at the very moment you were born. As the earth turns, a different sign rises over the horizon every two hours. This explains why other babies who were born in the same place, but later or earlier on the same day, would have a different chart. Even though the planets would be in the same signs, the rising sign would be earlier or later. Therefore, the planets would be in another place, or house, in their horoscopes, emphasizing different areas of their lives.

If you have read the description of the houses in chapter 3 of this book, you'll know that the houses are twelve stationary divisions of the horoscope, which represent areas of life. The sign moving over the boundary (cusp) of each house describes that area of life.

The rising sign rules the first house, which is the physical body, your outward appearance, your style, tastes, health, and physical environment (where you are most comfortable working and living). After the rising sign is determined, then each of the next eleven houses in the chart will be influenced by the signs following in sequence.

When we know the rising sign of a chart, then we know where to put each planet. Without a valid rising sign, your collection of planets would have no homes.

Once the rising sign is established, it becomes possible

to analyze a chart accurately because the astrologer knows in which house or area of life the planets will operate. For instance, if Mars is in Gemini and your rising sign is in Taurus, then Mars will most likely be active in the second house, the house of finances, of your chart. If you were born later in the day and your rising sign is Virgo, then Mars will be positioned at the top of your chart, energizing your tenth house, the house of career.

Many astrologers insist on knowing the exact time of a client's birth before they will analyze a chart. The more exact your birth time, the more accurately an astrologer can position the planets in your chart.

Your rising sign has an important relationship with your sun sign. Some will complement the sun sign; others hide it under a totally different mask, as if playing an entirely different role, making it difficult to guess the person's sun sign from outer appearances. This may be the reason why you might not look or act like your sun sign's archetype. For example, a Leo with a conservative Capricorn ascendant would come across as much more serious than a Leo with a fiery Aries or Sagittarius ascendant.

It is usually the rising sign that creates the first impression you make. However, if the sun sign is accompanied by other planets in the same sign, this might overpower the impression of the rising sign. For instance, a Leo sun plus a Leo Venus and Leo Jupiter would counteract the more conservative image that would otherwise be conveyed by the person's Capricorn ascendant.

Rising signs change every two hours with the earth's rotation. Those born early in the morning when the sun was on the horizon will be most likely to project the image of their sun sign. These people are often called a "double Aries" or a "double Virgo" because the same sun sign and ascendant reinforce each other.

Look up your rising sign from the chart at the end of this chapter. Since rising signs change every two hours, it is important to know your birth time as close to the minute as possible. Even a few minutes' difference could change the rising sign and therefore the setup of your chart. If you are unsure about the exact time, but know within a few hours, check the following descriptions to see which is most like the personality you project.

Aries Rising: High Energy

You are the most aggressive version of your sun sign, with boundless energy that can be used productively if it's channeled in the right direction. Watch a tendency to overreact emotionally and blow your top. You come across as openly competitive, a positive asset in business or sports. Be on guard against impatience, which could lead to head injuries. Your walk and bearing could have the telltale head-forward Aries posture. You may wear more bright colors, especially red, than others of your sign. You may also have a tendency to drive your car faster.

FAMOUS EXAMPLES: Barbara Streisand, Bette Midler

Taurus Rising: Earthbound

You're slow-moving, with a beautiful (or distinctive) speaking or singing voice that can be especially soothing or melodious. You probably surround yourself with comfort, good food, luxurious environments, and other sensual pleasures. You prefer welcoming others into your home to gadding about. You may have a talent for business, especially in trading, appraising, and real estate. A Taurus ascendant gives a well-padded physique that gains weight easily. This ascendant can also endow females with a curvaceous beauty.

FAMOUS EXAMPLE: Liza Minnelli

Gemini Rising: The Communicator

You're naturally sociable, with lighter, more ethereal mannerisms than others of your sign, especially if you're female. You love to communicate with people, and express your ideas and feelings easily. You may have a talent for writing or public speaking. You thrive on variety, a constantly changing scene, and a lively social life. However, you may relate to others at a deeper level than might be suspected. And you will be far more sympathetic and caring than you project. You will probably travel widely, changing partners and jobs several times (or juggle two at once). Physically, your nerves are quite sensitive. Occasionally, you would benefit from a calm, tranquil atmosphere away from your usual social scene.

FAMOUS EXAMPLE: British prime minister Tony Blair

Cancer Rising: Nurturing

You are naturally acquisitive, possessive, private, a money-maker. You easily pick up others' needs and feelings—a great gift in business, the arts, and personal relationships. But you must guard against overreacting or taking things too personally, especially during full moon periods. Find creative outlets for your natural nurturing gifts, such as helping the less fortunate, particularly children. Your insights would be helpful in psychology. Your desire to feed and care for others would be useful in the restaurant, hotel, or child-care industries. You may be especially fond of wearing romantic old clothes, collecting antiques, and, of course, dining on exquisite food. Since your body may retain fluids, pay attention to your diet. To relax, escape to places near water.

FAMOUS EXAMPLES: Bill Gates, Michael Bloomberg

Leo Rising: Scene Player

You may come across as more poised than you really feel. However, you play it to the hilt, projecting a proud royal presence. A Leo ascendant gives you a natural flair for drama, and you might be accused of stealing the spotlight. You'll also project a much more outgoing, optimistic, sunny personality than others of your sign. You take care to please your public by always projecting your best star quality, probably tossing a luxuriant mane of hair, sporting a striking hairstyle, or dressing to impress. Females often dazzle with spectacular jewelry. Since you may have a strong parental nature, you could well be the regal family matriarch or patriarch.

FAMOUS EXAMPLES: Marilyn Monroe, George W. Bush

Virgo Rising: Discriminating

Virgo rising masks your inner nature with a practical, analytical outer image. You seem neat, orderly, more particular than others of your sign. Others in your life may feel they must live up to your high standards. Though at times you may be openly critical, this masks a well-meaning desire to have only the best for loved ones. Your sharp eye for details could be used in the financial world, or your literary skills could draw you to teaching or publishing. The healing arts, health care, and service-oriented professions attract many with a Virgo ascendant. You're likely to take good care of yourself, with great attention to health, diet, and exercise. Physically, you may have a very sensitive digestive system.

FAMOUS EXAMPLES: Woody Allen, Madonna

Libra Rising: Charming and Social

Libra rising gives you a charming, social public persona. You tend to avoid confrontations in relationships, preferring to smooth the way or negotiate diplomatically rather than give in to an emotional reaction. Because you are interested in all aspects of a situation, you may be slow to reach decisions. Physically, you'll have good proportions and symmetry. You will move with natural grace and balance. You're likely to have pleasing, if not beautiful, facial features, with a winning smile. You'll show natural good taste and harmony in your clothes and home decor. Legal, diplomatic, or public relations professions could draw your interest.

FAMOUS EXAMPLES: Bill Clinton, JFK, Cary Grant

Scorpio Rising: Mysterious Charisma

You project an intriguing air of mystery with this ascendant, as the Scorpio secretiveness and sense of underlying power combines with your sun sign. There's more to you than meets the eye. You seem like someone who is always in control and who can move comfortably in the world of power. Your physical look comes across as intense. Many of you have remarkable eyes, with a direct, penetrating gaze. But you'll never reveal your private agenda, and you tend to keep your true feelings under wraps (watch a tendency toward paranoia). You may have an interesting romantic history with secret love affairs. Many of you heighten your air of mystery by wearing black. You're happiest near water and should provide yourself with a seaside retreat.

FAMOUS EXAMPLES: Jacqueline Kennedy Onassis, Grace Kelly

Sagittarius Rising: The Wanderer

You travel with this ascendant. You may also be a more outdoor, sportive type, with an athletic, casual, outgoing air. Your moods are camouflaged with cheerful optimism or a philosophical attitude. Though you don't hesitate to speak your mind, you can also laugh at your troubles or crack a joke more easily than others of your sign. A Sagittarius ascendant can also draw you to the field of higher education or to spiritual life. You'll seem to have less attachment to things and people, and may travel widely. Your strong, fast legs are a physical bonus.

FAMOUS EXAMPLE: Ted Turner

Capricorn Rising: Serious Business

This rising sign makes you come across as serious, goal-oriented, disciplined, and careful with cash. You are not one of the zodiac's big spenders, though you might splurge occasionally on items with good investment value. You're the traditional, conservative type in dress and environment, and you might come across as quite normal and businesslike. You'll function well in a structured or corporate environment where you can climb to the top. (You are always aware of who's the boss.) In your personal life, you could be a loner or a single parent who is "father and mother" to your children.

FAMOUS EXAMPLES: Rupert Murdoch, Jane Fonda

Aquarius Rising: One of a Kind

You come across as less concerned about what others think and could even be a bit eccentric. Your appearance is sure to be unique and memorable. You're more at ease with groups of people than others in your sign, and you may be attracted to public life. Your appearance may be unique, either unconventional or unimportant to you. Those of you whose sun is in a water sign (Cancer, Scorpio, Pisces) may exercise your nurturing qualities with a large group, an extended family, or a day-care or community center.

FAMOUS EXAMPLE: Jay Leno

Pisces Rising: Romantic Roles

Your creative, nurturing talents are heightened and so is your ability to project emotional drama. And your dreamy eyes and poetic air bring out the protective instinct in others. You could be attracted to the arts, especially theater, dance, film, and photography, or to psychology, spiritual practice, and charity work. You are happiest when you are using your creative ability to help others. Since you are vulnerable to mood swings, it is especially important for you to find interesting, creative work where you can express your talents and heighten your self-esteem. Accentuate the positive. Be wary of escapist tendencies, particularly involving alcohol or drugs to which you are supersensitive.

FAMOUS EXAMPLES: Whitney Houston, Antonio Banderas

RISING SIGNS-A.M. BIRTHS

	1 AM	2 AM	3 AM	4 AM	5 AM	6 AM	7 AM	8 AM	9 AM	10 AM	11 AM	12 NOON
Jan 1	Lib	Sc	Sc	Sc	Sag	Sag	Cap	Cap	Aq	Aq	Pis	Ar
Jan 9	Lib	Sc	Sc	Sag	Sag	Sag	Cap	Cap	Aq	Pis	Ar	Tau
Jan 17	Sc	Sc	Sc	Sag	Sag	Cap	Cap	Aq	Aq	Pis	Ar	Tau
Jan 25	Sc	Sc	Sag	Sag	Sag	Cap	Cap	Aq	Pis	Ar	Tau	Tau
Feb 2	Sc	Sc	Sag	Sag	Cap	Cap	Aq	Pis	Pis	Ar	Tau	Gem
Feb 10	Sc	Sag	Sag	Sag	Cap	Cap	Aq	Pis	Ar	Tau	Tau	Gem
Feb 18	Sc	Sag	Sag	Cap	Cap	Aq	Pis	Pis	Ar	Tau	Gem	Gem
Feb 26	Sag	Sag	Sag	Cap	Aq	Aq	Pis	Ar	Tau	Tau	Gem	Gem
Mar 6	Sag	Sag	Cap	Cap	Aq	Pis	Pis	Ar	Tau	Gem	Gem	Can
Mar 14	Sag	Cap	Cap	Aq	Aq	Pis	Ar	Tau	Tau	Gem	Gem	Can
Mar 22	Sag	Cap	Cap	Aq	Pis	Ar	Ar	Tau	Gem	Gem	Can	Can
Mar 30	Cap	Cap	Aq	Pis	Pis	Ar	Tau	Tau	Gem	Can	Can	Can
Apr 7	Cap	Cap	Aq	Pis	Ar	Ar	Tau	Gem	Gem	Can	Can	Leo
Apr 14	Cap	Aq	Aq	Pis	Ar	Tau	Tau	Gem	Gem	Can	Can	Leo
Apr 22	Cap	Aq	Pis	Ar	Ar	Tau	Gem	Gem	Gem	Can	Leo	Leo
Apr 30	Aq	Aq	Pis	Ar	Tau	Tau	Gem	Can	Can	Can	Leo	Leo
May 8	Aq	Pis	Ar	Ar	Tau	Gem	Gem	Can	Can	Leo	Leo	Leo
May 16	Aq	Pis	Ar	Tau	Gem	Gem	Can	Can	Can	Leo	Leo	Vir
May 24	Pis	Ar	Ar	Tau	Gem	Gem	Can	Can	Can	Leo	Leo	Vir
June 1	Pis	Ar	Tau	Gem	Gem	Can	Can	Can	Leo	Leo	Vir	Vir
June 9	Ar	Ar	Tau	Gem	Gem	Can	Can	Leo	Leo	Leo	Vir	Vir
June 17	Ar	Tau	Gem	Gem	Can	Can	Can	Leo	Leo	Vir	Vir	Vir
June 25	Tau	Tau	Gem	Gem	Can	Can	Leo	Leo	Leo	Vir	Vir	Lib
July 3	Tau	Gem	Gem	Can	Can	Can	Leo	Leo	Vir	Vir	Vir	Lib
July 11	Tau	Gem	Gem	Can	Can	Leo	Leo	Leo	Vir	Vir	Lib	Lib
July 18	Gem	Gem	Can	Can	Can	Leo	Leo	Vir	Vir	Vir	Lib	Lib
July 26	Gem	Gem	Can	Can	Leo	Leo	Vir	Vir	Vir	Lib	Lib	Lib
Aug 3	Gem	Can	Can	Can	Leo	Leo	Leo	Vir	Vir	Vir	Lib	Sc
Aug 11	Gem	Can	Can	Leo	Leo	Leo	Vir	Vir	Lib	Lib	Lib	Sc
Aug 18	Can	Can	Can	Leo	Leo	Vir	Vir	Vir	Lib	Lib	Sc	Sc
Aug 27	Can	Can	Leo	Leo	Leo	Vir	Vir	Lib	Lib	Lib	Sc	Sc
Sept 4	Can	Can	Leo	Leo	Leo	Vir	Vir	Vir	Lib	Lib	Sc	Sc
Sept 12	Can	Leo	Leo	Leo	Vir	Vir	Lib	Lib	Lib	Sc	Sc	Sag
Sept 20	Leo	Leo	Leo	Vir	Vir	Vir	Lib	Lib	Lib	Sc	Sc	Sag
Sept 28	Leo	Leo	Leo	Vir	Vir	Lib	Lib	Lib	Sc	Sc	Sag	Sag
Oct 6	Leo	Leo	Vir	Vir	Vir	Lib	Lib	Sc	Sc	Sc	Sag	Sag
Oct 14	Leo	Vir	Vir	Vir	Lib	Lib	Lib	Sc	Sc	Sag	Sag	Cap
Oct 22	Leo	Vir	Vir	Lib	Lib	Lib	Sc	Sc	Sc	Sag	Sag	Cap
Oct 30	Vir	Vir	Vir	Lib	Lib	Sc	Sc	Sc	Sag	Sag	Cap	Cap
Nov 7	Vir	Vir	Lib	Lib	Lib	Sc	Sc	Sc	Sag	Sag	Cap	Cap
Nov 15	Vir	Vir	Vir	Lib	Lib	Sc	Sc	Sc	Sag	Sag	Cap	Aq
Nov 23	Vir	Lib	Lib	Lib	Sc	Sc	Sag	Sag	Sag	Cap	Cap	Aq
Dec 1	Vir	Lib	Lib	Sc	Sc	Sc	Sag	Sag	Cap	Cap	Aq	Aq
Dec 9	Lib	Lib	Lib	Sc	Sc	Sag	Sag	Sag	Cap	Cap	Aq	Pis
Dec 18	Lib	Lib	Sc	Sc	Sc	Sag	Sag	Cap	Cap	Aq	Aq	Pis
Dec 28	Lib	Lib	Sc	Sc	Sag	Sag	Sag	Cap	Aq	Aq	Pis	Ar

RISING SIGNS—P.M. BIRTHS

	1 PM	2 PM	3 PM	4 PM	5 PM	6 PM	7 PM	8 PM	9 PM	10 PM	11 PM	12 MIDNIGHT
Jan 1	Tau	Gem	Gem	Can	Can	Can	Leo	Leo	Vir	Vir	Vir	Lib
Jan 9	Tau	Gem	Gem	Can	Can	Leo	Leo	Leo	Vir	Vir	Vir	Lib
Jan 17	Gem	Gem	Can	Can	Can	Leo	Leo	Vir	Vir	Vir	Lib	Lib
Jan 25	Gem	Gem	Can	Can	Leo	Leo	Leo	Vir	Vir	Lib	Lib	Lib
Feb 2	Gem	Can	Can	Can	Leo	Leo	Vir	Vir	Vir	Lib	Lib	Sc
Feb 10	Gem	Can	Can	Leo	Leo	Leo	Vir	Vir	Lib	Lib	Lib	Sc
Feb 18	Can	Can	Can	Leo	Leo	Vir	Vir	Vir	Lib	Lib	Sc	Sc
Feb 26	Can	Can	Leo	Leo	Leo	Vir	Vir	Lib	Lib	Lib	Sc	Sc
Mar 6	Can	Leo	Leo	Leo	Vir	Vir	Vir	Lib	Lib	Sc	Sc	Sc
Mar 14	Can	Leo	Leo	Vir	Vir	Vir	Lib	Lib	Lib	Sc	Sc	Sag
Mar 22	Leo	Leo	Leo	Vir	Vir	Lib	Lib	Lib	Sc	Sc	Sc	Sag
Mar 30	Leo	Leo	Vir	Vir	Vir	Lib	Lib	Sc	Sc	Sc	Sag	Sag
Apr 7	Leo	Leo	Vir	Vir	Lib	Lib	Lib	Sc	Sc	Sc	Sag	Sag
Apr 14	Leo	Vir	Vir	Vir	Lib	Lib	Sc	Sc	Sc	Sag	Sag	Cap
Apr 22	Leo	Vir	Vir	Lib	Lib	Lib	Sc	Sc	Sc	Sag	Sag	Cap
Apr 30	Vir	Vir	Vir	Lib	Lib	Sc	Sc	Sc	Sag	Sag	Cap	Cap
May 8	Vir	Vir	Lib	Lib	Lib	Sc	Sc	Sag	Sag	Sag	Cap	Cap
May 16	Vir	Vir	Lib	Lib	Sc	Sc	Sc	Sag	Sag	Cap	Cap	Aq
May 24	Vir	Lib	Lib	Lib	Sc	Sc	Sag	Sag	Sag	Cap	Cap	Aq
June 1	Vir	Lib	Lib	Sc	Sc	Sc	Sag	Sag	Cap	Cap	Aq	Aq
June 9	Lib	Lib	Lib	Sc	Sc	Sag	Sag	Sag	Cap	Cap	Aq	Pis
June 17	Lib	Lib	Sc	Sc	Sc	Sag	Sag	Cap	Cap	Aq	Aq	Pis
June 25	Lib	Lib	Sc	Sc	Sag	Sag	Sag	Cap	Cap	Aq	Pis	Ar
July 3	Lib	Sc	Sc	Sc	Sag	Sag	Cap	Cap	Aq	Aq	Pis	Ar
July 11	Lib	Sc	Sc	Sag	Sag	Sag	Cap	Cap	Aq	Pis	Ar	Tau
July 18	Sc	Sc	Sc	Sag	Sag	Cap	Cap	Aq	Aq	Pis	Ar	Tau
July 26	Sc	Sc	Sag	Sag	Sag	Cap	Cap	Aq	Pis	Ar	Tau	Tau
Aug 3	Sc	Sc	Sag	Sag	Cap	Cap	Aq	Aq	Pis	Ar	Tau	Gem
Aug 11	Sc	Sag	Sag	Sag	Cap	Cap	Aq	Pis	Ar	Tau	Tau	Gem
Aug 18	Sc	Sag	Sag	Cap	Cap	Aq	Pis	Pis	Ar	Tau	Gem	Gem
Aug 27	Sag	Sag	Sag	Cap	Cap	Aq	Pis	Ar	Tau	Tau	Gem	Gem
Sept 4	Sag	Sag	Cap	Cap	Aq	Pis	Pis	Ar	Tau	Gem	Gem	Can
Sept 12	Sag	Sag	Cap	Aq	Aq	Pis	Ar	Tau	Tau	Gem	Gem	Can
Sept 20	Sag	Cap	Cap	Aq	Pis	Pis	Ar	Tau	Gem	Gem	Can	Can
Sept 28	Cap	Cap	Aq	Aq	Pis	Ar	Tau	Tau	Gem	Gem	Can	Can
Oct 6	Cap	Cap	Aq	Pis	Ar	Ar	Tau	Gem	Gem	Can	Can	Leo
Oct 14	Cap	Aq	Aq	Pis	Ar	Tau	Tau	Gem	Gem	Can	Can	Leo
Oct 22	Cap	Aq	Pis	Ar	Ar	Tau	Gem	Gem	Can	Can	Leo	Leo
Oct 30	Aq	Aq	Pis	Ar	Tau	Tau	Gem	Can	Can	Can	Leo	Leo
Nov 7	Aq	Aq	Pis	Ar	Tau	Tau	Gem	Can	Can	Can	Leo	Leo
Nov 15	Aq	Pis	Ar	Tau	Gem	Gem	Can	Can	Can	Leo	Leo	Vir
Nov 23	Pis	Ar	Ar	Tau	Gem	Gem	Can	Can	Leo	Leo	Leo	Vir
Dec 1	Pis	Ar	Tau	Gem	Gem	Can	Can	Leo	Leo	Leo	Vir	Vir
Dec 9	Ar	Tau	Tau	Gem	Gem	Can	Can	Leo	Leo	Leo	Vir	Vir
Dec 18	Ar	Tau	Gem	Gem	Can	Can	Can	Leo	Leo	Vir	Vir	Vir
Dec 28	Tau	Tau	Gem	Gem	Can	Can	Leo	Leo	Vir	Vir	Vir	Lib

CHAPTER 6

Learn the Glyphs to Decipher Your Horoscope Chart like a Pro

To read a horoscope chart (or to use one of the popular astrology programs on your computer), you must first learn to read the universal symbols of astrology, the mysterious glyphs that appear on every astrology chart. At first, they seem like a strange foreign language. But once you learn the secret behind the glyphs, which contain clues to the meaning of the sign or planet they represent, it's easy!

Since there are only twelve signs and ten planets (not counting a few asteroids and other space objects some astrologers use), it's a lot easier than learning to read a foreign language. Here's a code cracker for the glyphs, beginning with the glyphs for the planets. To those who already know their glyphs, don't just skim over the chapter. These familiar graphics have hidden meanings you will discover!

The Glyphs for the Planets

The glyphs for the planets are easy to learn. They're simple combinations of the most basic visual elements: the circle, the semicircle or arc, and the cross. However, each component of a glyph has a special meaning in relation to the other parts of the symbol.

The circle, which has no beginning or end, is one of

the oldest symbols of spirit or spiritual forces. All of the early diagrams of the heavens—spiritual territory—are shown in circular form. The never-ending line of the circle is the perfect symbol for eternity. The semicircle or arc is an incomplete circle, symbolizing the receptive, finite soul, which contains spiritual potential in the curving line.

The vertical line of the cross symbolizes movement from heaven to earth. The horizontal line describes temporal movement, here and now, in time and space. Combined in a cross, the vertical and horizontal planes symbolize manifestation in the material world.

The Sun Glyph ☉

The sun is always shown by this powerful solar symbol, a circle with a point in the center. The center point is you, your spiritual center, and the symbol represents your infinite personality incarnating (the point) into the finite cycles of birth and death.

The sun has been represented by a circle or disk since ancient Egyptian times when the solar disk represented the Sun god, Ra. Some archaeologists believe the great stone circles found in England were centers of sun worship. This particular version of the symbol was brought into common use in the sixteenth century after German occultist and scholar Cornelius Agrippa (1486–1535) wrote a book called the *Die Occulta Philosophia*, which became accepted as the authority in the field. Agrippa collected many medieval astrological and magical symbols in this book, which have been used by astrologers since then.

The Moon Glyph ☽

The moon glyph is the most recognizable symbol on a chart, a left-facing arc stylized into the crescent moon. As part of a circle, the arc symbolizes the potential fulfillment of the entire circle, the life force that is still incomplete. Therefore, it is the ideal representation of the reactive, receptive, emotional nature of the moon.

The Mercury Glyph ☿

Mercury contains all three elemental symbols: the crescent, the circle, and the cross in vertical order. This is the "Venus with a hat" glyph (compare with the symbol of Venus). With another stretch of the imagination, can't you see the winged cap of Mercury the messenger? Think of the upturned crescent as antennae that tune in and transmit messages from the sun, reminding you that Mercury is the way you communicate, the way your mind works. The upturned arc is receiving energy into the spirit or solar circle, which will later be translated into action on the material plane, symbolized by the cross. All the elements are equally sized because Mercury is neutral; it doesn't play favorites! This planet symbolizes objective, detached, unemotional thinking.

The Venus Glyph ♀

Here the relationship is between two components: the circle of spirit and the cross of matter. Spirit is elevated over matter, pulling it upward. Venus asks, "What is beautiful? What do you like best? What do you love to have done to you?" Consequently, Venus determines both your ideal of beauty and what feels good sensually. It governs your own allure and power to attract, as well as what attracts and pleases you.

The Mars Glyph ♂

In this glyph, the cross of matter is stylized into an arrowhead pointed up and outward, propelled by the circle of spirit. With a little imagination, you can visualize it as the shield and spear of Mars, the ancient god of war. You can deduce that Mars embodies your spiritual energy projected into the outer world. It's your assertiveness, your initiative, your aggressive drive, what you like to do to others, your temper. If you know someone's Mars, you know whether they'll blow up when angry or do a slow burn. Your task is to use your outgoing Mars energy wisely and well.

The Jupiter Glyph ♃

Jupiter is the basic cross of matter, with a large stylized crescent perched on the left side of the horizontal, temporal plane. You might think of the crescent as an open hand, because one meaning of Jupiter is "luck," what's handed to you. You don't have to work for what you get from Jupiter; it comes to you, if you're open to it.

The Jupiter glyph might also remind you of a jumbo jet plane, with a huge tail fin, about a take off. This is the planet of travel, mental and spiritual, of expanding your horizons via new ideas, new spiritual dimensions, and new places. Jupiter embodies the optimism and enthusiasm of the traveler about to embark on an exciting adventure.

The Saturn Glyph ♄

Flip Jupiter over, and you've got Saturn. This might not be immediately apparent because Saturn is usually stylized into an "h" form like the one shown here. The principle it expresses is the opposite of Jupiter's expansive tendencies. Saturn pulls you back to earth: the receptive arc is pushed down underneath the cross of matter. Before there are any rewards or expansion, the duties and obligations of the material world must be considered. Saturn says, "Stop, wait, finish your chores before you take off!"

Saturn's glyph also resembles the sickle of old "Father Time." Saturn was first known as Chronos, the Greek god of time, for time brings all matter to an end. When it was the most distant planet (before the discovery of Uranus), Saturn was believed to be the place where time stopped. After the soul departed from earth, it journeyed back to the outer reaches of the universe and finally stopped at Saturn, or at "the end of time."

The Uranus Glyph ♅

The glyph for Uranus is often stylized to form a capital *H* after Sir William Herschel who discovered the planet. But the more esoteric version curves the two pillars of the H into crescent antennae, or "ears," like satellite disks receiving signals from space. These are perched on the horizontal material line of the cross of matter and pushed from below by the circle of the spirit. To many sci-fi fans, Uranus looks like an orbiting satellite.

Uranus channels the highest energy of all, the white electrical light of the universal spiritual force that holds the cosmos together. This pure electrical energy is gathered from all over the universe. Because Uranus energy doesn't follow any ordinary celestial drumbeat, it can't be controlled or predicted (which is also true of those who are strongly influenced by this eccentric planet). In the symbol, this energy is manifested through the balance of polarities (the two opposite arms of the glyph) like the two polarized wires of a lightbulb.

The Neptune Glyph ♆

Neptune's glyph is usually stylized to look like a trident, the weapon of the Roman god Neptune. However, on a more esoteric level, it shows the large upturned crescent of the soul pierced through by the cross of matter. Neptune nails down, or materializes, soul energy, bringing impulses from the soul level into manifestation. That is why Neptune is associated with imagination or "imagining in," making an image of the soul. Neptune works through feelings, sensitivity, and mystical capacity to bring the divine into the earthly realm.

The Pluto Glyph ♀

Pluto is written two ways. One is composite of the letters *PL*, the first two letters of the word Pluto and coincidentally the initials of Percival Lowell, one of the planet's discoverers. The other, more esoteric symbol is a small circle above a large open crescent that surmounts the cross of matter. This depicts Pluto's power to regenerate. Imagine a new little spirit emerging from the sheltering cup of the soul. Pluto rules the forces of life and death. After this planet has passed a sensitive point in your chart, you are transformed, reborn in some way.

Sci-fi fans might visualize this glyph as a small satellite (the circle) being launched. It was shortly after Pluto's discovery that we learned how to harness the nuclear forces that made space exploration possible. Pluto rules the transformative power of atomic energy, which totally changed our lives and from which there is no turning back.

The Glyphs for the Signs

On an astrology chart, the glyph for the sign will appear after that of the planet. For example, when you see the moon glyph followed first by a number and then by another glyph representing the sign, this means that the moon was passing over a certain degree of that astrological sign at the time of the chart. On the dividing lines between the houses on your chart, you'll find the symbol for the sign that rules the house.

Because sun sign symbols do not contain the same basic geometric components of the planetary glyphs, we must look elsewhere for clues to their meanings. Many have been passed down from ancient Egyptian and Chaldean civilizations with few modifications. Others have been adapted over the centuries.

In deciphering many of the glyphs, you'll often find that the symbols reveal a dual nature of the sign, which is not always apparent in the usual sun sign descriptions. For instance, the Gemini glyph is similar to the Roman numeral for two, and reveals this sign's longing to discover a twin soul. The Cancer glyph may be interpreted as resembling either the nurturing breasts or the self-protective claws of a crab, both symbols associated with the contrasting qualities of this sign. Libra's glyph embodies the duality of the spirit balanced with material reality. The Sagittarius glyph shows that the aspirant must also carry along the earthly animal nature in his quest. The Capricorn sea goat is another symbol with dual emphasis. The goat climbs high, yet is always pulled back by the deep waters of the unconscious. Aquarius embodies the double waves of mental detachment, balanced by the desire for connection with others in a friendly way. Finally, the two fishes of Pisces, which are forever tied together, show the duality of the soul and the spirit that must be reconciled.

The Aries Glyph ♈

Since the symbol for Aries is the Ram, this glyph is obviously associated with a ram's horns, which characterize one aspect of the Aries personality—an aggressive, me-first, leaping-headfirst attitude. But the symbol can be interpreted in other ways as well. Some astrologers liken it to a fountain of energy, which Aries people also embody. The first sign of the zodiac bursts on the scene eagerly, ready to go. Another analogy is to the eyebrows and nose of the human head, which Aries rules, and the thinking power that is initiated by the brain.

One theory of this symbol links it to the Egyptian god Amun, represented by a ram in ancient times. As Amun-Ra, this god was believed to embody the creator of the universe, the leader of all the other gods. This relates easily to the position of Aries as the leader (or first sign) of the zodiac, which begins at the spring equinox, a time of the year when nature is renewed.

The Taurus Glyph ♉

This is another easy glyph to draw and identify. It takes little imagination to decipher the bull's head with long curving horns. Like its symbol the Bull, the archetypal Taurus is slow to anger but ferocious when provoked, as well as stubborn, steady, and sensual. Another association is the larynx (and thyroid) of the throat area (ruled by Taurus) and the eustachian tubes running up to the ears, which coincides with the relationship of Taurus to the voice, song, and music. Many famous singers, musicians, and composers have prominent Taurus influences.

Many ancient religions involved a bull as the central figure in fertility rites or initiations, usually symbolizing the victory of man over his animal nature. Another possible origin is in the sacred bull of Egypt, who embodied the incarnate form of Osiris, god of death and resurrection. In early Christian imagery, the Taurus Bull represented St. Luke.

The Gemini Glyph ♊

The standard glyph immediately calls to mind the Roman numeral for two (II) and the Twins symbol, as it is called, for Gemini. In almost all drawings and images used for this sign, the relationship between two persons is emphasized. Usually one twin will be touching the other, which signifies communication, human contact, the desire to share.

The top line of the Gemini glyph indicates mental communication, while the bottom line indicates shared physical space.

The most famous Gemini legend is that of the twin sons, Castor and Pollux, one of whom had a mortal father while the other was the son of Zeus, king of the gods. When it came time for the mortal twin to die, his grief-stricken brother pleaded with Zeus, who agreed to let them spend half the year on earth in mortal form and half in immortal life, with the gods on Mount Olympus. This reflects a basic duality of humankind, which possesses an immortal soul yet is also subject to the limits of mortality.

The Cancer Glyph ♋

Two convenient images relate to the Cancer glyph. It is easiest to decode the curving claws of the Cancer symbol, the Crab. Like the crab, Cancer's element is water. This sensitive sign also has a hard protective shell to protect its tender interior. The crab must be wily to escape predators, scampering sideways and hiding under rocks. The crab also responds to the cycles of the moon, as do all shellfish. The other image is that of two female breasts, which Cancer rules, showing that this is a sign that nurtures and protects others as well as itself.

In ancient Egypt, Cancer was also represented by the scarab beetle, a symbol of regeneration and eternal life.

The Leo Glyph ♌

Notice that the Leo glyph seems to be an extension of Cancer's glyph, with a significant difference. In the Cancer glyph, the lines curve inward protectively. The Leo glyph expresses energy outwardly. And there is no duality in the symbol, the Lion, or in Leo, the sign.

Lions have belonged to the sign of Leo since earliest times. It is not difficult to imagine the king of beasts with his sweeping mane and curling tail from this glyph. The upward sweep of the glyph easily describes the positive energy of Leo: the flourishing tail, their flamboyant qualities. Another analogy, perhaps a stretch of the imagination, is that of a heart leaping up with joy and enthusiasm, also very typical of Leo, which also rules the heart. In early Christian imagery, the Leo Lion represented St. Mark.

The Virgo Glyph ♍

You can read much into this mysterious glyph. For instance, it could represent the initials of "Mary Virgin," or a young woman holding a staff of wheat, or stylized female genitalia, all common interpretations. The M shape might also remind you that Virgo is ruled by Mercury. The cross beneath the symbol reveals the grounded, practical nature of this earth sign.

The earliest zodiacs link Virgo with the Egyptian goddess Isis who gave birth to the god Horus, after her husband Osiris had been killed, in the archetype of a miraculous conception. There are many ancient statues of Isis nursing her baby son, which are reminiscent of medieval Virgin and Child motifs. This sign has also been associated with the image of the Holy Grail, when the Virgo symbol was substituted with a chalice.

The Libra Glyph ♎

It is not difficult to read the standard image for Libra, the Scales, into this glyph. There is another meaning, however, that is equally relevant: the setting sun as it descends over the horizon. Libra's natural position on the zodiac wheel is the descendant, or sunset position (as the Aries natural position is the ascendant, or rising sign). Both images relates to Libra's personality. Libra is always weighing pros and cons for a balanced decision. In the sunset image, the sun (male) hovers over the horizontal earth (female) before setting. Libra is the space between these lines, harmonizing yin and yang, spiritual and material, male and female, ideal and real worlds. The glyph has also been linked to the kidneys, which are ruled by Libra.

The Scorpio Glyph ♏

With its barbed tail, this glyph is easy to identify as the Scorpion for the sign of Scorpio. It also represents the male sexual parts, over which the sign rules. From the arrowhead, you can draw the conclusion that Mars was once its ruler. Some earlier Egyptian glyphs for Scorpio represent it as an erect serpent, so the Serpent is an alternate symbol.

Another symbol for Scorpio, which is not identifiable in this glyph, is the Eagle. Scorpios can go to extremes, either in soaring like the eagle or self-destructing like the scorpion. In early Christian imagery, which often used zodiacal symbols, the Scorpio Eagle was chosen to symbolize the intense apostle St. John the Evangelist.

The Sagittarius Glyph ♐

This is one of the easiest to spot and draw: an upward pointing arrow lifting up a cross. The arrow is pointing skyward, while the cross represents the four elements of the material world, which the arrow must convey. Elevating materiality into spirituality is an important Sagittarius quality, which explains why this sign is associated with higher learning, religion, philosophy, travel—the aspiring professions. Sagittarius can also send barbed arrows of frankness in the pursuit of truth, so the Archer symbol for Sagittarius is apt. (Sagittarius is also the sign of the supersalesman.)

Sagittarius is symbolically represented by the centaur, a mythological creature who is half man, half horse, aiming his arrow toward the skies. Though Sagittarius is motivated by spiritual aspiration, it also must balance the powerful appetites of the animal nature. The centaur Chiron, a figure in Greek mythology, became a wise teacher who, after many adventures and world travels, was killed by a poisoned arrow.

The Capricorn Glyph ♑

One of the most difficult symbols to draw, this glyph may take some practice. It is a representation of the sea goat: a mythical animal that is a goat with a curving fish's tail. The goat part of Capricorn wants to leave the waters of the emotions and climb to the elevated areas of life. But the fish tail is the unconscious, the deep chaotic psychic level that draws the goat back. Capricorn is often trying to escape the deep, feeling part of life by submerging himself in work, steadily ascending to the top. To some people, the glyph represents a seated figure with a bent knee, a reminder that Capricorn governs the knee area of the body.

An interesting aspect of this glyph is the contrast of the sharp pointed horns—which represent the penetrating, shrewd, conscious side of Capricorn—with the swishing tail—which represents its serpentine, unconscious, emotional force. One Capricorn legend, which dates from Roman times, tells of the earthy fertility god, Pan, who tried to save himself from uncontrollable sexual desires by jumping into the Nile. His upper body then turned into a goat, while the lower part became a fish. Later, Jupiter gave him a safe haven as a constellation in the skies.

The Aquarius Glyph ≈

This ancient water symbol can be traced back to an Egyptian hieroglyph representing streams of life force. Symbolized by the Water Bearer, Aquarius is distributor of the waters of life—the magic liquid of regeneration. The two waves can also be linked to the positive and negative charges of the electrical energy that Aquarius rules, a sort of universal wavelength. Aquarius is tuned in intuitively to higher forces via this electrical force. The duality of the glyph could also refer to the dual nature of Aquarius, a sign that runs hot and cold and that is friendly but also detached in the mental world of air signs.

In Greek legends, Aquarius is represented by Ganymede, who was carried to heaven by an eagle in order to become the cupbearer of Zeus and to supervise the annual flooding of the Nile. The sign later became associated with aviation and notions of flight.

The Pisces Glyph)(

Here is an abstraction of the familiar image of Pisces, two Fishes swimming in opposite directions yet bound together by a cord. The Fishes represent the spirit—which yearns for the freedom of heaven—and the soul—which remains attached to the desires of the temporal world. During life on earth, the spirit and the soul are bound together. When they complement each other, instead of pulling in opposite directions, they facilitate the Pisces creativity. The ancient version of this glyph, taken from the Egyptians, had no connecting line, which was added in the fourteenth century.

In another interpretation, it is said that the left fish indicates the direction of involution or the beginning of a cycle, while the right fish signifies the direction of evolution, the way to completion of a cycle. It's an appropriate grand finale for Pisces, the last sign of the zodiac.

CHAPTER 7

Join the Astrology Community

Have you caught the astrology bug? Whether you're new to astrology or already hooked, you'll find the more you get involved, the more you'll be fascinated by its accuracy and relevance to your life. You'll soon discover that there's no end to the fascinating techniques and aspects of our age-old art. And there's a vast community of astrology fans ready to welcome you. You need only type the word *astrology* into any Internet search engine and watch hundreds of listings of astrology-related sites pop up. There is computer software available for all levels of astrological expertise, which makes calculating horoscopes a breeze. There are local meetings and international conferences where you can connect with other astrologers, and books and tapes to help you study at home.

To help you sort out the variety of options available, here are our top picks for the Internet and the astrological community at large.

Nationwide Astrology Organizations and Conferences

National Council for Geocosmic Research (NCGR)

Whether you'd like to know more about such specialties as financial astrology or techniques for timing events, or if you'd prefer the psychological or mythological approach, you'll meet the top astrologers at conferences sponsored by the National Council for Geocosmic Research. NCGR is dedicated to providing quality education, bringing astrologers and astrology fans together at conferences, and promoting fellowship. Their course structure provides a systematized study of the many facets of astrology. The organization sponsors educational workshops, taped lectures, conferences, and a directory of professional astrologers. For an annual membership fee, you get their excellent publications and newsletters, plus the opportunity to network with other astrology buffs at local chapter events (there are chapters in twenty states).

To join NCGR for the latest information on upcoming events and chapters in your city, consult their Web site: www.geocosmic.org.

American Federation of Astrologers (AFA)

Established in 1938, this is one of the oldest astrological organizations in the United States. AFA offers conferences, conventions, and a thorough correspondence course. If you are looking for a reading, their interesting Web site will refer you to an accredited AFA astrologer.

AFA
6535 South Rural Road
Tempe, AZ 85283-3746
Phone: (888) 301-7630 or (480) 838-1751
Fax: (480) 838-8293
Web site: www.astrologers.com

Association for Astrological Networking (AFAN)

Did you know that astrologers are still being harassed for practicing astrology? AFAN provides support and legal information, and works toward improving the public image of astrology. AFAN's network of local astrologers links with the international astrological community. Here are the people who will go to bat for astrology when it is attacked in the media. Everyone who cares about astrology should join!

AFAN
8306 Wilshire Boulevard
PMB 537
Beverly Hills, CA 90211
Phone: (800) 578-2326
E-mail: info@afan.org
Web site: www.afan.org

International Society for Astrology Research (ISAR)

An international organization of professional astrologers dedicated to encouraging the highest standards of quality in the field of astrology with an emphasis on research. Among ISAR's benefits are a quarterly journal, a weekly e-mail newsletter, and a free membership directory.

ISAR
P.O. Box 38613
Los Angeles, CA 90038
Fax: (805) 933-0301
Web site: www.isarastrology.com

Astrology Software

Astrolabe

One of the top astrology software resources. Check out the latest version of their powerful Solar Fire software for Windows. It's a breeze to use and will grow with your increasing knowledge of astrology to the most sophisticated levels. This company also markets a variety of programs for all levels of expertise and a wide selection of computer-generated astrology readings. A good resource for innovative software as well as applications for older computers.

The Astrolabe Web site is a great place to start your astrology tour of the Internet. Visitors to the site are greeted with a chart of the time you log on. You can download a free demo sample of their Solar Fire program. And you can get your chart calculated, also free, with a short interpretation e-mailed to you.

Astrolabe
P.O. Box 1750-R
Brewster, MA 02631
Phone: (800) 843-6682
Web site: www.alabe.com

Matrix Software

A wide variety of software in all price ranges, demo disks (student and advanced level), and interesting readings. Check out Winstar Express, a powerful but reasonably priced program suitable for all skill levels. The Matrix Web site offers lots of fun activities for Web surfers, such as free readings from the *I Ching*, the runes, and the tarot. Here's where to connect with news groups and online discussions. Their online almanac helps you schedule the best day to sign on the dotted line, ask for a raise, or plant your tomatoes.

Matrix Software
126 S. Michigan Avenue
Big Rapids, MI 49307
Phone: (800) 416-3924
Web site: www.Astrologysoftware.com

Astro Communications Services (ACS)

Books, software for Mac and IBM compatibles, individual charts, and telephone readings are offered by this California company. Find technical astrology materials here such as the American Ephemeris and PC atlases. ACS will calculate and send charts to you, a valuable service if you do not have a computer.

ACS Publications
5521 Ruffin Road

San Diego, CA 92123
Phone: (800) 888-9983
Fax: (858) 492-9917
Web site: www.astrocom.com

Air Software

Here you'll find powerful, creative astrology software. Financial astrology programs for stock market traders are a specialty.

Air Software
115 Caya Avenue
West Hartford, CT 06110
Phone: (800) 659-1247
Web site: www.alphee.com

Time Cycles Research (for Mac Users)

Here's where Mac users can find astrology software that's as sophisticated as it gets. If you have a Mac, you'll love their beautiful graphic IO Series programs.

Time Cycles Research
P.O. Box 797
Waterford, CT 06385
Fax: (860) 442-0625
Web site: www.timecycles.com

Halloran Software (A Super Shareware Program)

Check out Halloran Software's Web site (www.halloran.-com), which offers several levels of Windows astrology software. Beginners should consider their Astrology for Windows shareware program, which is available in un-registered demo form as a free download and in regis-tered form for a very reasonable price.

Astrolog

If you're computer-savvy, you can't go wrong with Walter Pullen's amazingly complete astrology program, which is offered absolutely free at the site. The Web address is www.astrolog.org/astrolog.htm.

Astrolog is an ultrasophisticated program with all the features of much more expensive programs. It comes in versions for all formats—DOS, Windows, Mac, UNIX—and has some cool features such as a revolving globe and a constellation map. If you are looking for astrology software with bells and whistles that doesn't cost big bucks, this program has it all!

Astroscan

Surf to www.astroscan.ca for a free program called Astroscan. Stunning graphics and ease of use make this basic program a winner. Astroscan has a fun list of celebrity charts you can call up with a few clicks.

Astrology Magazines

In addition to articles by top astrologers, most have listings of astrology conferences, events, and local happenings.

American Astrology
Dept. 4
P.O. Box 2021
Marion, OH 43306-8121

Dell Horoscope
P.O. Box 54097
Boulder, CO 80322-4907

The Mountain Astrologer

A favorite magazine of astrology fans! *The Mountain Astrologer* also has an interesting Web site featuring the latest news from an astrological point of view, plus feature articles from the magazine.

The Mountain Astrologer
P.O. Box 970
Cedar Ridge, CA 95924
Web site: www.mountainastrologer.com

Astrology College

Kepler College of Astrological Arts and Sciences

A degree-granting college, which is also a center of astrology, has long been the dream of the astrological community and is a giant step forward in providing credibility to the profession. Therefore, the opening of Kepler College in 2000 was a historical event for astrology. It is the only college in the western hemisphere authorized to issue B.A. and M.A. degrees in Astrological Studies.

Kepler College of Astrological Arts and Sciences
4630 200th Street SW
Suite A-1
Lynnwood, WA 98036
Phone: (425) 673-4292
Fax: (425) 673-4983
Web site: www.kepler.edu

Our Top Web Sites

It's a daunting task to choose from the thousands of astrological Web sites that come and go on the Internet. Here are some favorites which have stood the test of time and are likely to still be operating when this book is published.

Astrodienst (www.astro.com)

Don't miss this fabulous international site that has long been one of the best astrology resources on the Internet. It's also a great place to view and download your own astrology chart. The world atlas on this site will give you the accurate longitude and latitude of your birthplace for setting up your horoscope. Then you can print out your free chart in a range of easy-to-read formats. Other attractions: a list of famous people born on your birth date, a feature that helps you choose the best vacation spot, plus articles by world-famous astrologers.

AstroDatabank (www.astrodatabank.com)

When the news is breaking, you can bet this site will be the first to get accurate birthdays of the headliners. The late astrologer Lois Rodden was a stickler for factual information and her meticulous research is being continued, much to the benefit of the astrological community. The Web site specializes in charts of current newsmakers, political figures, and international celebrities. You can also participate in discussions and analysis of the charts and see what other astrologers have to say about them. Their AstroDatabank program, which you can purchase at the site, provides thousands of verified birthdays sorted into categories. It's an excellent research tool.

StarIQ (www.stariq.com)

Find out how top astrologers view the latest headlines at the must-see StarIQ site. Many of the best minds in astrology comment on the latest news, stock market ups and downs, political contenders. You can sign up to receive e-mail forecasts at the most important times keyed to your individual chart. (This is one of the best of the many online forecasts.)

Astrology Books (www.astroamerica.com)

The Astrology Center of America sells a wide selection of books on all aspects of astrology, from the basics to the most advanced, at this online bookstore. Also available are many hard-to-find and recycled books.

History and Mythology Site (www.elore.com)

Be sure to visit the astrology section of this gorgeous site, dedicated to the history and mythology of many traditions. Beautifully designed and presented.

Astrology Scholars' Sites

See what one of astrology's great teachers, Robert Hand, has to offer on his site: www.robhand.com. A leading expert on the history of astrology, he's on the cutting edge of the latest research.

The Project Hindsight group of astrologers is devoted to restoring the astrology of the Hellenistic period, the primary source for all later Western astrology. There are fascinating articles for astrology fans on this site, www.projecthindsight.com.

Financial Astrology Sites

Financial astrology is a hot specialty, with many tipsters, players, and theorists. There are online columns, newsletters, specialized financial astrology software, and mutual funds run by astrology seers. One of the more respected financial astrologers is Ray Merriman, whose column on www.stariq.com is a must read for those following the bulls and bears. Other top financial astrologers offer tips and forecasts at the www.afund.com and www.alphee.com sites.

CHAPTER 8

Do You Need a Personal Reading?

If you are interested in astrology, at some point you'll consider having a personal reading. For instance, an important date is coming up, perhaps a wedding or the start of a new business, and you're wondering if an astrologically picked date could influence the outcome. You've fallen in love and must know if it will last forever. Your partnership is not going well, and you're not sure if you can continue to work together. You're in a downslide when problems seem insurmountable. Or you simply want to have your chart interpreted by an expert.

But what kind of reading should you have? There are so many options for readings that sorting through them can be a daunting task. Besides individual one-on-one readings with a professional astrologer, there are telephone readings, Internet readings, tapes, computer-generated reports, and celebrity-sponsored readings. Here's what to look for and some cautionary notes.

Done by a qualified astrologer, the personal reading can be an empowering experience if you want to reach your full potential, size up a lover or business situation, or find out what the future has in store. There are astrologers who are specialists in certain areas such as finance or medical astrology. And, unfortunately, there are many questionable practitioners who range from streetwise gypsy fortune-tellers to unscrupulous scam artists.

The following basic guidelines can help you sort out your options to find the reading that's right for you.

One-on-One Consultations with a Professional Astrologer

Nothing compares to a one-on-one consultation with a professional astrologer who has analyzed thousands of charts and can pinpoint the potential in yours. During your reading, you can get your specific questions answered. For instance, how to get along better with your mate or coworker. There are many astrologers who now combine their skills with training in psychology and are well-suited to help you examine your alternatives.

To give you an accurate reading, an astrologer needs certain information from you: the date, time, and place where you were born. (A horoscope can be cast about anyone or anything that has a specific time and place.) Most astrologers will then enter this information into a computer, which will calculate a chart in seconds. From the resulting chart, the astrologer will do an interpretation.

If you don't know your exact birth time, you can usually locate it at the Bureau of Vital Statistics at the city hall or county seat of the state where you were born. If you still have no success in getting your time of birth, some astrologers can estimate an approximate birth time by using past events in your life to determine the chart. This technique is called *rectification*.

How to Find an Astrologer

Choose your astrologer with the same care as any trusted adviser such as a doctor, lawyer, or banker. Unfortunately, anyone can claim to be an astrologer—to date, there is no licensing of astrologers or universally established professional criteria. However, there are nationwide organizations of serious, committed astrologers that can help you in your search.

Good places to start your investigation are organizations such as the American Federation of Astrologers (AFA) or the National Council for Geocosmic Research (NCGR), which offer a program of study and certification. If you live near a major city, there is sure to be an active NCGR chapter or astrology club in your area; many are listed in astrology magazines available at your local newsstand. In response to many requests for referrals, both the AFA and the NCGR have directories of professional astrologers listed on their Web sites; these directories include a glossary of terms and an explanation of specialties within the astrological field. Contact the NCGR and AFA headquarters for information (see chapter 7 in this book).

Warning Signals

As a potentially lucrative freelance business, astrology has always attracted self-styled experts who may not have the knowledge or the counseling experience to give a helpful reading. These astrologers can range from the well-meaning amateur to the charlatan or street-corner gypsy who has for many years given astrology a bad name. Be very wary of astrologers who claim to have occult powers or who make pretentious claims of celebrated clients or miraculous achievements. You can often tell from the initial phone conversation if the astrologer is legitimate. He or she should ask for your birthday time and place, then conduct the conversation in a professional manner. Any astrologer who gives a reading based only on your sun sign is highly suspect.

When you arrive at the reading, the astrologer should be prepared. The consultation should be conducted in a private, quite place. The astrologer should be interested in your problems of the moment. A good reading involves feedback on your part. So if the reading is not relating to your concerns, you should let the astrologer know. You should feel free to ask questions and get clarifications of technical terms. The more you actively participate, rather than expecting the astrologer to carry the reading or come forth with oracular predictions, the more meaningful your experience will be. An astrologer should help you validate your current experience and be frank about possible negative happenings, but also suggest a positive course of action.

In their approach to a reading, some astrologers may be more literal, others more intuitive. Those who have had counseling training may take a more psychological approach. Though some astrologers may seem to have an almost psychic ability, extrasensory perception or any other parapsychological talent is not essential. A very accurate picture can be drawn from the data in your horoscope chart.

An astrologer may do several charts for each client, including one for the time of birth and a *progressed chart,* showing the evolution from birth to the present time. According to your individual needs, there are many other possibilities, such as a chart for a different location if you are contemplating a change of place. Relationships between any two people, things, or events can be interpreted with a chart that compares one partner's horoscope with the other's. A composite chart, which uses the midpoint between planets in two individual charts to describe the relationship, is another commonly used device.

An astrologer will be particularly interested in transits, those times when cycling planets activate the planets or sensitive points in your birth chart. These indicate important events in your life.

Many astrologers offer tape-recorded readings, another option to consider, especially if the astrologer you choose lives at a distance. In this case, you'll be mailed a taped reading based on your birth chart. This type of reading is more personal than a computer printout and can give you valuable insights, though it is not equivalent to a live dialogue with the astrologer when you can discuss your specific interests and issues of the moment.

The Telephone Reading

Telephone readings come in two varieties: a dial-in taped reading, usually recorded in advance by an astrologer, or a live consultation with an "astrologer" on the other end of the line. The taped readings are general daily or weekly forecasts, applied to all members of your sign and charged by the minute. The quality depends on the astrologer. One caution: Be aware that these readings can run up quite a telephone bill, especially if you get into the habit of calling every day. Be sure that you are aware of the per-minute cost of each call beforehand.

Live telephone readings also vary with the expertise of the astrologer. Ideally, the astrologer at the other end of the line enters your birth data into a computer, which then quickly calculates your chart. This chart will be referred to during the consultation. The advantage of a live telephone reading is that your individual chart is used and you can ask about a specific problem. However, before you invest in any reading, be sure that your astrologer is qualified and that you fully understand in advance how much you will be charged. There should be no unpleasant financial surprises later.

Computer-Generated Reports

Companies that offer computer programs (such as ACS, Matrix, Astrolabe) also offer a variety of computer-generated horoscope readings. These can be quite comprehensive, offering a beautiful printout of the chart plus many pages of detailed information about each planet and aspect of the chart. You can then study it at your convenience. Of course, the interpretations will be general, since there is no personal input from you, and may not cover your immediate concerns. Since computer-generated horoscopes are much lower in cost than live consultations, you might consider them as either a supplement or a preparation for an eventual live reading. You'll then be more familiar with your chart and able to plan specific questions in advance. They also make a terrific gift for astrology fans. There are several companies, listed in chapter 7, that offer computerized readings prepared by reputable astrologers.

Whichever option you decide to pursue, may your reading be an empowering one!

CHAPTER 9

Dieting by the Stars: Let Astrology Help You Lose Those Extra Pounds This Year

Dieting has become a major health concern after it was recently discovered that nearly one-third of American adults are seriously overweight and more than half need to lose some weight. Diets abound—the Zone, the Atkins, the South Beach, the No-Grain, even the Cave Man diet—as do strategies such as cutting portion sizes or eliminating fat or carbohydrates. Because everyone's metabolism differs and diets have differing rates of success, why not take advantage of astrology's wisdom to help you find the right diet, as well as the best time to start your diet.

Timing your diet according to the moon's phase could help you get off to a good start. Usually the body tends to hold water as the moon waxes and lose it as the moon wanes, so beginning your diet from the last quarter moon until the new moon could help you drop the initial water weight. Since every body reacts differently, monitor your diet through the moon's phases to see if you plateau or gain near the full moon, then don't be discouraged if your body gets fuller as the moon waxes. Stay on track and you'll be pleasantly surprised to see the weight fall off as the moon wanes.

The moon's sign as you begin your diet could also have an effect on your diet's success. Choose a fire sign moon (look in the daily forecasts in this book), when you'll be energetic and motivated. A cool, disciplined

Capricorn moon is another option. The emotional water sign or easily distracted air sign moons could weaken your resolve. Avoid the moons in Taurus and Cancer—signs known for their love of food in quantity.

Another prime time to diet is when Saturn is favorably aspecting your sign, either in the same sign or element. Since Saturn is in Cancer until July, when it moves into Leo, both of these signs should have more discipline and resolve this year. Saturn can be tough in other areas of your life, but this taskmaster of the zodiac will work for you when you need to stick to your diet.

On the other hand, Jupiter, the planet of expansion and abundance, is usually considered the planet of luck, but not so for Jupiter-favored dieters. This planet creates a devil-may-care attitude that you crave more of everything—especially your favorite culinary treats. It may be difficult for Libra dieters to lose weight until October, when Jupiter moves into Scorpio. Then it'll be the Scorpios who fight the battle of the bulge. If you're blessed by Jupiter this year, however, don't give up. One strategy would be to give yourself an abundance of fresh, healthy food (rather than refined carbohydrates) and find a diet that does not leave you feeling deprived!

Some signs have an easier time keeping weight off. These are the most active signs of Aries, Gemini, Sagittarius, disciplined Capricorn and health-conscious Virgo. More sedentary, self-indulgent food-loving signs like Taurus, Cancer, Pisces, Leo, and Libra have a more difficult time. Aquarius tends to go on fad diets, can yo-yo up and down, while Scorpio goes to extremes—feast or famine. Here are some tips for each sign, plus celebrity gurus to inspire you!

Aries: Fast Food Fixes

On-the-go Aries is usually one of the skinny signs. Thanks to your hyperactive Mars-ruled lifestyle, you're sometimes too busy to bother with healthy meals in a calm atmosphere. You're more likely to grab carbohydrate-laden, calorie-packed fast foods on the run, which give you fast energy, but could pack on the pounds if you do it too often. You need a regimen that gives you sustained energy, rather than a quick fix or a caffeine-fueled jump start. Aim for small, frequent meals and carry healthy snacks with you to recharge your batteries. Protein and fruit smoothies in the morning might provide you with a quick, healthy head start to the day.

Taurus: Downsize Portions

You're not all Audrey Hepburn! Of the signs, yours is probably the one with the most weight issues. Taurus loves food, all kinds of food, in quantity. Especially rich, creamy desserts and fried goodies. (Once you start eating rich food, you find it almost impossible to stop.) Deprivation in any form is not going to work for you, so find a diet that allows you healthy variations of the foods you love most. Aim for smaller portions and fill up on skinny foods like salads. First, raid your refrigerator and eliminate any foods that are not on your diet. If it's there, you're likely to find it and eat it. The techniques for weight loss in ever-young Cher's diet books might inspire you.

Gemini: Weight Games

Gemini is another on-the-go sign that does not usually have a weight problem, as long as you keep moving. If life circumstances force you to be sedentary, however, you may eat out of boredom and watch the pounds pile on. Your active social life can also sabotage your weight with sumptuous party buffets and restaurant meals where you have to sample everything. Your challenge is to find a healthy eating system with enough variety so you won't get bored. Develop a strategy for eating out—at parties or restaurants—and fill up the buffet plates with salad or veggies before you sample the desserts. Sociable Geminis on a diet can benefit from group support in a system like Weight Watchers. Find a diet twin who'll support you and have fun losing weight together.

Cancer: The Emotional Eater

Dieting can be difficult for Cancers, who love good food, find emotional solace with goodies, and fill up with comfort foods in tough times. There are sure to be conflicts between the Cancer who wants to be fashionably thin, but also to please the family with Grandma's favorite dishes. Cancerian food conflicts sometimes lead to eating disorders, as with Princess Diana. Remember that you must be nurtured emotionally as well as physically. A diet therapy group might help you deal with issues surrounding food and give you the support you need to stick to a diet. Find nonfood ways to baby yourself: a visit to a spa, walks along the beach, or beauty treatments are ways to help you feel good about yourself while you lose weight. And challenge yourself to create diet-conscious variations of family recipes so the whole family can eat healthy.

Leo: The Dangers of the Good Life

Leo's diet downfall might be your preference for the finer things in life, like dining on gourmet food at the best restaurants. And a Leo that is not getting the love and attention you need can easily turn to food for consolation. Give yourself the royal treatment in nonfood ways and imagine how great you'll look in that sexy gold dress. Let the slim beauty Kim Cattrall of *Sex and the City* fame or bodacious Jennifer Lopez inspire you! Leos, like their lion namesake, often tend to be carnivores, so a low-carbohydrate, high-protein diet such as the Perricone or Atkins diets, might work best for you. If you're having trouble getting started on your diet, give yourself a jump start with a spa vacation. Some extra pampering, plus expert advice, could see you through the first difficult week and get you on the road to healthy eating.

Virgo: Find a Diet Coach

Since Virgo is associated with the digestive system, you can make quite an issue of food quality, preparation, and diet. Many of you will select a very detailed special diet to promote health, such as a macrobiotic diet. Potassium-rich vegetables are especially important, as is your relationships to whole grains. The mind-body connection to overweight has been emphasized by Virgo diet coach, Dr. Phil MacGraw. If you become overweight, it's usually from coping with emotional or work-related stress. To counteract this tendency, add activities to your life that promote peace of mind. Exercises that use mental as well as physical techniques could help you stay with your program.

Libra: Resist Sweet Temptations

One of the most famous diet doctors, Dr. Robert Atkins, was a Libra. A well-spoken gentleman, with a liking for sweets, he fit your sign's profile. At first, the low-carbohydrate diet he advocated was vilified by nutritional experts; however, in recent years, he has been vindicated, and the effectiveness of the Atkins Diet proven. It could be the perfect diet for Libras who often put on too much weight from indulging their famous sweet tooth. Because your sign rules the kidneys, it's no surprise that this diet advocates drinking plenty of water to cleanse the system as you reduce. Since you are one of the most social signs, you may entertain or be entertained often. Plan your food choices before you go out, so you'll know exactly what to eat. Then you'll be more likely to resist sweet temptations. Dieting with your mate or group of friends could provide the support you need and keep you on track when you go out to dinner.

Scorpio: Going to Extremes

Scorpios never do anything halfway and need to be fully committed to their diet. Some Scorpios will go to great lengths to be thin, even resorting to extreme means like stomach stapling or gastric bypass, as Roseanne Barr did. You are gifted with amazing focus and discipline and can stick with any diet, once you have made up your mind. The trick is to eliminate self-destructive food habits. Finding a diet plan you can live with for long periods, such as the South Beach Diet, which worked for Hillary Clinton, will help you avoid the yo-yo diet syndrome.

Sagittarius: Avoid the Quick Fix

Dieting is something Sagittarius does with great difficulty—there has to be more to it than just getting thin. Therefore, an eating plan that is part of a spiritually oriented lifestyle, such as vegetarianism, might have more appeal. Aim for long range benefits by balancing a sane, practical eating plan with plenty of exercise. Beware of fad diets that promise instant results and come with a high-pressure sales pitch. Avoid gimmicks, pills, or anything instant; these solutions are especially tempting to impatient Sagittarius. Exercise is the greatest antidote to overeating for your sports-loving sign, so follow your guru (Jane Fonda), go for the burn, and burn off those calories.

Capricorn: Disciplined Dieting

It was a Capricorn hostess and decorator, Lady Elsie de Wolfe Mendl, who introduced dieting to America, via the 1920s health guru Gayelord Hauser. Lady Mendl served very small portions of exquisitely prepared health food at her elegant dinner parties, a good tip for you who may need to downsize your portions. Another one of the skinny signs, Capricorn has amazing self-discipline, a big help in maintaining weight loss. Exercise or active sports should help you keep the pounds off without strenuous dieting. Food and mood are linked with Capricorn, so to avoid eating to console or comfort yourself; instead, choose upbeat, relaxed companions. Since you are likely to mix business with pleasure, plan your work-related lunches and dinners in advance, so you won't be led astray by the dessert tray.

Aquarius: Diet Trendsetter

Aquarius is a sign of reaching out to others, a cue to make your diet program a social one. Sharing your diet with friends might keep you interested and prevent boredom. It worked for Oprah Winfrey, an Aquarius whose yo-yo weight gains and losses became media events. If you know you'll be going public for a party or wedding, you'll be motivated to look your best. The trick is to segue from dieting to an ongoing healthy lifestyle. Otherwise you'll be back up the scale again. Try to find a flexible plan that adapts to individual personalities rather than one that imposes a rigid diet structure. Keep a diet diary or online blog to help monitor yourself—a tip from Oprah.

Pisces: Addictive Eaters

Pisces is a sign of no boundaries, one of the most difficult to discipline dietwise. You can get hooked on a fattening food like french fries (or alcohol), a habit like coffee with lots of sugar and a roll, and easily gain weight. Your water sign body may have a tendency to bloat and hold water weight at certain times, especially around the full moon. The key for you, as with so many others, is commitment and support. Don't try to go it alone. Get a partner, a doctor, a group, or one of the online diet-related sites to help. Since you're influenced by the atmosphere around you, choose to be with slim healthy friends and those who will support your efforts. Avoid those seemingly well-meaning diet saboteurs who say just one cookie won't do any harm. A seafood-based diet, like the Perricone Diet could be the right one for you. Your Pisces sisters—Queen Latifah, Liza Minnelli, Camryn Manheim, and Elizabeth Taylor—have slimmed down, and so can you!

CHAPTER 10

The Astro Dating and Mating Guide

This year the planet of luck, Jupiter, is traveling through Venus-ruled Libra, the sign of relating (and marriage), so what better time to explore the zodiac to find your twin soul, a romantic playmate, or a lifetime companion? Astrology gives you a powerful tool for discovering why you are attracted to a certain person and how that person might act and react toward you.

Some sign combinations used to be treated like champagne and tomato juice—never the twain should meet. Others were blessed by the stars as perfectly compatible. Today's astrologers are more realistic, realizing that too many long-lasting relationships happen between so-called incompatible signs. There's really no combination that is totally unworkable. We've gone beyond stereotyping to respecting and enjoying the differences between people and using astrology to help us get along with them. Besides, at certain times in life, you might need the stimulation of a sign that thinks and operates in a completely different way.

Even under optimum aspects, astrology can't guarantee that you'll have a problem-free relationship, but it can give you a romantic road map to guide you over the rough spots and reveal what you might expect in the future with your partner, after the initial glow has given way to day-to-day reality. Working in your favor is the fact that no one totally embodies any one sign; we're a combination of all the signs in different proportions. So

146

there will always be some naturally compatible (as well as incompatible) aspects between two people's charts.

Here's a three-step technique for determining if your lover is the right one for a lasting relationship.

How to Predict Your Romantic Success

Consider the other planets in your lover's chart, not just the sun sign (you can look up most of them using the charts in this book). Venus will tell what attracts you both. Mars reveals your temper and sex drive, Mercury how you'll communicate, and the moon your emotional nature. (For the moon and Mercury signs, you can consult one of the free charts available on the Internet, which we recommend in chapter 7.)

Step One: Size Up the Overall Relationship

To do an instant take on your relationship, compare the elements of the sun, moon, Mercury, Mars and Venus, each a key planet in compatibility, in both charts. The interaction of elements (earth, air, fire, water) is the fastest way to size up a relationship. Planets of the same element will have the smoothest chemistry together.

Earth element: Taurus, Virgo, Capricorn
Air element: Gemini, Libra, Aquarius
Fire element: Aries, Leo, Sagittarius
Water element: Cancer, Scorpio, Pisces

When your partner has the same planet in the same element as your planet in question, the energy will flow freely. Complementary elements (fire signs with the air signs or earth signs with water signs) also get along easily.

What if many planets are in other combinations? That's where you'll probably have to work at the relationship. There is tension and possible combustion between fire and water signs or earth and air signs. Taking the analogy literally, fire brings water to a boil, earth and air create a dust storm or tornado. If both your Venus signs are clashing, you will probably have very different tastes, something that could adversely affect a long-term relationship. However, challenges can be stimulating as well, adding spice to a relationship, especially when planets of sexual attraction—Mars relating to Venus—are involved.

Step Two: Find Out How the Individual Planets Relate

Find out and compare how each planet operates in both your horoscopes (sun, moon, Mercury, Mars, and Venus) by comparing its quality or mode. Planets in cardinal signs are active, assertive; planets in fixed signs are tenacious, stubborn; planets in mutable signs are adaptable, easily changeable. Two planets of the same quality (but different signs) do not easily relate—there is usually a conflict of interests— but they can challenge each other to be more flexible or they can open up new areas in each other's lives. This is where you have to make compromises to reconcile different points of view. You'll have to be flexible or give in often.

Cardinal signs (active): Aries, Cancer, Libra, Capricorn
Fixed signs (static): Taurus, Leo, Scorpio, Aquarius
Mutable signs (changeable): Gemini, Virgo, Pisces, Sagittarius

Step Three: Rate Your Overall Compatibility

The planets closest to the earth (sun, moon, Mercury, Mars, Venus) are those most likely to affect close rela-

148

tionships. Where possible, look up your planets and those of your partner in this book and grade them as follows. (The more A's and B's, the better! Y's and Z's indicate where you'll have to compromise to work things out.)

Grade A: for the same element (earth, air, fire, water)
Grade B: for complementary elements (air with fire, earth with water)
Grade Y: for challenging elements (air with water, earth with fire)
Grade Z: for the same quality, but different signs

By now, you should have a good idea of where your relationship stands, astrologically. A further check of the individual planets can answer some all-important questions.

Here's what the individual planets in your charts can reveal about your relationship:

ARE YOU BASICALLY ATTRACTED? COMPARE SUN SIGNS.

The sun sign gives the big picture. Though it is not the whole story, and can be modified by other factors, the sun sign will always have an overall effect.

ARE YOU EMOTIONALLY COMPATIBLE? CHECK YOUR MOON SIGNS.

Emotional compatibility is strong enough to offset many other stressful factors in your horoscopes. Compare moon and sun signs, too. There is an especially strong bond if your partner's moon is in your sun sign or vice versa.

HOW WELL DO YOU COMMUNICATE? CHECK MERCURY.

Mercury in the same quality (cardinal, fixed, or mutable) could give you mental stimulation or irritation. Mercury in the same sign or element could be a meeting of minds.

DO YOU HAVE SIMILAR TASTES? CHECK VENUS.

An incompatible Venus relationship can be very difficult over the long run, if other factors do not balance this out, because it has so much to do with the kind of atmosphere that makes you happy. One of you likes modern, the other likes traditional. One of you has an elegant style, the other is casual. It can be difficult to find the middle ground where you both win. Sometimes you just don't want to compromise that much.

SEXUALLY SIZZLING OR FIZZLING? CHECK MARS.

It is also useful to compare both Mars and Venus signs. Mars and Venus in the same sign or element is strong chemistry. Your partner's Mars or Venus in your sun sign is another big plus. Sometimes, if Mars and Venus are in different modes, it can add sizzle to the relationship.

WILL YOUR PARTNER BE FAITHFUL?

Some sun signs tend to more monogamous than others. Fixed signs like a steady relationship, tend not to have multiple lovers. However, if a fixed sign is unhappy, it will tend to have lovers on the side. The chief culprit here is the sign of Leo, which needs to be treated like royalty or else it will exercise royal rights elsewhere. Mutable signs tend to be the least monogamous. Gemini, Sagittarius, and Pisces are difficult to tie down and more difficult to hold. Sharing common interests and providing a stable home base can be a big help here, especially with Gemini.

WHERE CAN YOU MEET THE SIGN OF YOUR DREAMS?

If you have a sun sign in mind, here are places where they are likely to be (and like to go):

ARIES

A sports event, martial arts display, action movie, cooking school, adventure sports vacation, the trendy new hot spot in town, the jogging or bike path.

TAURUS
A gourmet restaurant, auction house, farm, flower show, garden shop, art classes, stores—especially food or jewelry stores.

GEMINI
Working for a newspaper or radio station, at parties or social events, writing courses, lectures, sociable watering holes where there's good talk.

CANCER
Family dinners, boat shows, cruises, at the beach, at seafood dinners, cooking schools, gourmet food stores, photography classes, art exhibits.

LEO
Big parties, country clubs, golfing, tanning salons, acting classes, theatrical events, movie showings, dancing, nightclubs, fine department stores, classy restaurants, VIP lounges at the airport, first-class hotels.

VIRGO
Craft shows and flea markets, adult education courses, your local college, libraries, bookstores, health food stores, doctor's offices, volunteering at your local hospital or medical centers, health lectures, concerts, fine art events.

LIBRA
Art shows, fine restaurants, shopping centers, tennis, social events, fashionable stores, exhibits of beautiful objects, antique shows, decorating centers, ballet and the theater.

SCORPIO
Banks, tax-preparation offices, police stations, sports events, motorcycle rallies, the beach or swimming pool, the gym, action or mystery movies, psychic fairs.

SAGITTARIUS
Comedy club or film, horse races or horse shows, pet stores, night courses at your local college, political debates, traveling to an exotic place, car shows, mountain climbing, jogging, skiing, discussion groups.

CAPRICORN
Country music shows, decorator show house, investment seminar, prestigious country club, exclusive resort, mountain climbing, self-improvement courses.

AQUARIUS
Political rallies, sci-fi conventions, restaurants off the beaten path, union meetings, working for a worthy cause, fund-raising, flying lessons or airports.

PISCES
Waterside places, the theater or acting class, arts class, dancing, ballet, swimming pool, seafood restaurant, psychic event, church or other spiritual gathering, hospitals, local watering holes.

For your sun sign's compatibility with every other sign, see chapter 18.

How to Keep Your Relationship Sizzling

The Aries Lover

To keep your Aries mate red-hot, be sure to maintain your own energy level. This is one sign that shows little sympathy for aches, pains, and physical complaints. Curb any tendency toward self-pity—whining is one sure Aries turnoff (water signs take note). This is an open, direct sign. Don't expect your lover to probe your innermost needs. Intense psychological discussions that would thrill a Cancer or Scorpio only make Aries restless. Aries is not the stay-at-home type. This sign is sure to have plenty of activities going on at once. Share them or they'll find someone else who will!

Always be a bit of a challenge to your Aries mate—this sign loves the chase almost as much as the conquest. So don't be too easy or accommodating—let them feel a sense of accomplishment when they've won your heart.

Stay up-to-date in your interests and appearance. You can wear the latest style off the fashion show runway with an Aries, especially if it's bright red. Aries is a pioneer, an adventurer. Play up your frontier spirit. Present the image of the two of you as an unbeatable team, one that can conquer the world, and you'll keep this courageous sign at your side.

Since they tend to idealize their lovers, Aries is especially disillusioned when their mates flirt. So tone down your roving eye to make sure they always feel like number one in your life.

The Taurus Lover

Taurus is an extremely sensual, affectionate, nurturing lover, but can be quite possessive. Taurus likes to own you. Don't hold back with them or play power games. If you need more space in the relationship, be sure to set clear boundaries, letting them know exactly where they stand. When ambiguity in a relationship makes Taurus uneasy, they may go searching for someone more solid and substantial. A Taurus romance works best where the limits are clearly spelled out.

Taurus needs physical demonstrations of affection—don't hold back on hugs. Together you should create an atmosphere of comfort, good food, and beautiful surroundings. In fact, Taurus is often seduced by surface physical beauty alone. Their five sense are highly susceptible, so find ways to appeal to all of them! Your home should be a restful haven from the outside world. Get a great sound system and some comfortable furniture to sink into, and keep the refrigerator stocked with treats. Most Taureans would rather entertain on their own turf than gad about town, so it helps if you're a good host or hostess.

Taurus likes a calm, contented, committed relationship. This is not a sign to trifle with. Don't flirt or tease if you want to please. Don't rock the boat or try to make this sign jealous. Instead, create a steady, secure environment with lots of shared pleasures.

The Gemini Lover

Keeping Gemini faithful is like walking a tightrope. This sign needs stability and a strong home base to accomplish their goals. But they also require a great deal of personal freedom.

A great role model is Barbara Bush, a Gemini married to another Gemini. This is a sign that loves to communicate. Sit down and talk things over. Don't interfere. Be interested in your partner's doings, but have a life of your own and ideas to contribute. Since this is a gad-about social sign, don't insist on quiet nights at home when your Gemini is in a party mood.

Gemini needs plenty of rope but a steady hand. Focus on common goals and abstract ideals. Gemini likes to share—be a twin soul, do things together. Keep up on their latest interests. Stay in touch mentally and physically, use both your mind and your hands to communicate.

Variety is the spice of life to this flirtatious sign. Guard against jealousy—it is rarely justified. Provide a stimulating sex life—this is a very experimental sign. Most of all, sharing lots of laughs together can make Gemini take your relationship very seriously.

The Cancer Lover

This is probably the water sign that requires the most care. Cancers tend to be very private people who may take some time to open up. They are extremely self-protective and will rarely tell you what is truly bothering them. They operate indirectly, like the movements of the crab. You may have to divine their problem by following subtle clues. Draw them out gently and try to voice any criticism in the most tactful, supportive way possible.

Family ties are especially strong for Cancer. They will rarely break a strong family bond. Create an intimate family atmosphere, with emphasis on food and family get-togethers. You can get valuable clues to Cancer appeal from their mothers and their early family situation. Whatever you do, don't compete with their mother! Get her to teach you the favorite family recipes, take her out to dinner. If your lover's early life was unhappy, it's even more important that Cancer feels there is now a close family with you.

Encouraging their creativity can counter Cancer's moodiness, which is also a sure sign of emotional insecurity. Find ways to distract them from negative moods. Calm them with a good meal or a trip to the seashore. Cancers are usually quite nostalgic and attached to the past. So be careful not to throw out their old treasures or photos.

The Leo Lover

Whether the Leo is a sunny, upbeat partner or reveals catlike claws could depend on how you handle the royal Leo pride. A relationship is for two people—a fact that ego-centered Leo can forget. You must gently remind them. Appearances are important to Leo. So try to always look your best.

Leo thinks big—so don't you be petty or miserly. Remember special occasion with a beautifully wrapped gift or flowers. Make an extra effort to treat them royally. Keep a sense of fun and playfulness and loudly applaud Leo's creative efforts. React, respond, be a good audience! If Leo is ignored, this sign will seek a more appreciative audience—fast! Cheating Leos are almost always looking for an ego boost.

Be generous with compliments. You can't possibly overdo it here. Always accentuate the positive. Make them feel important by asking for advice and consulting them often. Leo enjoys a charming sociable companion, but be sure to make them the center of attention in your life. If you have a demanding job or outside schedule, make a point to pull out all the stops once in a while.

The Virgo Lover

Virgo may seem cool and conservative on the surface, but underneath, you'll find a sensual romantic. Think of Raquel Welch, Sophia Loren, Jacqueline Bisset, and Greta Garbo! It's amazing how seductive this practical sign can be!

They are idealists, however, looking for someone who meets their high standards. If you measure up, they'll do anything to serve and please you. Virgos love to feel needed, so give them a job to do in your life. They are great fixer-uppers. Take their criticism as a form of love and caring, of noticing what you do. Bring them out socially—they're often very shy. Calm their nerves with good food, a healthy environment, trips to the country.

Mental stimulation is a turn-on to this Mercury-ruled sign. An intellectual discussion could lead to romantic action, so stay on your toes and keep well-informed. This sign often mixes business with pleasure so it helps if you share the same professional interests—you'll get to see more of your busy mate. With Virgo, the couple who works as well as plays together, stays together.

The Libra Lover

Libra enjoys life with a mate and needs the harmony of a steady relationship. Outside affairs can throw them off balance. However, members of this sign are natural charmers who love to surround themselves with admirers, and this can cause a very possessive partner to feel insecure. Most of the time, Libras, who love to be the belles of the ball, are only testing their allure with harmless flirtations and will rarely follow through, unless they are not getting enough attention or there is an unattractive atmosphere at home.

Mental compatibility is what keeps Libra in tune. Unfortunately this sign, like Taurus, often falls for physical beauty or someone who provides an elegant lifestyle, rather than someone who shares their ideals and activities, which is the kind of sharing that will keep you together in the long run.

Do not underestimate Libra's need for beauty and harmony. To keep them happy, avoid scenes. Opt for a calm, impersonal discussion of problems (or a well-reasoned debate) over an elegant dinner. Pay attention to the niceties of life. Send little gifts on Valentine's Day and don't forget birthdays and anniversaries. Play up the romance to the hilt, but tone down intensity and emotional drama (Aries and Scorpio, take note). Libra needs to be surrounded by a physically tasteful atmosphere.

The Scorpio Lover

Scorpios are often deceptively cool and remote on the outside, but don't be fooled. This sign always has a hidden agenda and feels very intensely about most things. The disguise is necessary because Scorpio does not trust easily; but when they do, they are devoted and loyal. You can lean on this very intense and focused sign. The secret is in first establishing that basic trust through mutual honesty and respect.

Scorpio is fascinated by power and control in all its forms. They don't like to compromise—it's all or nothing. Therefore they don't trust or respect anything that comes too easily. Be a bit of a challenge, keep them guessing. Maintain your own personal identity, in spite of Scorpio's desire to probe your innermost secrets.

Sex is especially important to this sign, which will de-

157

mand fidelity from you (though they may not plan to deliver it themselves), so communication on this level is critical. Explore Scorpio's fantasies together. Scorpios rarely flirt for the fun of it themselves. There is usually a strong motive behind their actions.

Scorpio has a fascination with the dark, mysterious side of life. If unhappy, they are capable of carrying on a secret affair. So try to emphasize the positive, constructive side of life with them. Don't fret if they need time alone to sort out problems. They may also prefer time alone with you to socializing with others, so plan romantic getaways together to a private beach or a secluded wilderness spot.

The Sagittarius Lover

Be a mental and spiritual traveling companion. Sagittarius is a footloose adventurer whose ideas know no boundaries—so don't try to fence them in! Sagittarius resents restrictions of any kind. For a long-lasting relationship, be sure you are in harmony with Sagittarius' ideals and spiritual beliefs. They like to feel that their life is constantly being elevated, taken to a higher level. Since down-to-earth matters often get put aside in the Sagittarius scheme of things, get finances under control (money matters upset more relationships with Sagittarius than any other problem), but try to avoid becoming the stern disciplinarian in this relationship (find a good accountant to do this chore).

Sagittarius is not generally a homebody (unless there are several homes). Be ready and willing to take off on the spur of the moment, or they'll go without you. Sports, outdoor activities, and physical fitness are important—stay in shape with some of Sagittarius Jane Fonda's tapes. Dress with flair and style—it helps if you look especially good in sportswear. Sagittarius men like beautiful legs, so play yours up. And this is one of the great animal lovers, so try to get along with their dog, cat, or horse.

The Capricorn Lover

These people are ambitious, even if they are the stay-at-home partner in your relationship. They will be extremely active, have a strong sense of responsibility to their partner, and take commitments seriously. However, they might look elsewhere if the relationship becomes too dutiful. They also need romance, fun, lightness, humor, adventure!

Generation gaps are not unusual in Capricorn romances, where the older Capricorn partner works hard all through life and seeks pleasurable rewards with a young partner, or the young Capricorn gets a taste of luxury and instant status from an older lover. This is one sign that grows more interested in romance as they age! Younger Capricorns often tend to put business way ahead of pleasure.

Capricorn is impressed by those who entertain well, have class, and can advance their status in life. Keep improving yourself and cultivate relationships with important people. Stay on the conservative side. Extravagant or frivolous loves don't last—Capricorn keeps an eye on the bottom line. Even the wildest Capricorns, such as Elvis Presley, Rod Stewart, or David Bowie, show a conservative streak in their personal lives. It's also important to demonstrate a strong sense of loyalty to your family, especially older members. This reassures Capricorn, who'll be happy to grow old along with you!

The Aquarius Lover

Aquarius is one of the most independent, least domestic signs. Finding time alone with this sign may be one of your greatest challenges. They are everybody's buddy, usually surrounded by people they collect, some of whom may be old lovers who are now just friends. However, it is unlikely that old passions will be rekindled if you become Aquarius' number one best friend as well as lover, and if you get actively involved in other important aspects of Aquarius' life, such as the political or charitable causes they believe in.

Aquarius needs a supportive backup person who encourages them, but is not overpossessive when their natural charisma attracts admirers by the dozen. Take a leaf from Joanne Woodward, whose marriage to perennial Aquarius heartthrob Paul Newman has lasted more than thirty years. Encourage them to develop their original ideas. Don't rain on their parade if they decide suddenly to market their spaghetti sauce and donate the proceeds to their favorite charity, or drive racing cars. Share their goals, be their fan, or you'll never see them.

You may be called on to give them grounding where needed. Aquarius needs someone who can keep track of their projects. But always remember, it's basic friendship—with the tolerance and common ideals that implies—that will hold you together.

The Pisces Lover

To keep a Pisces hooked, don't hold the string too tight! This is a sensitive, creative sign that may appear to need someone to manage their lives or point the direction out of their Neptunian fog; but if you fall into that role, expect your Pisces to rebel against any strong-arm tactics. Pisces is more susceptible to a play for sympathy than a play for power. They are suckers for a sob story. More than one Pisces has been seduced and held by someone who plays the underdog role.

They are great fantasists and extremely creative lovers, so use your imagination to add drama and spice to your times together. You can let your fantasies run wild with this sign—and they'll go you one better! They enjoy variety in lovemaking, so try to never let it become routine.

Long-term relationships work best if you can bring Pisces down to earth and, at the same time, encourage their creative fantasies. Deter them from escapsim into alcohol or substance abuse by helping them to get counseling, if needed. Pisces will stay with the lover who gives positive energy, self-confidence, and a safe harbor from the storms of life, as well as one who is their soul mate.

CHAPTER 11

Astrology Reveals the Secrets of the Rich and Powerful: 12 Rules of Success from Every Sign's Billionaires

If you have dreams of running a business that will bring financial and personal satisfaction, some advice from those who achieved phenomenal success could help you make those dreams a reality. Every sign has representative billionaires who have followed certain proven wealth-building secrets that you can apply in your own life. Let astrology help you reach your true money-making potential with these tips from tycoons of each sign.

The Aries Secret: Be a Pioneer

Follow the career of self-made Aries billionaire Sam Walton to learn the first secret of success: Don't be afraid to take a new idea and run with it. Walton took an idea and revolutionized the way we shop. He was a pioneer in setting up megastores, becoming the nation's largest retailer, and where others failed, his operations have remained successful. Today, there are thousands of Wal-Mart stores across the country. He is the perfect example of the Aries innovative spirit.

The Taurus Secret: Be Persistent

Taurus are natural empire builders who go into business for long-term gains. Yours is the sign of staying power that rarely switches careers. William Randolph Hearst, who founded a newspaper empire, and Hollywood's Aaron Spelling, who developed TV series like *Dynasty,* are good examples.

The Gemini Secret: Practice the Art of the Deal

Gemini's naturally analytical mind and way with words can be used to wheel and deal your way to the top. Master deal maker and real estate tycoon Donald Trump has written two books on his techniques, which should make fascinating reading for ambitious Geminis. Be inspired and entertained by this colorful tycoon, who changed the skyline of New York.

The Cancer Secret: Give the People What They Want

Cancer's emotional sensitivity is their greatest strength and enables them to connect with what the public wants and needs. Richard Branson's Virgin Records began when he saw an opportunity to sell pop records at a discount. Later he started Virgin Airlines when he sensed that the public wanted more personal services at reasonable prices than other airlines were providing. Estée Lauder is a self-made cosmetics tycoon who had a finger on the pulse of women's needs. Cancers often create a family business or bring their own family into their successful business, as Estée Lauder did.

The Leo Secret: Think Big, Watch Your Image, and Make Your Own Rules

The current Leo prototype in business is billionaire Larry Ellison, the founder of Oracle software. His enormous risks and daring moves made him one of the greatest success stories of the Internet era. In an industry dominated by poorly dressed geeks, Ellison truly looks the part of a Leo leader with his tailor-made Italian suits and shirts, flamboyant lifestyle, expensive yachts, and private jets. His drive, character, and success inspired a biography titled *The Difference Between God and Larry Ellison*. In the Leo mogul tradition of Adnan Khashoggi and the late Malcolm Forbes, Ellison believes in living the royal lifestyle to the hilt—with all the perks. Another larger-than-life Leo is the self-made billionaire George Soros, known for great generosity as well as risk-taking financial tactics.

The Virgo Secret: Look for Value

The perfect example is Virgo sage Warren Buffet, who, as of 2003, was the second-richest man in the world. Widely hailed as an investing genius, Buffett puts his Virgo discrimination and critical qualities to work sizing up companies, amassing his fortune from a technique called value investing. Like the bargain hunter, the value investor tries to find those items that are valuable but not quite recognized as such by the majority of other buyers. Buffet's practical down-to-earth attitude extends to his understated lifestyle. He doesn't live in a huge house, collect cars, or take a limousine to work. Yet the witty and savvy pronouncements of the Oracle of Omaha are the most eagerly followed in the financial world.

The Libra Secret: Find Your Own Brand and Market It Well

Libra designer Ralph Lauren marketed his own classic personal style into a billion-dollar company and one of the most recognizable and consistently popular brands in the world. He sold his style not only in clothing, but followed it through to home furnishings. An astute businessman, he has managed to adapt to consumers' changing needs and the fickle fashion world, yet retain the elegant, classic image of his brand. That's quite a Libra balancing act! Probably everyone reading this chapter has at least one item—whether it a polo shirt, an evening gown, a dinner plate, or even a towel—bearing his name.

The Scorpio Secret: Stick with It Through Tough Times

Scorpios are survivors. You needn't go farther than Microsoft's Bill Gates, GE's Jack Welch, or CNN's Ted Turner to find businessmen who have weathered great storms and emerged with megasuccess through shrewd career maneuvers and careful planning. You are capable of taking on great responsibility, but may do so from behind the scenes or with a quiet unassuming demeanor. Scorpios specialize in transforming the lives of others: Ted Turner through his charitable donations and transformation of television news through CNN; Bill Gates through his foundations combating disease in Africa and his contributions to education; Jack Welch through his management of General Electric.

The Sagittarius Secret: Be Inspiring

The Sagittarius success is the one who is inspired and inspiring. Walt Disney made America wish upon a star to make their dreams come true. By turning dreams into reality, he transformed the entertainment industry into what we know today. He pioneered the field of animation, and found new ways to combine entertainment with education. No small part of Disney's success came from his Sagittarius quality of vision; he tapped into America's past, connected it to the future, and created a separate Disney World, where life is more fun for everyone. Another visionary in the Disney tradition is film director Steven Speilberg. Actress and fitness guru Jane Fonda became rich and famous from her motivational videos and books.

The Capricorn Secret: Get in on the Ground Floor and Climb to the Top

The Capricorn success story is the one who started at the bottom and worked his way to the top. You keep your eye on the top of the mountain all the way. And you have a great talent for spotting potential business opportunities. Diane von Furstenberg saw a little wrap dress as the perfect dress for the modern career woman and then made her fortune with it. Capricorn moves carefully, according to a plan, and often sees opportunity where others see none. For inspiration, there's the career of Capricorn Jeff Bezos, who took a loan from his parents to start Amazon.com, which became the paradigm of e-commerce. Bezos believed in the Internet and saw retailing possibilities far ahead of everyone else. He has weathered the ups and downs of the Internet to become an established success.

The Aquarius Secret: Be Original

For Aquarius inspiration, look to Oprah Winfrey, who has broken rules of gender and race to become one of America's most powerful women. Oprah translated her natural Aquarius ability to bring people together and to act as a bridge between cultures into a multifaceted entertainment and magazine business. Another great Aquarius success story, media mogul Michael Bloomberg founded a highly original business news network, and since that wasn't enough, he embarked on a demanding political career as mayor of New York City. Barry Diller, the entertainment tycoon, has had a colorful business career, spotting the hot trends before anyone else and capitalizing on them.

The Pisces Secret: Use Your Sensitive Antennae

Though Pisces is not usually considered a business-savvy sign, one look at the list of Pisces moguls easily proves this assumption wrong. Pisces' secret is their sensitivity put to good use. It helps them psyche out the competition, divine the consumer mood, and understand the hidden agendas of coworkers. Teamed with the creativity of this water sign, it's a formidable combination. There are many inspiring examples of successful Pisces, such as billionaire Michael Dell, who dropped out of college to start Dell Computers, a pioneer in direct-to-customer computer sales. At age twenty-seven, he became the youngest CEO of a Fortune 500 company in history. Steven Jobs, cofounder of Apple Computers, developed the Macintosh with an easy-to-use graphic interface that made it the first user-friendly computer—the PC of choice for creative work. It continues to be at the forefront of design and creativity. Pisces also thrive in the management side of show business, as evidenced by Michael Eisner of Disney and David Geffen of Dreamworks, both of whom have molded the entertainment business. Sanford Weill and Walter Annenberg are legendary Pisces entrepreneurs who flourished in the worlds of finance and publishing.

CHAPTER 12

The Great Debate: Fate Versus Free Will

Are we in control of our destiny, or do the stars control us? That is one of the biggest questions of astrology, one which each astrologer—and student of astrology—must wrestle with and answer for himself.

Astrology does not provide a set answer. It is actually a specialized study of cycles, one that links happenings in our own lives with the forces of the universe at large. But most enlightened astrologers believe that you are in charge of your destiny and can use the planetary forces at your disposal as you wish, especially if you understand the nature of upcoming cycles. It's not unusual to compare two charts in which one person has developed in a positive way and another, with similar aspects, has become a criminal. Or as recently happened in New York City, twin teenage girls who were separated as babies in Mexico were reunited by chance when a casual observer mistook one twin for the other. As the girls got to know each other, they were astonished by the similarities in their lives.

In its fundamental assumption that a given moment in time embodies the forces going on at that instant in the solar system, astrology does link us to a divine plan or design. When man first looked toward the heavens, it was in a wish to communicate with God, whether from a Babylonian ziggurat or a Mayan pyramid. The character of each sign of the zodiac was developed in a very systematic way, linking elements, qualities, and polarities. And the influence of the planets was determined after much observation. It is interesting that Mars, in all the various systems of astrology around the world, still embodies the same aggressive force; Venus is still the same kind of benevolent energy; and from the time of the lunar goddesses of Babylonia, Phrygia, and Greece, to modern psychological interpretations, the moon has represented our instinctive emotional self.

Many religious people are threatened by astrologers, because they equate all astrology with that practiced by many charlatans of the past or because they feel that someone interested in astrology will turn away from religion. However, as anyone who has delved seriously into astrology can attest, the study of astrology tends to bring one closer to a spiritual understanding of the interchange between a universal design, the material world and man's place in it. Astrology can, in a very practical way, help man keep in balance with the forces of the universe.

Scientists, on the other hand, attack astrology as a pseudoscience for its supposed lack of factual evidence. We are forever hearing comparisons between astrology and astronomy, which is really more of a parent-child relationship, since astronomy grew out of astrology. History has conveniently forgotten that four of the most famous astronomers of all time were astrologers: Copernicus, Galileo, Tycho Brahe, and Johannes Kepler.

Most scientists have not studied astrology, nor do they approach it scientifically. They do not respect astrology as a discipline in its own right, thereby missing the point of astrology. It is not concerned with linear facts, but with linking man to the cosmos, linking the universe without to the universe within. The rise of quantum physics could bridge the gap between science and astrology, as scientists begin to explore a different reality beyond the mechanistic, materialistic view. Scientists are realizing that their own theories of natural phenomena are creations of the mind itself, depending on the position of the observer and the observed, and by means the last word. When science begins to look within, perhaps the parent-child respect can be renewed and, once again, science and astrology can be part of the same family.

The great psychologist Carl Jung is responsible for creating quite a different attitude, one of partnership, between astrology and psychology. Jung had great respect for astrology and used it in his practice to clarify points which he said would otherwise have been unable to understand. "Astrology represents the summation of all the psychological knowledge of antiquity," he explained. Today, there are many psychologists who use astrology to help them penetrate in depth into the authentic personality of their clients. In turn, astrologers have benefitted by psychological counseling techniques, using them to guide their clients toward personal growth and find positive ways to handle the trends evident in their birth chart.

In this millennium, when the Aquarius Age takes root, we'll be looking for ways to expand our lives. Perhaps in this era, a new, positive relationship will be forged between astrology and science and between astrology and religion, as we find these disciplines more complementary than competitive.

Meanwhile, astrology bashing has gone on in this country for many years. Early in the last century, the proper Bostonian descendent of two American presidents stood on trial for practicing astrology. Evangeline Adams acquitted herself with style, proving her skills with a penetrating analysis of a mystery chart, which turned out to be that of the judge's son. Reported in national media, this marked the beginning of astrology consciousness in this country on a mass level. Thanks to Evangeline Adams, astrology was publicly recognized as much more than fortune-telling, and a legitimate practice in its own right.

Since that time, astrology has grown in popularity, with daily horoscopes now a familiar feature in most newspapers. Where once it was difficult to find an astrologer, practitioners now advertise in newspapers and yellow pages. Some are highly qualified professionals, with years of study and proven expertise. Others simply dispense canned horoscopes from one of the many computer programs available. Still others give readings which depend more on supposed psychic talents than astrological technique.

One debunker of astrology was French statistician Michel Gauquelin, who set out back in 1953 to disprove astrology by correlating astrological data for thousands of doctors, politicians, athletes, and soldiers. He concluded that, indeed, it rested upon verifiable premises. Among his findings, he showed that Mars and Saturn contacts held true throughout the horoscopes of military leaders, and Mars propelled the horoscope of athletes. He also confirmed planetary links between parent and child.

Though astrology has never claimed to be a science, a religion, or a psychology, it has links to all three in their mutual origin in man's search for truth and for his real purpose in life. We might say that astrology is the place where science, spirit, and psyche meet. Astrology has deep roots in all religions and can be found embedded in the spiritual history of every race. However, when religion became linked to doctrine and dogma, astrology, which has been accessible to everyone who wishes to study the planets, parted company with religion. In the Christian tradition, astrology was perceived as a threat to the established church, and astrologers were driven underground or persecuted. But the study of the planets and their relationship to the affairs of men continued, though astrology gained an unsavory reputation as fortune-telling, a connection that still lingers in the minds of those who try to discredit it.

There are still parts of the country where, at this writing, well-organized groups work against the practice of astrology. To assist astrologers in dealing with astrology bashers of all types, the Association for Astrological Networking (AFAN) was formed. AFAN legal committees keep constant watch over those prejudiced against astrology who try to spread misinformation and prevent astrologers from practicing. The organization also works to educate the public about astrological issues and create a network of astrology supporters who are interested in moving astrology forward and advancing the cause of professional freedom. Membership is open to the general public, as well as the professional astrological community, and it's an excellent way to participate in creating a better climate for astrology, as well as protect our individual rights. See pages 124–25 for more information about AFAN.

CHAPTER 13

Star-Quality Style: Let Astrology Help You Find the Perfect Look in Hot Fashion Trends

Styling your wardrobe by the stars is one of the secrets to projecting your sun sign's personality. There's a current look that's right for you—just follow your sun sign designers and celebrities this year and you won't go wrong.

The Trends, Colors, and Looks for 2005

Libra Style: Elegance!

This is sure to be one of the most style-conscious years ever, with Jupiter, the planet of luck and abundance, in fashionable Libra for most of the year. The key to Libra style is balance, elegance, and harmony. Even the most seductive Libra looks are never blatantly sexy or uncoordinated. Hair should be soft—no punk streaks or shaved heads. The wild gelled and moussed manes of recent years will take a backseat to more formal romantic, pretty looks. Libra is creative with accessories and jewelry, so expect some stunning new handbags, shoes, and baubles this year.

Libra Colors: Soft and Harmonious

Libra is associated with soft shades, especially delicate pale pinks and airy blues. It is especially important that the color blend throughout your outfit. Mismatching and jarring colors should be very out this year.

Libra Designers and Celebrities

Libra designers Ralph Lauren and Donna Karan have this sign's special flair. They are known for their total head-to-toe styling, which extends to perfume, lingerie, and home furnishings. That way, there's no chance that a single element can be off-balance. Libra female celebrities like Catherine Deneuve and Gwyneth Paltrow embody this sign's ideal of balance, femininity, classic beauty, and elegant style.

Scorpio Style: The New Sexy

In November, the fashion story becomes more dramatic, intense as the sign of Scorpio moves into the spotlight. Scorpio designers are known for either purity of line or avant-garde trendiness. Gender-bending fashion—skirts for men, masculine looks for women—is very Scorpio. Indulge in sexy accessories like leather stiletto boots and hot lingerie to show your passionate nature. Black leather and fur, biker styling, studs, grommets, strapping, and belts will replace the toned-down look of previous seasons. The look will be very sexy, from subtle hints to blatant display.

Scorpio Colors: Deep and Passionate

Deep passionate colors, especially black and burgundy, will be evident. The more subtle Scorpio look comes in luscious fleshy neutrals á la Calvin Klein. Ocean blues are a good spring and summer color choice.

Scorpio Designers and Celebrities

Calvin Klein created a fashion style that is pure Scorpio, with a streamlined, uncluttered look from head to toe.

He often experimented with androgyny, putting women in male-inspired underwear, for instance. Stars who wear his look well are Jodie Foster, Lauren Hutton, and Julia Roberts. The avante-garde side of Scorpio is shown by Rei Kawakubo of Comme des Garçons, very extreme and slightly shocking. This look, worn by stars such as Bjork and Chloë Sevigny, is a sure attention getter aimed at breaking the rules of what to wear. We may not have liked it, but Björk's "swan dress" worn at the Academy Awards was unforgettable!

How to Interpret Fashion Trends for Your Sign

ARIES
You truly have fun with fashion. Don't take it too seriously. You're always on top of the latest trends and celebrities who influence fashion always include Aries— think of Sarah Jessica Parker of *Sex and the City,* and Reese Witherspoon, who have influenced designers recently. With the emphasis in your opposite sign, Libra, for most of this year, which means a more ladylike, pretty look, you may decide to tone down your flair for drama a bit. But do use your creativity with interesting accessories, especially hats. Go for one stunning piece and keep the rest of your outfit simple and harmonious.

TAURUS
You have developed your own look over the years, be it dramatic (Cher) or classic (Michelle Pfeiffer and Penelope Cruz), and you tend to stick with it. You rarely change your look to be part of the scene. However, you can pull off the pretty, feminine style with flair this year. For those who can wear the more bodacious looks favored by Cate Blanchett or Uma Thurman, there will be more daring exposure of the lower back (associated with

Libra). The hot Taurus designer is Donatella Versace, always on the cutting edge of hot new trends.

GEMINI
Since you have such a changeable personality, you'll probably experiment before you find the style that has your name on it. Some Geminis go for the shockingly sexy like Liz Hurley or Angelina Jolie; others prefer to look superelegant like Nicole Kidman. Whatever you wear is sure to get people talking. This year, follow the looks of designer Anna Sui or the fashion team of Dolce and Gabbana. Double-duty clothes that change personality with a scene-stealing accessory or two are ideal for your gadabout life. A hairstyle that can be worn several different ways would satisfy your need for constant change. Be sure to accent your expressive hands with gloves and fabulous rings.

CANCER
Some of the greatest fashion personalities of all time were born under your sign (Babe Paley, Slim Keith, Princess Diana, Nancy Reagan, Bill Blass, to name only a few). You seem to understand intuitively how to use a trend to suit your personality. This year's soft colors and ladylike styling should suit this sign's romantic nature well. Wear silver and pearls, wavy hair and filmy iridescent fabrics to emphasize your water sign femininity. As this sign is associated with the breast, many celebrities emphasize theirs with plunging necklines (Pamela Anderson, Lil' Kim). Cancer designers Giorgio Armani and Vera Wang understand how to convey your natural elegance.

LEO
Leos are great entrance makers, thriving in the spotlight. In this elegant year, follow the example of superstar style makers like Halle Berry, Charlize Theron, and the late Jacqueline Kennedy Onassis, who have favored simple styles in fabulous colors. Be careful not to overplay your

hand this season. Go for elegance, rather than glitz. Make the most of your fabulous lion's mane, your best accessory, by streaking it with gold, like Jennifer Lopez. Look to the retro designs of Chanel and St. Laurent, who understood how to be glamorous, comfortable, and practical at all times.

VIRGO
Simplicity suits Virgo best. Be inspired by the great screen goddesses Lauren Bacall, Greta Garbo, and Ingrid Bergman, who looked fabulous in beautifully cut classics, many of which could be worn today. Look for timeless, uncluttered designs in neutral colors and navy. Be careful of elaborate evening wear—choose flowing, but not fussy, looks. Even the most curvaceous Virgos like Salma Hayek and Sophia Loren avoid ruffles and flourishes. Virgo fashion designers Tom Ford and Karl Lagerfeld are on your wavelength.

LIBRA
This should be your best year, fashion-wise. Rather than drama, go for elegance in your clothes. Hair should be soft. Makeup should be just enough to give definition to your features. You look your best in beautiful party clothes, formal gowns and wedding dresses, so don't hesitate to dress up. You have an innate sense of balance when you select the perfect accessories and harmonious colors. Stick to the paler shades—nobody looks better than you in pink! Ralph Lauren and Donna Karan are your designers to watch. Be inspired by Catherine Deneuve, Gwyneth Paltrow, and Hillary Duff.

SCORPIO
In November, it's your time to shine. The best look for Scorpio is strong and intense, with deep colors or neutrals. Pull out your favorite little black dress, black leather jacket, and high heels. Scorpio can pull off the sexiest or most extreme styles, ones that would be shocking on another sign; however, most Scorpios should avoid

contrived, complicated clothing. Stick to the pure, simple, classic lines of designers like Calvin Klein. Think of vintage Scorpio revisited: Grace Kelly, the cool kind of Scorpio beauty; Vivien Leigh, the fiery type; or the sultry sexpot Hedy Lamarr in *Algiers*.

SAGITTARIUS
You're hip to the latest trends and know how to adapt them to your lifestyle. Because sports are usually a big part of your life, active sportswear often goes from the playing field to your working life. Usually you prefer casual jeans looks to more formal wear. Choose clothing that travels well, is carefree, and moves with your body. Stay away from fussy ruffles or too many accessories. Britney Spears and Christina Aguilera are Sagittarius to watch. Be sure to show off your spectacular legs, a perk of your sign. Swinging retro fifties styles are trends suited to your sign.

CAPRICORN
No-nonsense Capricorn usually chooses clothing for longevity and avoids trends. Your clothes must project the look that is appropriate for your job or social requirements and be of the highest quality affordable. This Libra year should give you many classic wardrobe choices for work and social life. Designer Carolina Herrera is the summit of Capricorn high-fashion style, while Diane von Furstenberg creates sensual but practical clothing that is ideal for the working woman. Model Christy Turlington creates sporty exercise wear for Capricorn workouts and yoga classes.

AQUARIUS
You're a trendsetter rather than a follower, often as a result of exaggerating your unusual features rather than trying to distract from them. However, your look is always interesting and attention-getting. You can be sensual like Jennifer Aniston, classic all-American like Cybill Shepherd, or as far-out as Christina Ricci. You

can carry off unique clothes that would look all wrong on anyone else. In the rather formal trend this season, opt for the romantic look which is embodied by Jane Seymour. Look to Italian designer Krizia for unusual patterns and carefree knits. The French designer Ungaro does sexy dresses in mixes of bright colors and patterns.

PISCES

Pisces enjoys the role-playing aspect of fashion. You'll switch with ease from crisp, efficient office clothes to romantic evening wear or casual sporty weekend clothes. But you are in your element when you wear glamorous clothes with a theatrical flair. Like Sharon Stone, you can look like a mermaid in simple sequins, or wear a Gap T-shirt to a formal party with a few diamonds added for sparkle. Or take on another personality in tweeds. Your makeup should play up your beautiful eyes to the max! Since Pisces is associated with the feet, shoes should be your special fashion indulgence. Play up your dancing feet with sexy strappy sandals or decorated pumps. Collect boots for all occasions. Invest in stylish walking shoes to protect your posture. For fashion inspiration, some of the most beautiful models are Pisces: Cindy Crawford, Ester Canadas, Eva Herzigova, and Nadja Auermann.

CHAPTER 14

Understanding Your Virgo Self

Understanding how your own sun sign is defined and following its prototype through all the roles you may play in life is an excellent way to connect with astrology. Virgo coincides with the time of harvest in the northern hemisphere, which is conveyed by the symbol for Virgo (sometimes interpreted as a virgin holding a sheaf of wheat). The Virgo personality reflects this time of productivity, of utilizing the fruits of the earth. Therefore, Virgo is associated with daily work, service, health maintenance, usefulness, cleanliness, routine, and order. Virgo occupies the sixth position in the zodiac, where we organize and prepare ourselves for meeting life's challenges. Virgo is also defined by the element of earth, which endows practical common sense and a ruling planet, Mercury, the planet of communication, intellect, analytical thinking. Virgo's polarity is feminine, reactive, yin and its mutable modality (the way it operates) is adaptable, flexible, changeable, transitional. Everything about Virgo is earth-oriented, practical, mentally inclined, concerned with how well things work.

The Virgo Man: The Thinking Man

Contradicting the virgin symbol of your sign is one of the pleasures of being a Virgo man, some of whom have been dubbed the "sexiest man in the world." You are the type who becomes even more attractive with age, like Sean Connery, Richard Gere, and Jeremy Irons. Maturity looks wonderful on you.

Part of the Virgo man's appeal is his subtlety. You never come on too strong. You are more likely to have a modest facade and to be as interested in a woman's mind as in her body. You usually let the opposite sex do the chasing. Though you may be sexually skilled, you prefer to keep your feelings under wraps, leave grand passion to others, and remain tantalizingly out of reach.

The Virgo man is not always as practical, health-conscious, aloof, and appraising as he appears. Underneath, you have a vivid fantasy life, full of adventure, like the world of James Bond, populated by perfect love partners (although the dream may get blurry at this point). You are never quite sure what the perfect partner is, but you know what she is *not*.

Virgo has extremely high standards in life and love. You reach your potential by seeing that everything is well run. Virgo usually chooses the functional over the flamboyant, mistrusting anything or anyone that seems uncontrollable. Your negative side is simply your good side carried to extremes. That happens when too-high standards make you overly critical of others, when concern for health becomes hypochondria, when extreme neatness and organization make you difficult to live with, and when careful budgeting turns into penny-pinching.

Virgo feels impelled to right whatever is not functioning or at least to point it out. Some Virgos, like Michael Jackson, actually create their own isolated perfect worlds, where the real world is excluded. This is one reason why the Virgo male is often called the bachelor of the zodiac. No one quite lives up to that fantasy image.

When forced to deal with the real world, Virgo becomes the efficiency expert, the demanding perfectionist, or the teacher in some way. You are best when you are improving someone in body or in mind—being the doctor or the teacher, and sometimes both at the same time.

In a Relationship

The Virgo man can be a devoted partner when you find a mate who meets your high standards. Like everything else, you work hard at your relationships, though you may not express your tender romantic side easily. You like to have your house in order, and will expect your partner to stick to your agenda. You will tolerate her having a career, as long as she also maintains the home as a well-ordered refuge from the outside world. However, a Virgo's woman is well advised to look beneath the surface of her man and encourages him to express his erotic sensual side, those hidden "Agent 007" fantasies. Otherwise, as the Virgo man ages, he may decide to take a risk and live out some of his fantasies with a younger playmate. Some Virgos leave their sensible mates for a glamorous, far riskier partner who provides them with the taste or adventure they've been missing. As one aging Virgo entrepreneur described his glamorous second wife, "She spends all my money, but she's worth it!"

The Virgo Woman: A Sensible Romantic

Like your male counterpart, the Virgo woman is a paradox. You're renowned for being a schoolmarm type, obsessed with neatness and tidiness. However, some of the world's most seductive women were born under the sign of the virgin—Raquel Welch, Sophia Loren, Cameron Diaz, and Salma Hayek, for example. Looking more deeply into the lives of these beauties, we find women who are extremely health-conscious, devoted to their families, and discriminating about relationships. They have cool business heads and often run multiple business ventures. These are not party girls by any means! Virgo is oriented toward work, not play (the Personal Digital

Assistant must have been invented by a Virgo). You are the type who will turn down a glamorous spontaneous invitation, or an exciting man, if you have scheduled that time to do your laundry. And this will make you all the more desirable to your pursuer! Remember the legendary Virgo beauty Greta Garbo, who wanted to be left alone yet always had a pack of admirers in pursuit.

When you set a goal, you proceed in a very methodical and efficient way to attain it. Your analytical mind will take it apart, piece by piece, to discover where you can make improvements. You do this to people, too. (Caution: With your critical Virgo nature, you can win points but lose your friends.)

Beneath the cool Virgo surface, there's a romantic in hiding, one who'll risk all for love, as did Ingrid Bergman, who scandalized the nation by leaving her family to run off with an Italian film director. Greta Garbo specialized in portraying the women who lived life romantically, like Mata Hari and Anna Karenina, the direct opposite of the Virgo image, and had a controversial ménage à trois in her personal life. Virgo Lauren Bacall blazed with Humphrey Bogart on and off screen, in spite of their considerable age difference. Many Virgos choose men who are contrary to the expectations of others. Someone from an entirely different race, age group, or culture may tempt you to drop your careful plans and take a chance on love!

In a Relationship

The Virgo woman appeals to both mind and body, but even though you may appear supersensual, you are rarely promiscuous. You are more interested in commitment, in finding the perfect mate.

Virgo often has a high-strung temperament that zeroes in on your partner's weak points and doesn't rest until they are corrected. This constant nagging and faultfinding can make you difficult to live with. A better approach is to use your talent and charm to provoke others to take action or to set a good example for others to follow.

Once committed, you're an excellent companion and one of the most helpful mates in the zodiac. Since you have been very careful about giving away your heart, you'll be an adoring wife. You are the perfect partner for a man who needs a helping hand and someone to take care of details. Many Virgos are in business with their husbands, blending work and home life perfectly. You will pull your weight in the relationship, stick by him in difficult times, and even support him financially if necessary. Needless to say, his life will get organized and his diet improved. Virgo is not sparing of a man's ego, however, and must be careful not to let criticism degenerate into nagging. When you let go and allow laughter and fun to enter your relationship, you may indeed achieve the perfect marriage.

Virgo in the Family

The Virgo Parent

Virgo, who enjoys providing useful service, makes a very effective parent, expressing love through devotion and caring attention. Your special strength is in practical matters that prepare your child for survival on his or her own, such as teaching useful skills and providing health care and the best education possible. You'll also develop your child's basic common sense and organizational skills.

Virgo's tendency to worry and be overly critical is better soft-pedaled with sensitive children, who need to develop inner confidence. You'll be more comfortable with the mental side of parenting than with the emotional demands of a needy child. You may have to compromise your overly high standards to give affection and praise, as well as criticism. Though you naturally focus on perfecting details, be sure to give your child room to grow. Realize that making mistakes and taking risks are an important part of education that will help prepare your child for solo flights.

The Virgo Stepparent

Your Virgo objectivity and teaching skill will come in handy as a new stepparent. You'll keep the home running smoothly and deal with your extended family with intelligence and objectivity. You'll allow time for the children to adjust before you make friendly moves, never forcing the relationship. But you may have to tone down your tendency to give advice for their own good. Build up their confidence first by showing warmth, caring, and encouragement. In time, the children will respect your well-considered advice and come to you for constructive, analytical opinions.

The Virgo Grandparent

The perennial Virgo curiosity and interest in all things will serve you well in your senior years. You're likely to remain mentally sharp and as alert as ever! You'll know what's going on and have a well-considered opinion to offer. And, surprise, more people are paying attention now! Maybe that's because you are more relaxed, open, and warmer than ever, and your self-confidence is justified by years of experience. You're especially attractive to youngsters. They come to you for advice because you're the one who knows what works and what doesn't. And you won't hesitate to tell it like it is. They'll consult with you about all manner of problems or hash over the world situation—you're right up with the latest news. Though you're still a worrier, you realize now how many imaginary problems never came to pass, and you've become more philosophical with age. You'll happily offer advice and zero in with sharp criticism when necessary, but now it's tempered with psychological wisdom that truly reflects your deep concern for the welfare of others.

CHAPTER 15

Living Well with Virgo

Does your home atmosphere make you feel comfortable the moment you walk into it? If not, then maybe you need to look to your sun sign for the colors, styles, places, and music that will help you do a makeover on your environment. On the following pages are cosmic tips for selecting the colors, sounds, and places that enhance your Virgo personality.

Virgo Home Decor

Earth-bound Virgos should have an environment that speaks calm and order. You make an art of creating a healthy home that is elegantly uncluttered. For that reason, many Virgos prefer modern architecture or Japanese-influenced rooms. Whatever your style preference, aim for clean lines and provide efficient storage space. Use a subdued palette with lots of white, your special color, to reflect light and to set off the various shapes of your furniture.

Virgos have a special genius for organization and can make even the tiniest space functional and efficient. Antique secretaries, oak file cabinets, printer's trays, and closet organizers get pressed into service. Because you're a reader, there should be plenty of bookshelves and safe storage for your prized record collection. Beautiful compositions of objects you love, natural fibers, and a special air filtering system to provide you with the cleanest air possible would satisfy your Virgo instincts.

With the Virgo eye for detail, nothing shares your environment unless it passes muster. Like Greta Garbo, who even designed her own rugs, you may prefer to craft your own furniture or cabinets. Your kitchen should be especially well planned, perhaps in germ-resistant stainless steel, equipped with blenders, juicers, sprouters, and shelves for vitamins.

Virgo Music

Virgo musical artists, from Michael Jackson to Itzak Perlman, are known for their virtuoso style. Your discriminating taste in music makes you search out the definitive recordings of your favorites to be perfectly played on state-of-the-art sound equipment. In classical music, you might prefer string quartets, Puccini operas, or the Virgo composers Dvořák, Bruckner, and John Cage. Virgo conductor Leonard Bernstein had your passion for perfection. Some Virgo musicians and composers who might add variety to your collection are Michael Jackson, Elvis Costello, Maria Muldaur, Dinah Washington, Mel Tormé, Paul Winter, Itzak Perlman, Barry Gibb, Bobby Short, and Michael Feinstein. Rock fans will go for Beyonce Knowles, Pink, and Moby.

Virgo Colors

Elegant white and earth tones belong to Virgo. These versatile colors are always appropriate in any season. You also look chic in navy and white or in gray tones. Bright colors are tricky with Virgo, because the wrong shade or color combination might jar your nerves. Use brights as accents to your basic neutral palette.

The Healthy Virgo

Virgo is one of the most health-conscious signs in the zodiac. Virgo is the sign of self-maintenance, so caring for the health of yourself and others is usually a high priority with members of your sign. Many great doctors, nurses, and dieticians were born under Virgo, such as the noted heart surgeon Dr. Michael DeBakey.

You tend to troubleshoot your health, scheduling medical exams and appropriate diagnostic tests promptly. You have probably learned that running your life efficiently does much to eliminate health-robbing stress. It's a great comfort to know you've got a smooth health-maintenance routine in place to back you up.

Virgos benefit from exercises that stress the relationship of mind and body, such as yoga or tai chi. Sports that require a certain technical skill to master can also challenge Virgo. The key factor in Virgo-appealing exercises is to offer self-improvement on several levels simultaneously, not just a boring or repetitive routine.

Virgo Getaways

Planning a trip is part of the fun of travel for Virgo. You will stock up on guidebooks and research the Internet for the best values. You'll demand a beautiful setting that has some health or intellectual benefits. As the great teacher (and student) of the zodiac, why not combine a vacation with a learning experience? You might, while traveling in a foreign land, take a vacation course in a subject that fascinates you. Select a subject that is completely divorced from your business. Add a new language to your repertoire while you enjoy the pleasures of Mexico or Provence. Improve your culinary skills at a gourmet cooking school in Paris, or join an archaeological dig in Turkey.

Consider putting yourself in top condition at a health spa, either in the mountains here or in a fascinating foreign country. Switzerland as well as northern Italy has a variety of health resorts and hot springs to choose from. Choose one with a medical emphasis, as well as beauty and fitness.

Indulging your interest in history with visits to the historical landmarks or houses of the period that interests you would make another stimulating and interesting vacation. Tours of antebellum mansions or English country houses can easily be arranged in advance. Many universities offer tours guided by an expert in antiquities and in local culture.

Other possibilities are rock climbing in Colorado, hiking through Wordsworth country (the Lake District of England), or exploring Amsterdam by bicycle. Special Virgo-blessed places are Boston, Paris, Greece, and Washington D.C.—all places of learning with wonderful museums and a vibrant cultural life.

Your bags are probably well made and sturdy, as well as good-looking. Save yourself some time at the baggage claim by labeling your bags with brightly colored stickers. Save your meticulous and detailed packing lists from trip to trip. Then, when you revisit the same destination or climate, you'll know just what to take. Be sure to take along a good book or some stationery to make use of the inevitable delays.

CHAPTER 16

The Virgo Career

Your key word is "service," so your career should be involved with helping others improve themselves or with providing a practical, useful product. Glamour jobs that depend on a flashy presentation are not for you. Nor are you especially interested in public pizzazz. You are the efficiency expert who saves the company money and time, or who monitors quality control. Your meticulous neatness and concern for health make you a natural in the fitness, health, medical, and nutrition fields. This is not to say that Virgo is not glamorous or creative! Who could forget Bergman, Bacall, Garbo! But even in the arts, you are a flawless performer who takes a craftsmanlike approach.

Mercury-ruled Virgos have a talent for communicating knowledge. You are the zodiac's most natural teacher, in the educational system or in some facet of your job. The Virgo eye for detail is put to good use in editorial work, accounting, science, literary criticism (or any kind of criticism), and law. Avoid jobs where too much diplomacy, hand-holding, or flattery is required. Political power plays also irritate your delicate nerves.

Virgo in Charge

The Virgo boss is a passionate perfectionist who expects others to meet his high standards. Your mind is systematic. You are always aware of how smoothly an organization is run. When you spot an error or something out of order, you are quick to report the misdeed or flaw. But you also are a wonderful teacher, known for developing your staff and eliciting peak performance. Though some may find your attention to detail irritating, others will benefit by your caring attention. You are always thinking of your subordinates' welfare; you will make sure they get requisite benefits, sick leave, vacation time. As a boss, however, you may place more emphasis on efficiency than creativity.

Virgo on a Team

The Virgo worker is an employer's dream: punctual, efficient, detail-oriented, hardworking, willing to put in long hours. You are modest and quiet (except when something's wrong!) and do meticulously neat and thorough work. You are the perfect right-hand person who troubleshoots for the boss. You are best when you can organize your job yourself rather than cope with the inefficiency and slipups of others. On a team, your critical attitude may cause friction with less scrupulous types. You'll have to learn to phrase your criticisms diplomatically—usually you will not hesitate to deflate a fragile ego! You shine in a position where others appreciate your dedication and attention to quality.

How to Succeed

Pick a job where your services are vitally needed, then show what you can do. Play up these Virgo talents:

- Analysis
- Your eye for significant detail
- Grace under pressure

- Constructive criticism
- Teaching ability
- Craftsmanship
- Organization
- Practicality

CHAPTER 17

Virgo Celebrities: Let Them Teach You About Your Sign

Want to learn the secrets of the rich and famous? Don't bother with the tabloids. Instead, check the celebrities' sun signs. And when the famous are born under the same sign as you, you'll find you have so much in common.

You'll come across stellar Virgo style in Lauren Bacall, Cameron Diaz, Beyoncé Knowles, Hugh Grant, and Richard Gere. Screen immortals Greta Garbo, Sophia Loren, Charles Boyer, and Ingrid Bergman are archetypal Virgos. The Virgo teacher-type is TV's Dr. Phil McGraw. Your money mentor is Warren Buffett.

If you really want to know your favorite Virgos better, check their planets as well by using the charts in this book. To find out what really turns them on, check their Venus. Or what sets off their temper (Mars) or shakes them up (Saturn). Compare similarities and differences between those who embody the typical Virgo sun sign traits and those who seem untypical. Further your education in astrology and learn what makes these Virgo stars shine brightly.

Virgo Celebrities

Kobe Bryant (8/23/78)
Gene Kelly (8/23/30)
Patricia McBride (8/23/42)

Shelley Long (8/23/49)
Rick Springfield (8/23/49)
River Phoenix (8/23/70)
Cesaria Evora (8/24/41)
Steve Guttenberg (8/24/58)
Marlee Matlin (8/24/65)
Walt Kelly (8/25/13)
Van Johnson (8/25/16)
Mel Ferrer (8/25/17)
Leonard Bernstein (8/25/18)
Sean Connery (8/25/30)
Ann Archer (8/25/50)
Elvis Costello (8/25/54)
Geraldine Ferraro (8/26/35)
Macaulay Culkin (8/26/80)
Lyndon Johnson (8/27/1908)
Martha Raye (8/27/16)
Yasser Arafat (8/27/29)
Tuesday Weld (8/27/43)
Barbara Bach (8/27/49)
Pee Wee Herman (8/27/52)
Charles Boyer (8/28/1899)
Donald O'Connor (8/28/25)
Ben Gazzara (8/28/30)
David Soul (8/28/43)
Scott Hamilton (8/28/58)
Emma Samms (8/28/61)
Shania Twain (8/28/65)
Ingrid Bergman (8/29/15)
Sir Richard Attenborough (8/29/23)
Dinah Washington (8/29/24)
John McCain (8/29/36)
Elliott Gould (8/29/38)
William Friedkin (8/29/39)
Robin Leach (8/29/41)
Michael Jackson (8/29/58)
Rebecca De Mornay (8/29/61)
Shirley Booth (8/30/1907)

Warren Buffett (8/30/30)
Jean Claude Killy (8/30/43)
Peggy Lipton (8/30/47)
Cameron Diaz (8/30/72)
Frederic March (8/31/1897)
James Coburn (8/31/28)
Paul Winter (8/31/39)
Van Morrison (8/31/45)
Itzak Perlman (8/31/45)
Richard Gere (8/31/49)
Queen Rania of Jordan (8/31/70)
Yvonne DeCarlo (9/1/22)
Vittorio Gassman (9/1/22)
George Maharis (9/1/33)
Lily Tomlin (9/1/39)
Barry Gibb (9/1/46)
Dr. Phil McGraw (9/1/50)
Gloria Estefan (9/1/57)
Christa McAuliffe (9/2/48)
Mark Harmon (9/2/51)
Jimmy Connors (9/2/52)
Keanu Reeves (9/2/64)
Salma Hayek (9/2/68)
Kitty Carlisle (9/3/15)
Irene Pappas (9/3/26)
Valerie Perrine (9/3/43)
Charlie Sheen (9/3/65)
Mitzi Gaynor (9/4/30)
Beyoncé Knowles (9/4/81)
Bob Newhart (9/5/29)
Werner Erhard (9/5/35)
William Devane (9/5/37)
Raquel Welch (9/5/40)
Swoozie Kurtz (9/6/44)
Jane Curtin (9/6/47)
Carly Fiorina (9/6/54)
Queen Elizabeth I (9/7/1533)
Grandma Moses (9/7/1860)

Elia Kazan (9/7/1909)
Peter Lawford (9/7/25)
Buddy Holly (9/7/36)
Susan Blakely (9/7/48)
Corbin Bernsen (9/7/54)
Michael Feinstein (9/7/56)
Sid Caesar (9/8/22)
Peter Sellers (9/8/25)
Cliff Robertson (9/9/25)
Otis Redding (9/9/41)
Billy Preston (9/9/46)
Michael Keaton (9/9/51)
Hugh Grant (9/9/60)
Kristy McNichol (9/9/62)
Charles Kuralt (9/10/34)
Jose Feliciano (9/10/45)
Margaret Trudeau (9/10/48)
Amy Irving (9/10/53)
Colin Firth (9/10/60)
Ryan Phillipe (9/10/74)
Earl Holliman (9/11/28)
Brian dePalma (9/11/40)
Harry Connick, Jr. (9/11/67)
Linda Gray (9/12/40)
Maria Muldaur (9/12/42)
Barry White (9/12/44)
Mel Tormé (9/13/25)
Jacqueline Bisset (9/13/44)
Nell Carter (9/13/48)
Stella McCartney (9/13/71)
Fiona Apple (9/13/77)
Zoe Caldwell (9/14/33)
Harve Presnell (9/14/33)
Nicol Williamson (9/14/38)
Joey Heatherton (9/14/44)
Mary Frances Crosby (9/14/59)
Agatha Christie (9/15/1890)
Claudette Colbert (9/15/1903)

Jackie Cooper (9/15/22)
Bobby Short (9/15/24)
Tommy Lee Jones (9/15/46)
Oliver Stone (9/15/46)
Greta Garbo (9/16/1905)
Lauren Bacall (9/16/24)
B. B. King (9/16/25)
Peter Falk (9/16/27)
Ed Begley, Jr. (9/16/49)
David Copperfield (9/16/56)
Roddy McDowall (9/17/28)
Anne Bancroft (9/17/31)
Dorothy Loudon (9/17/33)
John Ritter (9/17/48)
Rossano Brazzi (9/18/16)
Jack Warden (9/18/20)
Frankie Avalon (9/18/40)
Jada Pinkett-Smith (9/18/71)
Frances Farmer (9/19/10)
Duke Snider (9/19/26)
David McCallum (9/19/33)
Jeremy Irons (9/19/48)
Twiggy (9/19/49)
Joan Lunden (9/19/51)
Sophia Loren (9/20/34)
Larry Hagman (9/21/31)
Leonard Cohen (9/21/34)
Stephen King (9/21/47)
Bill Murray (9/21/50)
Paul Muni (9/22/1895)
Shari Belafonte Harper (9/22/54)

CHAPTER 18

Virgo's Cosmic Compatibility: Deal Makers and Deal Breakers for Partnerships of All Kinds

Practical earth signs also have a romantic side and need supportive relationships. The first step is to understand each other's needs. Whether you're looking for a business partner or a life companion, this chapter will help you evaluate your partnership potential. Once you understand how your partner's sun sign is likely to view commitment and what each of you wants from a relationship, you'll be in a much better position to judge whether your cosmic combination has staying power. We've included some celebrity romances (current or past), costars, and lifetime mates to help you visualize each sun sign combination.

Virgo/Aries

THE DEAL MAKERS:
Aries sexual magnetism and positive energy warm you up. You both share high ideals in pursuit of love. Aries puts lovers on a pedestal; Virgo seeks the perfect lover. Aries honesty and directness earn your trust. And Aries needs your meticulous follow-through.

THE DEAL BREAKERS:
Aries can be recklessly impatient, which you will find a

serious weakness. Virgo dedication to selfless service gets no credit from self-centered Aries, who wants recognition for services rendered. Virgo may get tired and feel abused or martyred by Aries' relentless demands. Unsympathetic Aries will see Virgo as a downer.

SIGN MATES:
Virgo Ryan Phillipe and Aries Reese Witherspoon

Virgo/Taurus

THE DEAL MAKERS:
Taurus admires the Virgo analytical mind, while Virgo admires Taurus concentration and goal-orientation. Virgo feels secure with predicable Taurus. You enjoy taking care of each other. Relaxed, soothing Taurus brings out Virgo sensuality. Virgo brings the world of ideas home to Taurus.

THE DEAL BREAKERS:
Virgo nagging can cause Taurus self-doubt, which can show up in bullheaded stubbornness. The Taurus slow pace and ideal of deep-rooted comfort could feel like constraint to Virgo, who needs the stimulation of diversity and lively communication.

SIGN MATES:
Virgo Mel Ferrer and Taurus Audrey Hepburn

Virgo/Gemini

THE DEAL MAKERS:
Both Mercury-ruled, your deepest bond will be mental communication and appreciation of each other's intelli-

gence. The Virgo Mercury is earthbound and analytical, while the Gemini Mercury is a jack-of-all-trades. Gemini shows Virgo the big picture; Virgo takes care of the details. Your combined talents make a stimulating partnership. Virgo becomes the administrator here, Gemini the idea person.

THE DEAL BREAKERS:
Your different priorities can be irritating to each other. Virgo needs a sense of order. Gemini needs to experiment and is forever the gadabout. An older Gemini who has slowed down somewhat makes the best partner here.

SIGN MATES:
Virgo David Arquette and Gemini Courteney Cox

Virgo/Cancer

THE DEAL MAKERS:
You two vulnerable signs protect and nurture each other. Moody Cancer needs your cool analytical nature to refine and focus emotions creatively. You give Cancer protective care and valuable insight. The Cancer charming romantic tenderness nurtures your shy side. Here is the caring lover of your dreams. You'll have good communication on a practical level, respecting each other's shrewd financial acumen.

THE DEAL BREAKERS:
Cancer extreme self-protection could arouse your suspicion. Why must Cancer be so secretive? Virgo protectiveness could become smothering, making Cancer overly dependent. You must learn to offer suggestions instead of criticism, to coddle Cancer feelings at all times. (This is a sign that doesn't take criticism well, even if given with the best intentions.)

Sopranos costars Virgo James Gandolfini and Cancer Edie Falco

Virgo/Leo

THE DEAL MAKERS:
Leo confidence, sales power, and optimism, as well as aristocratic presence, are big draws for Virgo. Virgo will have a ready-made job efficiently running the mechanical parts of the Leo lifestyle, which Leo is only too happy to delegate. And Leo social poise brings Virgo into the public eye, which helps your shy sign bloom! Both are faithful and loyal signs who find much to admire in each other.

THE DEAL BREAKERS:
You may not appreciate each other's point of view. Virgo is more likely to dole out well-meaning criticism and vitamins than the admiration and applause Leo craves. Virgo will also protest leonine high-handedness with the budget. Virgo makes the house rules, but Leo is above them, a rule unto itself. Leo always looks at the big picture, Virgo at the nitty-gritty. You could dampen each other's spirits, unless you find a way to work this out early in the relationship.

SIGN MATES:
Virgo Guy Ritchie and Leo Madonna

Virgo/Virgo

THE DEAL MAKERS:
There's a strong mental turn-on, since you both approach love in an analytical and rather clinical way. Two Virgo

sign mates have a mutual respect and an intuitive communication that are hard to beat. You'll evolve a carefully ordered way of being together, which works especially well if you share outside projects or similar careers.

THE DEAL BREAKERS:
Be careful not to constantly test or criticize each other. You need to focus on positive values, and not forever try to meet each other's standards or get bogged down in details. Bring a variety of friends into your life to add balance.

SIGN MATES:
Virgos Sophia Loren and Sean Connery

Virgo/Libra

THE DEAL MAKERS:
You are intelligent companions with refined tastes, both perfectionists in different ways. The Libra charm and elegant style work nicely with Virgo clearheaded decision making.

THE DEAL BREAKERS:
Libra responds to admiration and can turn off to criticism or too much negativity. Virgo will need to use diplomacy to keep the Libra scales in balance. Virgo appreciates function as well as form, and sticks to a budget. Extravagant Libra spends for beauty alone, regardless of the price tag.

SIGN MATES:
Virgo Jada Pinkett Smith and Libra Will Smith

Virgo/Scorpio

THE DEAL MAKERS:
With Scorpio, Virgo encounters intense feelings too powerful to intellectualize or analyze. This could be a grand passion, especially when Scorpio is challenged to uncover the Virgo earthy, sensual side. Your penetrating minds are simpatico, and so is your dedication to do meaningful work (here is a fellow healer). Virgo provides the stability and structure that keeps Scorpio on the right track.

THE DEAL BREAKERS:
Virgo may cool off if Scorpio goes to extremes or plays manipulative games. Scorpio could find Virgo perfectionism irritating and the Virgo approach to sex too limited.

SIGN MATES:
Costars Virgo Hugh Grant and Scorpio Julia Roberts

Virgo/Sagittarius

THE DEAL MAKERS:
Sagittarius inspires Virgo to take risks and win, and brings fun, laughter, and mental stimulation to Virgo life. Virgo supplies a much needed support system, organizing and following through on Sagittarius ideas. These two signs fulfill important needs for each other.

THE DEAL BREAKERS:
Virgo won't relate to the Sagittarius happy-go-lucky financial philosophy and reluctance to make firm commitments. Sagittarius would rather deal with the big picture, and may resent Virgo preoccupation with details. Sexual fidelity could be a key issue if the Sagittarius casual ap-

proach to sex conflicts with the Virgo desire to have everything perfect.

SIGN MATES:
Virgo Sophia Loren and Sagittarius Carlo Ponti

Virgo/Capricorn

THE DEAL MAKERS:
This looks like a sure thing between two signs who have so much in common. You're good providers, and you both have a strong sense of duty and respect for order. You have similar conservative tastes and a basically traditional approach to relationships. You could accomplish much together.

THE DEAL BREAKERS:
You may be too similar! The strong initial chemistry could give way to boredom. Romance needs challenges to keep the sparks flying.

SIGN MATES:
Virgo Lauren Bacall and Capricorn Humphrey Bogart

Virgo/Aquarius

THE DEAL MAKERS:
Aquarius inspires Virgo to get involved in problem solving on a large scale. You are both analytical and inquisitive, and can both be detached emotionally. You'll appeal to each other's idealistic side, fueling interest with good mental communication.

THE DEAL BREAKERS:
Virgo has a basically traditional, conservative outlook while Aquarius likes to stay open to all possibilities and can swing into spur-of-the-moment action. Virgo nerves could be jangled by Aquarius unpredictability and constant need for company. Aquarius could feel confined by the Virgo structured, ordered approach and focus on details.

SIGN MATES:
Virgo Michael Jackson and Aquarius Lisa Marie Presley

Virgo/Pisces

THE DEAL MAKERS:
Virgo supplies what Pisces often needs most—clarity and order—while Pisces sensuality and creative imagination takes the Virgo lifestyle into fascinating new realms. If you can reconcile your opposing points of view, you'll have much to gain from this relationship.

THE DEAL BREAKERS:
There are many adjustments for both signs here. Virgo could feel over your head with Pisces emotions and seeming lack of control and become frustrated when makeover attempts fail. Pisces could feel bogged down with Virgo worries and deflated by negative criticism. Try to support, not change, each other.

SIGN MATES:
Virgo Richard Gere and Pisces supermodel Cindy Crawford

CHAPTER 19

Astrological Outlook for Virgo in 2005

About three years ago, you established new goals and now you're going to be solidifying the foundation you laid. With Saturn in your eleventh house, energies are focused inward, compelling you to reexamine your goals, aspirations, and dreams. Saturn, whether in direct or retrograde motion, urges you to join the tribe—team efforts at work, in your community, your place of worship, your political party. Saturn in your eleventh house can bring to fruition everything you've been working to achieve.

For most of the year, Jupiter, the Santa Claus of the zodiac, is in Libra, your second house. Jupiter has been in Libra since late September 2004, and you should already be feeling its expansiveness and luck in your finances. If not, you will shortly. Until October, Jupiter should bring you new moneymaking possibilities and opportunities. Your personal values are also expanding under this transit. Your worldview and spirituality may be expanding in new, exciting ways. Foreign cultures and individuals play an intrinsic part in your financial picture.

On October 25, Jupiter moves into Scorpio, a position that will be extremely comfortable for you, and will remain there well into 2006. This marks a time when your life unfolds smoothly, pleasantly. You think bigger; you are able to grasp the larger picture of whatever you're doing. It's favorable for earning more income. Your optimism attracts new people. Your relationships with siblings, relatives, and neighbors generally go smoothly. This transit also influences your communication abilities. If you're a writer, you may suddenly find that your opportunities for publication are expanding.

Uranus—the planet of sudden, unexpected changes—is in Pisces in your seventh house. It's been there since January 2004, so you should notice energy manifesting itself in your life. It influences your partnerships, both personal and professional. You may find that relationships begin and end suddenly. If you're uncommitted, your attraction to potential lovers will be sudden and unexpected, and their attraction to you will be the same. The relationships are likely to be exciting, stimulating, and totally unlike anything you've experienced before. If you're committed or married, your relationship may have sudden ups and downs, but it won't end as long as it satisfies both you and your partner.

Neptune remains in Aquarius in your sixth house. It's been there since 1998, so you're familiar now with its energy. Since it's in your house of health and work, it can confuse your daily work routine because quite often you don't have the full picture. In terms of health, always get a second opinion under this transit.

Your ruler Mercury will be in your sign from November 4 to November 20. Expect news and travel related to writing, social events, and communication in general. Other strong Mercury periods for you are January 9 to 29, when your creative pursuits will peak, and May 12 to 27, when publishing, promotion, higher education, and spiritual issues are highlighted.

Venus, which represents the arts, women, love, and romance, will be in your sign from July 22 to August 15. This is a great time for meeting someone, for strengthening bonds with a committed partner, and for pursuing artistic interests. Another good period for romance, when your sex appeal will be very high, falls between January 9 and February 1.

Keep track of your daily forecasts on the following pages. To be forewarned is to be forearmed. Listen, always, to your intuition.

CHAPTER 20

Eighteen Months of Day-by-Day Predictions—July 2004 to December 2005

Moon sign times are calculated for Eastern Standard Time and Eastern Daylight Time. Please adjust for your local time zone.

JULY 2004

Thursday, July 1 (Moon in Sagittarius to Capricorn 2:00 p.m.) You could be "amazed" by the way people act; this especially includes family members. If receptive, you will learn much, perhaps more than you care to know. Generally a favorable day, including greater financial security. A Cancer is involved.

Friday, July 2 (Moon in Capricorn) The full moon in Capricorn represents your fifth house. This accents children, change, variety, and sexual attraction. An older suitor could be involved. Choose with care. This relationship could be of a permanent nature. Social life will accelerate.

Saturday, July 3 (Moon in Capricorn to Aquarius 1:22 p.m.) A Saturday night to remember! Wear your hair and clothes in different styles. Don't be with people who take you for granted. You will hear someone comment: "You look so vibrant I could fall for you!" Lucky lottery: 5, 8, 13, 22, 43, 12.

Sunday, July 4 (Moon in Aquarius)   Include an oral reading of the Declaration of Independence in festivities. The holiday spirit could be enhanced by a young person who shows intellectual curiosity. Steer clear of dangerous fireworks; keep pets indoors. A Scorpio is in the picture.

Monday, July 5 (Moon in Aquarius to Pisces 2:27 p.m.)   Attention revolves around a domestic adjustment. Questions will concern where you live and your marital status. Win through diplomacy. Don't attempt to force issues. You will get a fair deal in connection with a controversial financial arrangement.

Tuesday, July 6 (Moon in Pisces)   Stay out of sight! Play the waiting game. Do your best work backstage. Visit someone temporarily confined to home or hospital. Your extrasensory perception will be honed to razor-sharpness. Choose number 7 to win. A Pisces and another Virgo are featured.

Wednesday, July 7 (Moon in Pisces to Aries 7:03 p.m.)   Fulfill obligations. Some loved ones will rely on you for their emotional and financial welfare. A relationship intensifies. If you are merely playing games, move on. The "other party" is serious and expects legal partnership or marriage. Have luck with number 8.

Thursday, July 8 (Moon in Aries)   Someone who once played an important role in your life will make a surprise appearance. Maintain your emotional equilibrium. Remember that the heart you break could be your own. The pressure is on, but you will be up to it. An Aries figures in this scenario.

211

Friday, July 9 (Moon in Aries)   The answer to your question: This is a good time to take the initiative, to start your own business. Money will be provided by one who prefers to be anonymous. Be ready for surprises. Maintain an aura of mystery, of intrigue. A Leo plays a dramatic role.

Saturday, July 10 (Moon in Aries to Taurus 3:50 a.m.)   A long-distance communication elevates your morale. Your words will be promoted and published. Focus on civic activities and the ability to locate someone who could represent your talent or product in a foreign land. Lucky lottery: 2, 12, 20, 11, 22, 5.

Sunday, July 11 (Moon in Taurus)   Focus on spiritual values, philosophy, and theology. You could fall in love, even if you attempt to resist it. You will be communicating with someone who speaks "another language." Gemini and Sagittarius figure in this scenario.

Monday, July 12 (Moon in Taurus to Gemini 3:44 p.m.)   Within 24 hours, events transpire to bring you "on top of the heap." Your life could be transformed from the humdrum to the excitement of adventure. You are going places—decide tonight on which direction to take. A Taurus edges into today's activities.

Tuesday, July 13 (Moon in Gemini)   There will be serious discussions about a "change of names." The Gemini moon represents your tenth house. This lunar position relates to your career, promotion, and elevation of prestige. You might wonder about the responsibility, but also remember that "you asked for it."

Wednesday, July 14 (Moon in Gemini)   A family member flashes the green light. Initial opposition is transformed into encouragement. The spotlight falls on where you live and your marital status. You will receive a luxury item that helps brighten your home. Music is likely to be involved; find your own rhythm.

Thursday, July 15 (Moon in Gemini to Cancer 4:40 a.m.) Some of your hopes and wishes come true in a "mysterious way." You learn that discretion truly is the better part of valor. Don't get in your own way; avoid self-deception. By tonight, you will learn the entire truth. A Pisces figures prominently.

Friday, July 16 (Moon in Cancer)   Your cycle continues high. You will prosper with an enterprise that you recently started. Your home environment becomes not only pleasant but also "stimulating." People you respect show confidence in you. By accepting a challenge, you win plaudits.

Saturday, July 17 (Moon in Cancer to Leo 4:55 p.m.)   The new moon in Cancer represents your eleventh house. This relates to the fulfillment of your hopes and wishes as well as luck in matters of speculation. Stick with number 9. Finish what you start. Don't give up the ship! Aries and Libra will play exciting roles.

Sunday, July 18 (Moon in Leo)   Light up the darker areas of your home; this also applies to lifestyle. Do not fear the unknown. Tell about it and write about it. A former president inspired the nation by declaring: "There is nothing to fear but fear itself!" An Aquarius will figure in today's activities.

Monday, July 19 (Moon in Leo)   You regain what had been lost. A secret will be disclosed, and you will benefit as a result. The feeling of being "confined" is temporary. Let people know you are alive and kicking. Capricorn and Cancer will play revelatory roles.

Tuesday, July 20 (Moon in Leo to Virgo 3:43 a.m.)   The moon in your sign means that you will be at the right place at a special moment, almost effortlessly. Your personality is emphasized. You exude an aura of sex appeal. Someone in a position of authority makes a move as if to be intimate. A Gemini figures in this scenario.

Wednesday, July 21 (Moon in Virgo)   You get the proverbial "lucky break." An obstacle is removed. The green light flashes for progress in your building. Correct minor mechanical defects. At home, plumbing needs attention. Taurus, Leo, and Scorpio play instrumental roles and have these initials in their names: D, M, V.

Thursday, July 22 (Moon in Virgo to Libra 12:37 p.m.)   Within 24 hours, you receive news that money owed will be paid. Protect your possessions. Refuse to give up something of value for nothing. Read and write, teach and learn. An exciting relationship could grow hot and heavy. Another Virgo is represented.

Friday, July 23 (Moon in Libra)   Mixing business with pleasure might be a good idea. You could be host to people in authoritative positions. Turn on your Virgo charm and provide the necessary information. Taurus, Scorpio, and Libra will play leading roles. Have luck with number 6.

Saturday, July 24 (Moon in Libra to Scorpio 7:07 p.m.)   Luxury items figure prominently. You receive a gift intended to be a "gift of love." Be receptive, without being obsequious. Focus on romance, illusion, flowers, and the ability to appreciate what you possess. A Pisces and another Virgo will play "stunning" roles.

Sunday, July 25 (Moon in Scorpio)   Your views are verified—this is your day of vindication! A Scorpio relative phones or visits to report the news. Nothing happens halfway, including relationships. Whether you are married or single, the pressure is on and you will handle it adroitly.

Monday, July 26 (Moon in Scorpio to Sagittarius 10:46 p.m.) A short trip is necessary; a relative is involved. A project you started will be completed, and your presence is required. Shortcuts will ultimately waste time, so stick to the familiar route. You will be concerned with the "true meaning of love." An Aries figures prominently.

Tuesday, July 27 (Moon in Sagittarius) The Sagittarius moon relates to your fourth house. This means you will be close to home. You will make repairs and settle differences with a family member. Be independent, without being arrogant. Highlight original thinking; do not follow others.

Wednesday, July 28 (Moon in Sagittarius to Capricorn 11:56 p.m.) On this Wednesday, you learn more about the basic values of possessions, including real estate and home. Don't sell yourself short! You have plenty to offer, and others will acknowledge the fact. Capricorn and Cancer will play major roles and have these letters in their names: B, K, T.

Thursday, July 29 (Moon in Capricorn) The pressure is relieved. You will experience more freedom of thought and of action. A love relationship prospers. You would be wise to start a diary. Take notes of your feelings and dreams. Gemini and Sagittarius will help you stage a coup.

Friday, July 30 (Moon in Capricorn to Aquarius 11:54 p.m.) On this Friday, you will be dealing with young persons who demand your attention. Revise, review, and rewrite. People want to read about you and listen to what you have to say. A "big business" deal is in the offing. Taurus, Leo, and Scorpio will be involved.

Saturday, July 31 (Moon in Aquarius)   On this last day of July, there will be a blue moon in Aquarius, your sixth house. This relates to your work and service to others, but especially to taking care of your own health. Events may not be as they appear on the surface. Make necessary changes—there is no need for an apology.

AUGUST 2004

Sunday, August 1 (Moon in Aquarius)   A family get-together is featured; it will involve a place of worship. Focus on entertainment and recognition of spiritual values. Events transpire that evoke this comment: "I sure did get a lucky break!" Gemini and Sagittarius will play meaningful roles.

Monday, August 2 (Moon in Aquarius to Pisces 12:35 a.m.)   Lie low—time is on your side. You can afford to play the waiting game. Don't neglect repair work that includes fixtures, roofing, and plumbing. You have the ability to transform a "losing proposition" into a profitable enterprise. Scorpio is represented.

Tuesday, August 3 (Moon in Pisces)   Be positive concerning instructions and directions. Get ideas and promises in writing. A flirtation is more serous than you anticipated. Be sure the coast is clear before attending a "special meeting." Gemini, Sagittarius, and another Virgo figure in this scenario.

Wednesday, August 4 (Moon in Pisces to Aries 3:59 a.m.)
Financial aid comes from a surprise source. Stick close to familiar ground, including your home. You will hear

216

the sound of music; find your rhythm and dance or march to your own tune. Wear shades of blue. Participate enthusiastically in planning the remodeling of your home.

Thursday, August 5 (Moon in Aries) Investigate areas that have an aura of mystery. You might learn more than you care to know! Your partner or mate reveals that money is available; this information relieves tension. A Pisces and another Virgo figure prominently. Avoid self-deception.

Friday, August 6 (Moon in Aries to Taurus 11:26 a.m.) Within 24 hours, you receive a long-distance communication. This elevates your morale, because your views will be vindicated. Focus on responsibility, promotion. Learn more about the stock market and how it gets that way. Investigate and invest!

Saturday, August 7 (Moon in Taurus) Look behind the scenes. Be alert to the fact that someone wants to "tell you something." The lunar aspect equates to the realization of who you are and your purpose in life. Participate in a humanitarian project. Lucky lottery: 9, 12, 18, 33, 36, 14.

Sunday, August 8 (Moon in Taurus to Gemini 10:32 p.m.) You will make the acquaintance of someone from a distant land. Be gracious, not obsequious. Be positive concerning the financial status of someone who fascinates you. Live and love but be sure you can live comfortably. A Leo will figure prominently.

Monday, August 9 (Moon in Gemini) Attention revolves around your civic activities as well as proposals that include partnership and marriage. Overcome a tendency to brood. Get off the bench and into the game— it could be the "game of your life." Capricorn and Cancer will figure in this revelatory scenario.

Tuesday, August 10 (Moon in Gemini)   At the track, choose number 3 post position in the third race. You will be lucky in matters of speculation. You could receive news of a promotion. Accent humor; entertain and be entertained. Give full play to your intellectual curiosity. Don't be afraid to ask questions!

Wednesday, August 11 (Moon in Gemini to Cancer 11:19 a.m.)   This will be a "mysterious day" for you. A Gemini is leaving town; the separation is temporary. Revise, review, and rewrite; correct measurements. Rebuilding is necessary. The opposition will represent a "healthy challenge." Do not fear competition.

Thursday, August 12 (Moon in Cancer)   Some of your fondest hopes and wishes will be fulfilled. You will have luck in matters of speculation, especially by sticking with number 5. Emotional involvement should be kept in proper perspective. Maintain your balance and equilibrium. Another Virgo is involved.

Friday, August 13 (Moon in Cancer to Leo 11:28 p.m.)   Despite the date, this will not be an unlucky day. Today's lunar position accents your power of persuasion. Events transpire to bring you closer to your goal. Home improvement will be worth your time, money, and effort. You soon will be receiving important visitors.

Saturday, August 14 (Moon in Leo)   Events will be shrouded in mystery. You gain access to confidential information; keep your secrets sacred. Do not tell all; don't confide or confess. Maintain an aura of exclusivity. Steer clear of a drunken individual who could insist on driving a car. Pisces is represented.

Sunday, August 15 (Moon in Leo)   Communicate with someone temporarily confined to home or hospital. By helping elevate the morale of a person who means

218

much to you, your own morale will be raised. Define terms; get promises in writing. A real estate proposal deserves serious consideration. A Capricorn is involved.

Monday, August 16 (Moon in Leo to Virgo 9:48 a.m.) Last night's new moon in Leo represents your twelfth house. This could equate to a "mysterious adventure." Do not fear the unknown; tell and write anecdotes. You have a ready-made audience; they want to hear what you say and read what you write. Aries is represented.

Tuesday, August 17 (Moon in Virgo) Shake off your emotional lethargy. Your cycle is high, so you will be at the right place at a critical moment. The key is to be analytical; use your reasoning power. Highlight your personality. Realize that you exude sex appeal. Leo and Aquarius will play dramatic roles. Your lucky number is 1.

Wednesday, August 18 (Moon in Virgo to Libra 6:08 p.m.) You receive proposals that involve business, career, and marriage. Speak from the heart. Follow a hunch. Exude confidence and optimism. You will experience a "different" kind of romance. Your security is enhanced. You'll get what you need. You'll also receive praise and financial aid.

Thursday, August 19 (Moon in Libra) You will be lucky if you stick with number 3. At the track, choose number 3 post position in the third race. Be up-to-date on the fashion news; you could be interviewed, tested, and challenged. People will find you intelligent, witty, and wise.

Friday, August 20 (Moon in Libra) The Libra moon relates to your second house. This means you will locate a lost article and will find ways to improve your income potential. Taurus, Leo, and Scorpio will play major roles

and could have these letters in their names: D, M, V.
Rewriting is necessary!

**Saturday, August 21 (Moon in Libra to Scorpio 12:35
a.m.)**   An exciting Saturday night! A Scorpio relative
helps you entertain and could introduce you to the future
"love of your life." A short trip is necessary; take special
care in traffic. Highlight versatility and humor. Express
"romantic feelings." Your lucky number is 5.

Sunday, August 22 (Moon in Scorpio)   On this Sunday, be at home with your family, if possible. Someone
you care about has a gift for you. Be surprised; don't
reveal that you read it here first! Focus on beauty, music,
luxury, and the fulfillment of "romantic notions." A
Libra figures in this scenario.

**Monday, August 23 (Moon in Scorpio to Sagittarius
5:07 a.m.)**   Pay attention to the sale or purchase of
property. Define terms. Avoid self-deception. Repeat this
axiom: "All that glitters is not gold!" It is not possible
for anyone to really fool you, but you can deceive yourself. Know it, and act accordingly.

Tuesday, August 24 (Moon in Sagittarius)   You get
results! You meditated 24 hours ago, and as a result the
answers have come from within. You feel more pressure
due to promotion and responsibility. A relationship intensifies, and could get too hot not to cool down. A
Capricorn will provide meaningful information.

**Wednesday, August 25 (Moon in Sagittarius to Capri-
corn 7:45 a.m.)**   A fast-talking individual tells you
story after story, and most will be based on fiction. Your
response: "Please don't patronize me. It embarrasses
me!" Remember, it can be fun to be fooled, but not to
be deceived. Aries and Libra will play stimulating roles.
Your lucky number is 9.

Thursday, August 26 (Moon in Capricorn)   Take the initiative. Make personal appearances. Be open-minded about a romantic relationship, but don't be naive. Wear bright colors, including silver and gold. Emphasize originality, take the initiative, and create your own tradition.

Friday, August 27 (Moon in Capricorn to Aquarius 9:07 a.m.)   You come down to earth! Focus on your home, security, partnership, and marriage. Your "services" will be required by more people; you will profit as a result. Cancer and Capricorn could become your valuable allies. Make a decision about your goals.

Saturday, August 28 (Moon in Aquarius)   This could be a lively Saturday night! Keep resolutions about your diet and intake of adult beverages. You are being observed and could be regarded as a "role model." Focus on your intellectual curiosity. Ask questions, show wit and humor. Have luck with number 3.

Sunday, August 29 (Moon in Aquarius to Pisces 10:33 a.m.)   Give an Aquarius credit for being innovative. However, avoid being obsequious. You could be invited to join a special group interested in metaphysics, including astrology. Taurus, Leo, and Scorpio will play intriguing roles and have these letters in their names: D, M, V.

Monday, August 30 (Moon in Pisces)   The full moon in Pisces last night represents your seventh house. The emphasis will be on how the public relates to you, legal matters, partnership, and marriage. Blend logic with impulsiveness. Dare to dream, but at the same time protect yourself in emotional clinches. A Gemini figures prominently.

Tuesday, August 31 (Moon in Pisces to Aries 1:46 p.m.)   Home and marriage figure prominently. You win via diplomacy. You lose by attempting to force issues or decisions. Music plays a role. Your own voice will be melodious, so sing in or out of the shower! Taurus, Libra, and Scorpio will play memorable roles.

SEPTEMBER 2004

Wednesday, September 1 (Moon in Aries)   You could learn more than you care to know! The emphasis is on the financial status of someone who would like to be your partner or mate. Don't be embarrassed to ask questions; you have the right to know. Taurus, Leo, and Scorpio play fascinating roles and have these letters in their names: D, M, V.

Thursday, September 2 (Moon in Aries to Taurus 8:16 p.m.)   Take notes regarding feelings and opinions. A flirtation lends spice and could become more serious than you anticipated. Try to remember a dream you had last night; it could, if properly interpreted, relate to your future. Gemini, Virgo, and Sagittarius will play fascinating roles.

Friday, September 3 (Moon in Taurus)   A family member makes a surprise announcement; it relates to philosophy or possibly a journey in connection with education. Remember recent resolutions about the wisdom of restraint. A domestic adjustment could include an actual change of residence or marital status. Libra is represented.

Saturday, September 4 (Moon in Taurus)   On this Saturday night, avoid self-deception. The moon is in Taurus, so someone could be "throwing you the bull." Look beyond the immediate. Learn more about what really interests you. The focus will be on romantic illusion and a philosophical way of getting at the truth.

Sunday, September 5 (Moon in Taurus to Gemini 6:24 a.m.)   This is your power play day! You get the backing of authorities. Financing will cease to be of concern. Although it is Sunday, you receive calls relating to your career and business. This could be a time of love and money. Tonight can feature love and laughter.

Monday, September 6 (Moon in Gemini)   Finish what you started two months ago. Fulfill a dream. Don't give up the ship! The emphasis is on participation in a humanitarian endeavor. An important relationship could start or finish. If realistic, you'll know where you are going and how to obtain your objective.

Tuesday, September 7 (Moon in Gemini to Cancer 6:49 p.m.)   You are on the precipice of fulfilling your hopes and wishes. Pay heed to your intuitive intellect. What appeared to be "out of reach" is closer than you expect. You might decipher this day as one of love, money, and improved health. Your lucky number is 1.

Wednesday, September 8 (Moon in Cancer)   Focus on your home, family, marriage, and an offer of business partnership. Someone you care about will prove loyal and sincerely wants to be of service. Capricorn and Cancer will play mysterious roles. Lucky lottery: 2, 12, 22, 13, 18, 5.

Thursday, September 9 (Moon in Cancer)   Your popularity is on the rise. People offer to wine and dine you. Be selective. Maintain an aura of exclusivity. Many of your hopes and wishes will be fulfilled. This will be a joyous day. In matters of speculation, stick with number 3. A Gemini figures in this scenario.

Friday, September 10 (Moon in Cancer to Leo 7:05 a.m.) Progress appears to be at a standstill, but this is only temporary. A mechanical defect will be corrected; take care of other repairs that include roofing and plumbing. A relationship will become controversial. Know it, and prepare accordingly.

Saturday, September 11 (Moon in Leo)   Get viewpoints and ideas on paper. Be sure to get credit for what you have achieved. It might be best to take notes in diary form. Gemini, Sagittarius, and another Virgo play significant roles and could have these letters in their names: E, N, W. Your lucky number is 5.

Sunday, September 12 (Moon in Leo to Virgo 5:15 p.m.)   The emphasis is on where you live and your marital status. Your cycle moves up, so circumstances will be turning in your favor. Don't force issues. If diplomatic, you gain an important advantage. You receive a gift, a luxury item; it is meant to be a "gift of love." A Taurus is involved.

Monday, September 13 (Moon in Virgo)   If you avoid self-deception, events will transpire to bring you closer to your goal. Your moon cycle is high, so you will be at the right place at a special moment. Your personality is almost overwhelming; you exude an aura of sex appeal. A Pisces will play a major role.

Tuesday, September 14 (Moon in Virgo)   The new moon in your sign clearly indicates that you must take the initiative. This could be your day for a "power play." A love relationship gets too hot not to cool down. Focus also on your career, business, and the ability to "move up the ladder." Capricorn is represented.

Wednesday, September 15 (Moon in Virgo to Libra 12:52 a.m.)   Circumstances are ripe for completing an important project. Emphasize universal appeal. Give and receive love. This will not be a "calm" day. You will, however, do what must be done, and you will advance accordingly. Lucky lottery: 15, 40, 32, 9, 18, 33.

Thursday, September 16 (Moon in Libra)   At the track, choose number 1 post position in the first race. The number 1 will appear in your activities more than by coincidence. Take the initiative; don't wait for others. Be confident and direct. Make it clear that you are starting on your own. A Leo is in the picture.

Friday, September 17 (Moon in Libra to Scorpio 6:24 a.m.)   Protect your possessions. You locate a lost article in a "mysterious" way. The spotlight is also on civic activities, partnership, and marriage. Decide upon your direction and motivation. If you meditate, the answers will come from within. A Cancer plays an important role.

Saturday, September 18 (Moon in Scorpio)   The light touch is necessary. Display humor, versatility, and intellectual curiosity. The Scorpio moon represents your third house. Take special care in traffic, and make a gesture of reconciliation to a relative. Gemini and Sagittarius will play outstanding roles. Your lucky number is 3.

Sunday, September 19 (Moon in Scorpio to Sagittarius 10:28 a.m.)   This is your "makeover" day. Wear your hair and clothes in a different style. Tear down in order to rebuild. Be sure that your base is solid and that tools are workable. What begins as routine could be transformed into a creative endeavor. A Scorpio figures prominently.

Monday, September 20 (Moon in Sagittarius)   Your living quarters become more comfortable. You feel secure enough to begin writing. The key is communication and selectivity where romance is concerned. Gemini, Sagittarius, and another Virgo play instrumental roles and have these letters in their names: E, N, W.

Tuesday, September 21 (Moon in Sagittarius to Capricorn 1:34 p.m.)   Attention revolves around where you live and your marital status. Don't play games with your emotions; the heart you break could be your own. Beautify your surroundings; make your home inviting and beautiful. You soon will be entertaining people important to you—make a good impression!

Wednesday, September 22 (Moon in Capricorn)   Focus on change, travel, and a variety of sensations. A relationship takes on an aspect of being permanent. Define terms. Get commitments in writing. Avoid self-deception. A real estate proposal is not what it seems to be. A Pisces plays a dynamic role.

Thursday, September 23 (Moon in Capricorn to Aquarius 4:09 p.m.)   You get things your way, and today your way is the right way. Focus on organization and getting your priorities in order. A relationship intensifies. If you are asking, "Is it serious?"—the answer is "Very serious!" Capricorn and Cancer play featured roles.

Friday, September 24 (Moon in Aquarius)   Do your job in a "different" way. Someone who held you back will be gone. Now the way is cleared for progress, so respond accordingly. You will attract people to you. You gain a reputation for solving problems and predicting the future. An Aries plays a role.

Saturday, September 25 (Moon in Aquarius to Pisces 6:55 p.m.)   On this Saturday, attention revolves around the excitement of a "new romance." Don't give up something of value for a temporary thrill. Avoid a heavy drinker. This will be a very significant Saturday night! Imprint your style; wear bright colors. Have luck with number 1.

Sunday, September 26 (Moon in Pisces)   Play the waiting game. Although it is Sunday, you will receive proposals that include business, career, and marriage. Focus on direction, motivation, and meditation. Interest in theology will increase. You will discern your purpose in life—why you are here and what to do about it.

Monday, September 27 (Moon in Pisces to Aries 10:57 p.m.)   Entertain and be entertained. You will be questioned about legal rights and permissions. Have your accounting books in order; be sure that you are on the right side of the law. Deception at this time will be clearly detected. Another Virgo is involved.

Tuesday, September 28 (Moon in Aries)   The full moon in Aries represents your eighth house. This equates to the financial status of your partner or mate. Be meticulous in checking details. You are due for a surprise that could be pleasant, if you so permit. An Aries will figure prominently.

Wednesday, September 29 (Moon in Aries)   Steer clear of people who take you for granted. Get promises in writing. Realize that a "mild flirtation" could become serious. Money and security are involved. Do not assume that someone who paints a rosy picture is sincere. A Gemini is represented.

Thursday, September 30 (Moon in Aries to Taurus 5:23 a.m.)   On this last day of September, be close to your home and family. You receive good news in connection with finances, cooperative efforts, and marriage. Your voice is melodious; permission is hereby granted for you to sing in or out of the shower. Your lucky number is 6.

OCTOBER 2004

Friday, October 1 (Moon in Taurus)   On this Friday, you possess the ability to analyze events and cycles and ultimately to predict the future. Meeting with someone of the opposite sex could be the start of something important. The key is to take notes, to read and write, to teach and learn. A Gemini plays a role.

Saturday, October 2 (Moon in Taurus to Gemini 2:55 p.m.)   On this Saturday, you find ways of living up to your potential. Discuss philosophy and theology with Taurus. A publishing opportunity exists, if you take the initiative. Attention revolves around your home, family, decorating, and remodeling; hang paintings and pictures on the walls.

Sunday, October 3 (Moon in Gemini)   The Gemini moon relates to your tenth house. This emphasizes your career, business, and a willingness to accept more responsibility with the pressure that goes with it. Spiritual values figure prominently; answers will come from within. Avoid self-deception.

Monday, October 4 (Moon in Gemini)   On this Monday, the realization hits home that you are doing something important and that many people rely on you for their emotional and financial welfare. A Gemini superior relates facts and figures, and also helps elevate your morale. Your lucky number is 8.

Tuesday, October 5 (Moon in Gemini to Cancer 2:53 a.m.)   What a Tuesday! The lunar position equates to surprises of a pleasant variety. This day will be lucky for you in money and in romance. Someone who had been holding back payment will have a change of heart. Aries and Libra will play major roles.

228

Wednesday, October 6 (Moon in Cancer) Take the initiative in making a fresh start in a new direction. Then many hopes and wishes could become realities. Elements of timing and of luck ride with you; stick with number 1. Wear bright colors and make personal appearances. A Leo will play a dramatic role.

Thursday, October 7 (Moon in Cancer to Leo 3:22 p.m.) Some of your associates, perhaps family members, are planning a surprise for you. A secret meeting is held, and at the conclusion your prestige will zoom upward. Proposals are received that include business, career, and marriage. A Cancer is involved.

Friday, October 8 (Moon in Leo) The emphasis is on personal possessions, your income potential, and the ability to locate a lost article. Emotions tend to dominate; give logic at least equal time. Social activities are highlighted; you could be the subject of a "surprise party." A Sagittarius will figure prominently.

Saturday, October 9 (Moon in Leo) Two people, both of them close to you, will argue about who owns what and what to do about it. Remain neutral, if possible. You do not have all the information; wait, observe, and listen. Be discreet; regard secrets as sacred. A Scorpio will have a temperamental outburst; calm soon prevails.

Sunday, October 10 (Moon in Leo to Virgo 1:58 a.m.) It's your lunar cycle high. You get the proverbial "lucky break." Circumstances are taking a dramatic turn in your favor, even as you read these lines. Romance begins to spark; this applies whether you are married or single. Gemini, Sagittarius, and another Virgo will play meaningful roles.

Monday, October 11 (Moon in Virgo) A major domestic adjustment could include a possible change of residence or marital status. Be gentle and diplomatic, if you want to win. By attempting to force issues, you lose credibility and money. Taurus, Libra, and Scorpio will be your personal "soldiers."

Tuesday, October 12 (Moon in Virgo to Libra 9:30 a.m.)-Don't fool yourself about grandiose promises—get commitments in writing. The moon leaves your sign. Pressure is relieved, and you will be given a clear picture of the immediate future. Pisces and another Virgo play top roles and push aside obstructions to your progress.

Wednesday, October 13 (Moon in Libra) On this Wednesday, you discover ways to increase profits. Focus on organization, recognition of priorities, and how to make the best use of them. A romantic relationship grows hot and heavy and could get too hot not to cool down. Lucky lottery: 8, 47, 12, 18, 2, 25.

Thursday, October 14 (Moon in Libra to Scorpio 2:09 p.m.) Last night's new moon and solar eclipse happened in Libra, your second house. There could be a shake-up of funds, especially savings. The number 9 numerical cycle marks the beginning or ending of a transaction. Aries and Libra will play pivotal roles and could have these letters in their names: I and R.

Friday, October 15 (Moon in Scorpio) A short trip is necessary in connection with a relative who seeks your counsel. Emphasize independence of thought and of action. Avoid heavy lifting. Imprint your style. Leo and Aquarius will play dramatic roles and could have these letters in their names: A, S, J. Your lucky number is 1.

Saturday, October 16 (Moon in Scorpio to Sagittarius 4:57 p.m.) A rare opportunity exists to make a choice of whether to remain at home or to embark on a journey. The number 2 numerical cycle relates to the moon, your family, home, and marriage. The moon in your third house means a short trip. Do not wander too far!

Sunday, October 17 (Moon in Sagittarius)   You learn more about your property values and the need for home repairs. Maintain a jovial attitude. People want to be with you, and some insist on wining and dining you. You will be active in the local political scene. Gemini and Sagittarius will play significant roles and have these letters in their names: C, L, U.

Monday, October 18 (Moon in Sagittarius to Capricorn 7:06 p.m.)   An excellent day for detail work, for repairs, for checking measurements. Be thorough, and you cannot possibly go wrong. However, if your attention skips vital details, you will go wrong. Rewrite and rebuild. Wear your hair and clothes in different styles. This is your "makeover" day.

Tuesday, October 19 (Moon in Capricorn)   You will be the "star of your own show." The emphasis is on creativity, style, and sex appeal. Be selective. Don't let just anyone enter your private circle. Express yourself in writing. Let the whole wide world know that you are alive and kicking.

Wednesday, October 20 (Moon in Capricorn to Aquarius 9:37 p.m.)   Today's scenario highlights children, challenge, and a variety of sensations. Stay close to home. The rules will bend to favor your endeavors. Turn on your Virgo charm. Win your way through diplomacy and generosity. Taurus, Libra, and Scorpio figure in this scenario. Your lucky number is 6.

Thursday, October 21 (Moon in Aquarius)   See people and relationships as they are, not merely as you wish they could be. Keep recent health resolutions that in-

231

clude exercise, diet, and nutrition. An Aquarius will play a role in this area, introducing you to someone who practices unorthodox medicine.

Friday, October 22 (Moon in Aquarius) Define terms. Be sure you get promises in writing. The moon in your sixth house indicates that your services will be in demand. Interest will be fanned in the mantic arts and sciences, including astrology. You learn more about "alternative medicine." A Pisces is involved.

Saturday, October 23 (Moon in Aquarius to Pisces 1:13 a.m.) Avoid snap decisions. Time is on your side. You don't have all the necessary information. Legal matters could be discussed. Be positive about rights and permissions. Many answers will be found behind the scenes. Someone wants to tell you something, but is shy about approaching you.

Sunday, October 24 (Moon in Pisces) On this Sunday, you will be inspired to pursue romance and spiritual endeavors. The question of marriage will loom large. Time remains on your side. You can afford to play the waiting game. Leo and Aquarius will play dramatic, memorable roles. Have luck with number 1.

Monday, October 25 (Moon in Pisces to Aries 6:24 a.m.) The Aries moon represents your eighth house. This tells of the assets of your partner or mate. The eighth house also relates to life and death, to the occult, and to what is hidden. Capricorn and Cancer play fascinating roles and are apt to have these letters in their names: B, K, T.

Tuesday, October 26 (Moon in Aries) Accent diversity. Experiment. Find ways to make people laugh. You could invent a game. You discover that what gives you pleasure also entertains others. You have many hidden talents, Virgo! Today, some of your artistic abilities surge forward.

Wednesday, October 27 (Moon in Aries to Taurus 1:37 p.m.)   Within 24 hours, you receive news that your work or your writings receive favorable notice. This does not necessarily make you rich, but it is great for your morale. Taurus, Leo, and Scorpio will figure in today's scenario. Look for these letters in their names: D, M, V.

Thursday, October 28 (Moon in Taurus)   The full moon and lunar eclipse last night occurred in Taurus. That is your ninth house, which deals with philosophy, theology, and a possible long journey. Check reservations and appointments. The key is to communicate, to write to establish your "true identity." Ideas will come "easy." Your lucky number is 5.

Friday, October 29 (Moon in Taurus to Gemini 11:11 p.m.)   People gather around you, expressing eagerness to hear what you say. The moon in your ninth house equates to theology, spirituality, and ways to make the abstract crystal clear. Taurus, Libra, and Scorpio figure prominently in today's activities.

Saturday, October 30 (Moon in Gemini)   Your prestige rises! You could be given a special honor on this Saturday night. Avoid being obsequious—you deserve what you get. You've done many things for many people in the recent past. Your judgment about movies and literature will be eagerly sought. Maintain your high standards.

Sunday, October 31—Daylight Saving Time Ends (Moon in Gemini)   On this Sunday, the last day of the month and also Halloween, there will be an "emotional rampage." You want to get into the spirit of the holiday, but you don't really agree with its meaning and manifestations. Capricorn and Cancer will "dress up" in Halloween costumes. Pay mild compliments. It will be made clear that you don't approve or disapprove.

NOVEMBER 2004

Monday, November 1 (Moon in Gemini to Cancer 9:53 a.m.) On this first day of November, stay close to home. You will receive an important call or communication having to do with your business or career. A major domestic adjustment could revolve around your income potential and marital status. A Libra figures prominently.

Tuesday, November 2 (Moon in Cancer) Do not equate delay with defeat; what you have been waiting for will arrive tonight. Someone who cares about you is singing your praises. You may find out about it, and if you do, be grateful. Pisces and another Virgo will play astonishing roles.

Wednesday, November 3 (Moon in Cancer to Leo 10:32 p.m.) What you wish for is likely to be granted. Don't ask for more than you can handle! A love relationship is too hot not to cool down. Questions concern business, basic priorities, and marriage. Capricorn and Cancer play essential roles. Your lucky number is 8.

Thursday, November 4 (Moon in Leo) What had been a dilemma will "dissolve." You learn a secret. You'll also deal with the unknown in a courageous way. It will be true that there is nothing for you to fear except fear itself. Finish an idealistic project; work with an Aries.

Friday, November 5 (Moon in Leo) Accent original thinking. Make a fresh start in a new direction. This is an excellent time to start a business. Imprint your own style; dress up your product and utilize showmanship. Avoid heavy lifting. Advertise and publicize. Have luck with number 1.

Saturday, November 6 (Moon in Leo to Virgo 10:00 a.m.)   At the track, choose number 2 post position in the second race. A family member confides in you, but fears your response. Exert your ability to understand. Avoid accusations; highlight wisdom. In this way, you will gain respect and love. A Cancer is involved.

Sunday, November 7 (Moon in Virgo)   Check historical records. Circumstances favor your efforts, and you could be asked to impart knowledge to those willing to learn. Define terms; outline boundaries. Work with Gemini and Sagittarius. In matters of speculation, stick with number 3.

Monday, November 8 (Moon in Virgo to Libra 6:23 p.m.)   It's your lunar cycle high, so events will transpire to help you reach your goal. You get the proverbial "lucky break." Accent diversity, versatility, and intellectual curiosity. What had been lost will be recovered. Taurus, Leo, and Scorpio figure in this scenario.

Tuesday, November 9 (Moon in Libra)   You could win a contest! Be ready for change, travel, variety, and the excitement of adventure. The Libra moon represents your second house. That section of your horoscope relates to payments, collections, and the location of a lost article. Don't give up the ship! You could be on the way to a "gravy train."

Wednesday, November 10 (Moon in Libra to Scorpio 11:06 p.m.)   A gift is received. It's a luxury item meant to be a "gift of love." Focus on the restoration of domestic harmony. Taurus, Libra, and Scorpio will play significant roles. Money that you recently "lost" will be recovered. Lucky lottery: 6, 12, 15, 18, 22, 7.

Thursday, November 11 (Moon in Scorpio) What appears to be a defeat could turn out be a "victory in disguise." All is not what it appears to be on the surface. All that glitters is not gold, but you could "find gold." A romantic illusion is fulfilled, if you avoid self-deception. Pisces is represented.

Friday, November 12 (Moon in Scorpio) The new moon in Scorpio is in your third house. This means that you will have a more positive view of relatives. A short trip is featured and could include Capricorn and Cancer. The pressure is on due to added responsibility. You will be up to it and could prosper as a result.

Saturday, November 13 (Moon in Scorpio to Sagittarius 12:57 a.m.) At the track, choose number 8 post position in the ninth race. Look beyond the immediate. You could receive an offer that takes you overseas. Get commitments in writing. Participate in a humanitarian project. Let go of previous notions. You can do the "impossible," if you so desire.

Sunday, November 14 (Moon in Sagittarius) Spiritual values surface. Light up dark corners of your home. Wear brighter colors when you make personal appearances. The numerical cycle is number 1, and you will be first in line on numerous occasions. A love relationship is hot and heavy—and serious.

Monday, November 15 (Moon in Sagittarius to Capricorn 1:34 a.m.) Be optimistic, especially in connection with a creative project and romance. The spotlight is on passion, children, and your marital status. Tonight, you learn about direction, motivation, and the value of

236

meditation. Capricorn and Cancer will play meaningful roles.

Tuesday, November 16 (Moon in Capricorn) Elements of "good fortune" are with you. Take a chance on romance. In matters of speculation, stick with number 3. You will be tested and challenged regarding views on fashion. Express yourself freely and bring forth artistic talents.

Wednesday, November 17 (Moon in Capricorn to Aquarius 2:40 a.m.) The Aquarius moon in your sixth house relates to work, employment, and general health. Keep resolutions concerning exercise, diet, and knowledge of nutrition. Taurus, Leo, and Scorpio will play prominent roles. A rebuilding process gets under way.

Thursday, November 18 (Moon in Aquarius) Free yourself of destructive ideas. Don't fear the unknown; tell anecdotes about it and write your opinions. You exude sex appeal, so be careful. Protect yourself at close quarters. Strive to maintain emotional equilibrium. A Sagittarius figures in today's scenario.

Friday, November 19 (Moon in Aquarius to Pisces 5:38 a.m.) Be diplomatic, lie low, and play the waiting game. Be sure of legal rights and permissions. Questions figure prominently regarding partnership and marriage. Domestic tranquility can be obtained, if you make reasonable concessions.

Saturday, November 20 (Moon in Pisces) Define terms. See people and relationships in the light of reality. One week ago, you made an error in calculation. Today, make an adjustment and correction. The emphasis is on whom you trust and how you express "inner feelings." A real estate deal is for real.

Sunday, November 21 (Moon in Pisces to Aries 11:12 a.m.)   Within 24 hours, you receive a "revelation" about a partnership, marriage, and money. The answers to questions could be found in metaphysical literature. You enter areas previously neglected. Dig deep for information. Don't give up the ship! A Capricorn plays the dominant role.

Monday, November 22 (Moon in Aries)   You will attract attention by putting into operation original concepts. Despite "admiration," some will claim you are in the "playground of the occult." Finish what you start. Deal with the unknown and realize there is nothing to fear but fear itself.

Tuesday, November 23 (Moon in Aries to Taurus 7:16 p.m.)   At the track, choose number 1 post position in the first race. Accent original thinking and your pioneering spirit. Take the initiative in making a fresh start, imprinting your own style. Use advertising and publicity in promoting your product. A Leo figures prominently.

Wednesday, November 24 (Moon in Taurus)   Lucky lottery: 2, 24, 11, 22, 14, 9. Focus on reaching beyond the immediate. You can perceive potential, if you meditate. Refuse to be distracted by someone who is drinking too much. Money and travel could play major roles. Capricorn and Cancer edge their way into today's scenario.

Thursday, November 25 (Moon in Taurus)   The meaning of Thanksgiving will be made crystal clear. A long-distance telephone call will give reason to be thankful. Someone far away has not forgotten you, and the call will prove it. Gemini and Sagittarius will figure prominently.

Friday, November 26 (Moon in Taurus to Gemini 5:25 a.m.)   The full moon in Gemini represents your tenth house. This relates to business, career, and recognition that adds to your prestige. Your innovative ideas will be appreciated, and you will be rewarded. Someone you once loved will make a surprise appearance. Scorpio is involved.

Saturday, November 27 (Moon in Gemini)   Focus on flirtation and creative writing. Your words will be quoted and your work analyzed. Be careful, because you will be exuding sex appeal. Don't play games with your emotions; the heart you break could be your own. Your lucky number is 5.

Sunday, November 28 (Moon in Gemini to Cancer 5:11 p.m.)   Within 24 hours, circumstances make a dramatic change in your favor. A wish will be fulfilled, and you will say to yourself: "My platter is full!" Tonight, have a heart-to-heart talk with a Libra family member. You will hear the sound of music!

Monday, November 29 (Moon in Cancer)   Despite a delay, wishes will come true. Don't ask for more than you can handle. Be wise in using your powers of persuasion. A promise that was broken will be mended. You might be humming, "Who could ask for anything more?" Another Virgo will be involved.

Tuesday, November 30 (Moon in Cancer)   You close out the month with optimism. You can make your future bright, if you avoid brooding about the past. Get off the bench and into the game—"the game of your life!" Let people know you are "for real." Exhibit staying power. Deal gingerly with a Capricorn. Your lucky number is 8.

DECEMBER 2004

Wednesday, December 1 (Moon in Cancer to Leo 5:50 a.m.)   On this Wednesday, strive to confirm your

239

"holiday plans." Be realistic in your appraisal of people and relationships. Avoid self-deception. Get a definition of terms in writing. Your intuitive intellect will serve as a reliable guide. A Pisces figures in this scenario.

Thursday, December 2 (Moon in Leo)   Efforts made 24 hours ago will pay dividends. You realize that you made the right decision; act accordingly. The emphasis is on power, authority, and pressure due to responsibility. A relationship is intense, and could get too hot not to cool down. Capricorn is represented.

Friday, December 3 (Moon in Leo to Virgo 6:01 p.m.)   Your cycle moves up. Trust a hunch, and you will be at the right place. What had been a secret will be revealed to your advantage. Finish what you start. Be idealistic and reach beyond the immediate. Expand your marketing plans. Find someone to represent your talent or product.

Saturday, December 4 (Moon in Virgo)   Your lunar cycle is high, so you will be at the right place at a crucial moment, almost effortlessly. Imprint your own style. Wear brighter colors and make personal appearances. You will be sought after socially and romantically. Leo and Aquarius will play dramatic roles. Your lucky number is 1.

Sunday, December 5 (Moon in Virgo)   You realize you are not alone. Attention revolves around partnership and marriage. Decide on your direction. Examine your motivation. Find time for meditation. Capricorn and Cancer will play "astounding roles." Pay attention to spiritual values.

Monday, December 6 (Moon in Virgo to Libra 3:47 a.m.)   Luck rides with you, and as a result, you could win a contest. In matters of speculation, stick with number 3. Gemini and Sagittarius will play special roles. Check the list of people you want to be with during holiday celebrations.

Tuesday, December 7 (Moon in Libra)   You obtain a "true picture" of your finances in connection with the purchase of a gift. Be thorough; correct any accounting errors. Rewrite and rebuild. What had been turned down could now be enthusiastically accepted. A Scorpio figures prominently.

Wednesday, December 8 (Moon in Libra to Scorpio 9:45 a.m.)   Be ready for change, travel, and a variety of experiences. A financial decision will be right for you. Someone you helped in the past will return the favor and the relationship once more gets under way. Gemini, Sagittarius, and another Virgo figure in today's scenario. Your lucky number is 5.

Thursday, December 9 (Moon in Scorpio)   At the track, choose number 6 post position in the sixth race. Beautify your surroundings; decorate and remodel your living quarters. A Scorpio relative does not have an ulterior motive; know it, and be cooperative. Your personal possessions are worth more than anticipated.

Friday, December 10 (Moon in Scorpio to Sagittarius 11:55 a.m.)   See people and relationships as they are, not merely as you wish they could be. A short trip is part of today's scenario; take special care in traffic. You could be disillusioned in romance, but be willing to give it another chance. A Pisces plays a role.

Saturday, December 11 (Moon in Sagittarius)   Be aware of the facts and figures in connection with real estate and the value of land. Assert your views in a positive manner. In personal activities, be serious about a relationship. Emotions are involved. Don't break hearts, because the heart you break might be your own.

Sunday, December 12 (Moon in Sagittarius to Capricorn 11:42 a.m.) The new moon in Sagittarius last night accents your fourth house. This places emphasis on your home, shelter, and a decision relating to marriage. You obtain a new outlook in connection with a long-range project. You are better known than might be imagined. An Aries plays an unusual role.

Monday, December 13 (Moon in Capricorn) You will exude an aura of sensuality and sex appeal. Your outlook undergoes a transformation. Romance and love enter your life. Your experience will refresh and revitalize. Take the initiative. Make a new start in a different direction. A Leo plays a dramatic role.

Tuesday, December 14 (Moon in Capricorn to Aquarius 11:10 a.m.) At the track, choose number 2 post position in the second race. The moon position emphasizes luck in matters of speculation. Maintain a carefree attitude, but avoid being "careless." Capricorn and Cancer play roles in today's "amazing" scenario.

Wednesday, December 15 (Moon in Aquarius) Lucky lottery: 3, 11, 22, 18, 5, 14. Social activities accelerate. Keep health resolutions; you will need vitality for the upcoming holidays. Work methods and employment undergo changes that will benefit you. Perceive the picture in its entirety; feel free to ask questions of superiors.

Thursday, December 16 (Moon in Aquarius to Pisces 12:24 p.m.) The moon in Aquarius represents your sixth house. This relates to special services that you provide or receive. The key is to be thorough and to check your working tools. Taurus, Leo, and Scorpio will play efficient roles.

242

Friday, December 17 (Moon in Pisces)   Lie low, play the waiting game. Utilize the written word to make significant gains. A flirtation lends spice, but know when to say, "Enough!" Don't give up something of value for a temporary thrill. Gemini, Sagittarius, and another Virgo will figure prominently.

Saturday, December 18 (Moon in Pisces to Aries 4:52 p.m.)   The number 6 will appear today more times than by mere coincidence. At the track, choose number 6 post position in the sixth race. Attention also revolves around a domestic adjustment that could include a change of residence or marital status. Libra is represented.

Sunday, December 19 (Moon in Aries)   On this Sunday, let spiritual values surface. A mystery is involved. Have fun with it; don't fear the unknown. Some persons could accuse you of being in the playground of the occult; don't take it too seriously. A Pisces plays a key role.

Monday, December 20 (Moon in Aries)   Nothing happens halfway! Today, it is all or forget it. A serious discussion with Capricorn is necessary. You have the power and authority to do things your way, and your way will be the right way. Have luck with number 8.

Tuesday, December 21 (Moon in Aries to Taurus 12:52 a.m.)   Look beyond the immediate. You will get news from someone temporarily living abroad. This could be the start of something big! You need representation for your talent and product. Strive to make a deal that will be fair to all.

Wednesday, December 22 (Moon in Taurus)   Lucky lottery: 24, 32, 47, 1, 13, 18. The answer to your question: Open the lines of communication. Take a cold plunge into your own destiny. Don't follow others. Let them follow you, if they so desire. The love spark reignites—whether you are married or single.

Thursday, December 23 (Moon in Taurus to Gemini 11:33 a.m.)   What seemed long ago and far away will be closer than you anticipated. Take notes; put original ideas and formats on paper. The focus is also on your partnership and marital status. Keep resolutions about your diet. Attend to a possible digestive problem.

Friday, December 24 (Moon in Gemini)   On this Christmas Eve, you will be saying to yourself, "This is really the best Christmas I've had in many years!" People with you will be sociable and generous. You'll be surprised by gifts that exceed your expectations. The true spirit of the holiday will be expressed.

Saturday, December 25 (Moon in Gemini to Cancer 11:39 p.m.)   Your dream of a white Christmas will be fulfilled. On this Christmas Day, you will be praised and will be aware of "the gift of love." Taurus, Leo, and Scorpio will play "magnificent" roles. Don't take chances with fire hazards!

Sunday, December 26 (Moon in Cancer)   The full moon in Cancer is in your eleventh house. This places emphasis on romance and luck in matters of speculation. Many of your wishes, especially in connection with your home and marriage, will be fulfilled. Gemini and another Virgo will figure in this scenario.

Monday, December 27 (Moon in Cancer)   Stick close to home, if possible. The grass is not necessarily greener somewhere else. You will receive an offer or invitation. Remember: "All that glitters is not gold." Your teacher in grade school told you that, and tonight you will remember it.

Tuesday, December 28 (Moon in Cancer to Leo 12:15 p.m.)   You still have time to fulfill a commitment to a loved one. Someone tells you, "There is no time!" However, time is on your side, so you need not heed statements based on panic. A Pisces and another Virgo figure in today's dynamic scenario.

Wednesday, December 29 (Moon in Leo)   A secret conference involves you and plans for New Year's Eve. Let others do their part; sit back and enjoy yourself. Avoid those who drink too much. Look forward to the coming year. Maintain an optimistic attitude. Your fortunate number is 8.

Thursday, December 30 (Moon in Leo)   Let go of an obligation you should not have assumed in the first place. You could be the center of attention and celebration. Look beyond the immediate. The focus will be on drama and showmanship. Aries and Libra will play outstanding roles.

Friday, December 31 (Moon in Leo to Virgo 12:34 a.m.)   This is New Year's Eve, and your cycle is high. You will enjoy the attention and love showered on you. Prestige will rise. You will know once and for all that you are dynamic, vibrant, and sexy. Leo and Aquarius will play scintillating roles.

HAPPY NEW YEAR!

JANUARY 2005

Saturday, January 1 (Moon in Virgo)   There's no better way to start the new year than with the moon in your sign. Your inner and outer selves are in complete agreement today. The picky voice that usually chatters away inside your head will be quiet.

Sunday, January 2 (Moon in Virgo to Libra 11:20 a.m.) As the moon joins Jupiter in your second house, your thoughts turn to money. Do you earn enough? How much is enough? Can you earn enough on your art to quit your day job? These questions are excellent, and even though it may take you most of the year to find the answers, Jupiter is there to help!

Monday, January 3 (Moon in Libra) Relationships. Flirtations. You may have trouble making up your mind today about a relationship. Are you really interested or are you just lonely? Be sure of the answer before you leap in.

Tuesday, January 4 (Moon in Libra to Scorpio 7:00 p.m.) You feel ambivalent about a personal issue for much of the day. This evening, your emotions become more intense and you try to figure out why you're feeling as you do. You may not find the answer tonight, but you feel better by the time you go to bed.

Wednesday, January 5 (Moon in Scorpio) Things work more smoothly today. Even though you may have intense and powerful feelings concerning a sibling or neighbor, you're generally on top of things at work and at home. You may investigate a topic or issue that relates to something you're writing. You don't give up until you find exactly what you're looking for.

Thursday, January 6 (Moon in Scorpio to Sagittarius 10:45 p.m.) You find the answers for whatever you have been investigating with such intensity. A sibling or a neighbor inadvertently leads you in the right direction.

Friday, January 7 (Moon in Sagittarius) This can be a problematic position of the moon for you. The Sagittarius moon sends a call to adventure and sometimes to chaos, but your Virgo sun likes the world to be grounded.

246

If you can combine the energies in some way, it will make for a happier time. Expand your learning by taking a class or attending a seminar, or get away for the weekend—even better, do both!

Saturday, January 8 (Moon in Sagittarius to Capricorn 11:11 p.m.)   Your focus is on home and family. Your Virgo sun loves this, but the Sagittarius moon is straining to get out and have some fun. Throw a party and include your kids.

Sunday, January 9 (Moon in Capricorn)   Your Virgo sun feels more comfortable when the moon is in an earth sign. Today, the moon is joined by both Mercury and Venus. Your focus is on creativity. Paint your living room or work on your novel—ground your energy by doing something that gives tangible results.

Monday, January 10 (Moon in Capricorn to Aquarius 10:07 p.m.)   As the moon prepares to move into Aquarius, you feel compelled to set aside your creative projects and dive into work. If these tasks aren't as much fun or as fulfilling, then perhaps it's time to start thinking about new work goals. Where would you like to be in the future?

Tuesday, January 11 (Moon in Aquarius)   When the visionary Aquarius moon is in your sixth house, ideas about your daily work and health seem to surface with little effort on your part. You find a way to make a routine job more exciting and mentally stimulating. Before the end of the day, you tackle a mystery that has puzzled you for some time.

Wednesday, January 12 (Moon in Aquarius to Pisces 9:51 p.m.)   There is always a period of instability when the moon makes its transition from one sign to another. Today, that instability may be related to your health. Perhaps you feel you don't have the energy you usually do. Sign up for a yoga class or head to the gym. By tonight, you feel improved.

Thursday, January 13 (Moon in Pisces)   Even though this moon position is opposed to your sun, it's a more comfortable element for your sun. You need to pay close attention to your partnerships today. Your romantic partner may need more attention than you've been giving. A night at home together wouldn't hurt.

Friday, January 14 (Moon in Pisces)   You're more emotional than usual. A positive frame of mind can be extremely helpful in a relationship. It encourages you to express what you feel. If you're not in a positive frame of mind, this moon position may lead to jealousy. Either way, the moon in the seventh house brings up relationship issues that need to be confronted.

Saturday, January 15 (Moon in Pisces to Aries 12:27 a.m.)   You wake this morning prepared to leap into a risky venture of some kind. But since it involves property or resources that you share with another—perhaps a spouse or significant other—it would be wiser to hold off until you and the other person discuss it. You may not reach a decision today, but that's fine. Wait until the moon moves into grounded Taurus before you make your move.

Sunday, January 16 (Moon in Aries)   Impatience and recklessness often ride tandem with this moon sign. Maintain your cool today. Think twice before you speak. A flirtation or romance is possible.

Monday, January 17 (Moon in Aries to Taurus 7:07 a.m.)   Finally, the moon is in a sign that feels very comfortable to you. The sensual, grounded Taurus moon awakens your thirst for knowledge and for mystical ideas.

You may start planning an overseas trip to a place you've never been before. Start saving your money!

Tuesday, January 18 (Moon in Taurus) You need a change of scenery today. If you have a flexible work schedule, leave time today for a trip to a new place, the gym, or even a seminar on something that interests you. Alter your usual routine so you can bring a fresher perspective to the rest of your life.

Wednesday, January 19 (Moon in Taurus to Gemini 5:25 p.m.) A domestic situation or issue may need your attention. News may be forthcoming that's connected to publicity, promotion, or publishing. Your dreams are especially vivid. Record them. They illuminate a concern that you have.

Thursday, January 20 (Moon in Gemini) As the moon moves into your tenth house, your career is highlighted. Expect news related to professional concerns or relationships. Even though the Gemini moon is an air sign, which isn't especially compatible with your earth sun, both Gemini and Virgo are ruled by Mercury; so your communication skills are especially strong.

Friday, January 21 (Moon in Gemini) A minor professional challenge surfaces. You use your gift of gab to settle whatever it is. Call on your extensive network of contacts today. You never know who may have ideas that will prove useful.

Saturday, January 22 (Moon in Gemini to Cancer 5:43 a.m.) Home, family, roots—all of these areas play a role in your affairs today. You get a lucky break related to your goals. Run with it.

Sunday, January 23 (Moon in Cancer) A nurturing parent is strategic in helping you to redefine a goal you have. Your intuition is always strong when the moon is in a water sign, and when it's in Cancer, your intuition speaks loudly and clearly. Heed the advice.

Monday, January 24 (Moon in Cancer to Leo 6:22 p.m.)   Okay, maybe you were a bit grumpy when you got up today. Try to put that mood on a back burner and pay attention to what's really going on inside of you. Then deal with it.

Tuesday, January 25 (Moon in Leo)   You may feel a bit withdrawn and secretive. There's nothing inherently wrong with that, unless your secrecy is keeping something from you. What are you hiding from? When the moon is in the twelfth house, issues and concerns that originated in childhood often surface.

Wednesday, January 26 (Moon in Leo)   You reach out today to someone else and, in reaching, discover what's been bothering you. It may not be a blinding epiphany, but it definitely sheds light on the situation.

Thursday, January 27 (Moon in Leo to Virgo 6:25 a.m.)   The moon is in your sign and you can certainly tell the difference! You feel invigorated and enthusiastic, and your head and heart work hand in hand. Not a bad way to wind down the month.

Friday, January 28 (Moon in Virgo)   You tend to details related to your general health and your appearance. Maybe a new hairstyle is in order or a brand-new wardrobe or some other kind of self-improvement. Whatever it is, make it happen.

Saturday, January 29 (Moon in Virgo to Libra 5:13 p.m.)   Your thoughts turn to money this afternoon, specifically to your financial security. Explore other income-making venues. Don't be afraid to take a risk.

Sunday, January 30 (Moon in Libra)   Mercury goes into Aquarius and your sixth house today. It will be there until mid-February, urging you to pay closer attention to your work schedule. Your communication skills are sharp. Use them.

Monday, January 31 (Moon in Libra)   Your financial relationships are your focus; accountants, stock brokers, or just a friend or partner whose opinion you trust. In the end, it all boils down to your decision.

FEBRUARY 2005

Tuesday, February 1 (Moon in Libra to Scorpio 1:51 a.m.)   As the moon moves into your second house early this morning, security issues dominate. You may feel more attached than usual to your possessions and your particular value system. Jupiter turns retrograde in your second house. During this retrograde period, which lasts until early June, you'll be rethinking your values.

Wednesday, February 2 (Moon in Scorpio)   You have intense experiences today involving your values. It could be that someone challenges an opinion you have, and you take this action as a personal affront. Don't. A more useful and positive way to use this energy is to examine the opinion that's being challenged and ask if it's your opinion or simply one that was handed down to you.

Thursday, February 3 (Moon in Scorpio to Sagittarius 7:22 a.m.)   This fire-sign moon may feel somewhat uncomfortable to your earth sun. However, the Sagittarius moon can shake up your normal routine, forcing you to see things in a newer, fresher perspective. Since it's in your fourth house, its influence will be felt most strongly in your home life.

Friday, February 4 (Moon in Sagittarius)   You're being too narrow-minded about a domestic issue, but that changes as the moon moves through your fourth house. Friends or family members who live overseas may visit, or there could be news about a publishing project.

Saturday, February 5 (Moon in Sagittarius to Capricorn 9:32 a.m.)   With Venus in Aquarius in your sixth house, an office flirtation or romance is possible. This person may be different from your coworkers. It's precisely this difference that attracts you.

Sunday, February 6 (Moon in Capricorn)   Mars joins the moon in your fifth house of creativity. It's a good day to build a creative project by laying down your strategy and realizing what you hope to accomplish. It's also a great day for lovemaking or solidifying a romance.

Monday, February 7 (Moon in Capricorn to Aquarius 9:27 a.m.)   This morning, the moon joins Neptune in your sixth house. If you have a health complaint, get a second opinion before you make a decision. A female coworker could be problematic today, but just ignore her. Neither of you has the full story.

Tuesday, February 8 (Moon in Aquarius)   You have visionary ideas related to your daily work routine. However, you may have to make some adjustments or do some minor fine-tuning before the ideas can be put into a practical context.

Wednesday, February 9 (Moon in Aquarius to Pisces 9:00 a.m.)   The Pisces moon is opposed to your sun now. This creates a tug-of-war between your self-expression and your emotions, between who you think you are and who you feel you are. But on a more positive note, the element of this moon is compatible with the element of your sun. It softens your tendencies to criticize others.

Thursday, February 10 (Moon in Pisces)   Your spouse or significant other needs more attention today. Your professional partnerships may also require some attention. You feel more vulnerable emotionally and your imagination may feed into that emotional excess.

Friday, February 11 (Moon in Pisces to Aries 10:22 a.m.)   As the moon moves into your eighth house, you make all the right decisions concerning jointly held property and assets. Of course, these decisions aren't just yours alone and your partner agrees with your assessment of the situation.

Saturday, February 12 (Moon in Aries)   If you have incomplete home improvement projects, finish them today. If you simply can't do it because the call to adventure is so strong, indulge the call and head out of town. Be sure to do something thrilling that you've never experienced before. That will satisfy the urges of the Aries moon.

Sunday, February 13 (Moon in Aries to Taurus 3:19 p.m.)   This moon is passionate, impatient, and restless. Throughout the morning, all those traits are exacerbated. By midafternoon, the moon moves into earthy Taurus, where it feels quite comfortable for you.

Monday, February 14 (Moon in Taurus)   Happy Valentine's Day. Okay, so the holiday is commercial glitz. But with the moon in earthy, sensual Taurus, you and your partner should consider eating dinner at a gourmet restaurant and then spending an intimate evening together.

Tuesday, February 15 (Moon in Taurus) Publishing, promotion, and advertising are today's highlights. You come up with a fresh, innovative way to advertise yourself, your product, or your company. If you're traveling, things may not go quite as you planned.

Wednesday, February 16 (Moon in Taurus to Gemini 12:19 a.m.) Your ruler, Mercury, moves into Pisces today, into your seventh house. Expect news about professional partnerships. You and your romantic partner have a heart to heart.

Thursday, February 17 (Moon in Gemini) Your career and professional partnerships are highlighted. Your communication skills in this area are excellent, so your writing and public speaking are well-received.

Friday, February 18 (Moon in Gemini to Cancer 12:13 p.m.) Even though the moon is square your sun, creating a challenge, both Gemini and Virgo are ruled by Mercury. So use your way with language to get out of a tight spot and then figure out what went wrong.

Saturday, February 19 (Moon in Cancer) As the moon joins Saturn in your eleventh house, you focus attention on your goals and aspirations once again. Something may not feel quite right in this area. Since the moon is in intuitive Cancer, allow your intuition to show you where you need to make adjustments.

Sunday, February 20 (Moon in Cancer) Children and domestic issues play a role in your affairs today. It could be that your kids need your advice and support or one of them has group activities that require your presence.

Monday, February 21 (Moon in Cancer to Leo 12:55 a.m.) A rather odd thing happens when the moon goes into Leo. Sometimes you feel neglected by your loved ones, other times you neglect them because your focus is inward. And other times, you use this lunar energy by working creatively behind the scenes. Which one is it going to be for today, Virgo?

Tuesday, February 22 (Moon in Leo) Whatever you're doing in secret should be kept so until Thursday, when the moon is firmly in your sign. Only then will your project be understood by the people who need to do so.

Wednesday, February 23 (Moon in Leo to Virgo 12:44 p.m.) Despite a brief period of instability early in the day, your mood and sex appeal will be high. You're so self-confident that you impress your bosses and attract the attention of a certain someone who has had his eye on you. Ready to leap in, Virgo?

Thursday, February 24 (Moon in Virgo) You're solidly grounded today. Pragmatism and problem-solving are your hallmarks. Get to work, Virgo.

Friday, February 25 (Moon in Virgo to Libra 10:59 p.m.) Until late tonight, it's a Virgo kind of day. You attend to details and tackle problems with the heart of the true workaholic. By this afternoon, you can see your way clear through the rest of the weekend.

Saturday, February 26 (Moon in Libra) As Venus joins Uranus in Pisces in your seventh house, you're definitely in the mood for romance and love. You may also be in the mood to spend money and should resist extravagance until the check has cleared.

Sunday, February 27 (Moon in Libra) You may add to your art collection today or to a collection that has artistic value of some kind. Be prudent, but not stingy. Whatever you buy will increase in value.

Monday, February 28 (Moon in Libra to Scorpio 7:21 a.m.) You may have an intense emotional experience today with a sibling, a relative, or a neighbor. Whatever the issue, you're able to resolve it by the end of the day. When the moon is in Scorpio, no one settles for easy answers.

MARCH 2005

Tuesday, March 1 (Moon in Scorpio) Straight talk with a sibling is due. If you don't have a sibling, then you can expect a relative or even a neighbor to be confrontational. You may have a powerful emotional reaction to this confrontation.

Wednesday, March 2 (Moon in Scorpio to Sagittarius 1:30 p.m.) This lunar sign probably feels a bit strange. While your Virgo sun wants to pad around the house in comfortable clothes and slippers, this moon urges you to find an adventure or a party. Relax. Look for the larger picture of your home life.

Thursday, March 3 (Moon in Sagittarius) You take a seminar or a workshop that expands your knowledge and wisdom. You then bring this knowledge home to your family and all of you work together to integrate this wisdom into your lives.

Friday, March 4 (Moon in Sagittarius to Capricorn 5:12 p.m.) Mercury moves into Aries today, placing your thoughts squarely on sex, your sexuality, and your love life. A flirtation or new romance may be sparked at a workshop or seminar or even a lecture on estate planning, taxes, or insurance.

Saturday, March 5 (Moon in Capricorn)   The moon joins Mars in Capricorn in your fifth house. This provides a major boost for your creativity. You are building on past successes one step at a time. You have the correct structure for a creative project.

Sunday, March 6 (Moon in Capricorn to Aquarius 6:50 p.m.)   It's a day to organize and tidy up. You know those home-improvement projects you've put off? Make a list of what you have to do. Delegate responsibility. The same goes with projects at work.

Monday, March 7 (Moon in Aquarius)   You need a change in your routine, Virgo. Because it's a workday, it may be difficult to just leave for a change of scenery. So eat at a new restaurant, call an old friend, or go see an art film—do something different.

Tuesday, March 8 (Moon in Aquarius to Pisces 7:34 p.m.)   A domestic issue needs your attention today. It may concern your spouse or partner. Perform a service for someone else today—a good deed, Virgo—and then take the aftermath of the glow home with you.

Wednesday, March 9 (Moon in Pisces)   Your imagination and intuition are running high today. You're able to use both to bypass your left brain and find what you need much more quickly. It's tricky to sift through right-brain images. Get the help of a psychic friend.

Thursday, March 10 (Moon in Pisces to Aries 9:04 p.m.)   You feel short-tempered, impatient. You can't tolerate routine today, and if you can take vacation time, do so. Then get out into the urban wilderness and discover new hangouts, or go out into the real wilderness and find a mountain to climb!

Friday, March 11 (Moon in Aries)   This is a good moon for the weekend, when your time is your own. Indulge yourself today. Let your passions propel you into uncharted regions of the mind, experience, and life. Visit a carnival and take the wildest roller-coaster ride possible. Go rock climbing. Eat spicy food at an exotic restaurant. Let this moon shake up your status quo.

Saturday, March 12 (Moon in Aries)   A great day for a flirtation, romance, sex, and love. Your patience may be short and impatience will rule the day. But if you're aware of the tendencies, you won't overlook any opportunities that come your way.

Sunday, March 13 (Moon in Aries to Taurus 1:06 a.m.)   As the moon enters sensual Taurus, you're in for a physically oriented day. Go to the gym, take a yoga class, or head into the woods for a long hike. Be aware of your body—listen to its language. News from abroad is possible.

Monday, March 14 (Moon in Taurus)   Your practicality rules the day. You're able to take abstract notions and make them useful to other people. You're able to solve problems in a grounded, efficient way. Apply this energy to work and home.

Tuesday, March 15 (Moon in Taurus to Gemini 8:45 a.m.)   It's a good day to focus on your career and professional partnerships. Although you may not feel that you're up to snuff today, your charisma is strong and anything you do to promote yourself, your product, or your company at this time is well-received.

Wednesday, March 16 (Moon in Gemini)   Your facility with language really shines today. Even if you're confronted with minor annoyances or challenges related to

258

your career, your ability to speak your mind saves the day. So start talking, Virgo!

Thursday, March 17 (Moon in Gemini to Cancer 7:44 p.m.)   Your goals and dreams are a kind of security blanket for you. But as the moon enters Cancer, you may be reevaluating what you really want and questioning whether your present goals were merely those you accepted because other people wanted them for you. This is an internal process with no quick resolution.

Friday, March 18 (Moon in Cancer)   Domestic issues or concerns related to your home are part of your dreams and goals. Your intuition is exceptional today, so apply it to any questions that arise concerning your long-range goals.

Saturday, March 19 (Moon in Cancer)   Mercury turns retrograde today, in your eighth house and doesn't go direct again until April 12. During this time, be sure that any travel arrangements are firm; check and double check e-mails and correspondence that you send to confirm that they've arrived. Try to go with the flow of sudden changes in other people's schedules—or your own.

Sunday, March 20 (Moon in Cancer to Leo 8:17 a.m.)   The moon moves into your twelfth house today, favoring work done behind the scenes. Mars moves into Aquarius, into your sixth house. If you have trouble with circulation or your ankles, this moon could exacerbate the problem. Take a yoga class today. It will get your blood moving!

Monday, March 21 (Moon in Leo)   Saturn turns direct again in your eleventh house. This should be something of a relief. Now you can apply what you've learned about your goals and aspiration to your life and make things happen. Lay out your strategy. Allow your intuition to guide you.

Tuesday, March 22 (Moon in Leo to Virgo 8:10 p.m.) Venus moves into Aries in your eighth house. This is a passionate placement for the Aries moon. Your existing relationship deepens and intensifies, and if you're married, your spouse may get a raise or a promotion. If a romantic relationship begins under this transit, which lasts until April 14, it will be intense, sexual, and may have an enduring influence on your life.

Wednesday, March 23 (Moon in Virgo) With the moon in Leo until later this evening, you may experience conflicts with your mother or other women. These conflicts are rooted in the past. It's a good time to meditate or engage in other spiritual practices.

Thursday, March 24 (Moon in Virgo) With the moon firmly in your sign today, you're in a winning mood. Your willpower is strong; you can easily convince others that your point of view is correct. Don't be overbearing about it. Despite your focus on yourself, it's also a day to listen to what other people feel and think.

Friday, March 25 (Moon in Virgo to Libra 6:00 a.m.) Other people may need nurturing; you're in a position to help. The nurturing may take various forms, but what's needed could involve a service that you perform or a problem that you solve for a loved one. Not a bad way to start a weekend!

Saturday, March 26 (Moon in Libra) Pluto turns retrograde today in your fourth house and doesn't turn direct again until September 2. In daily life, this means that you may be revisiting issues and situations that prevailed in your life between January and early June 2004.

Sunday, March 27 (Moon in Libra to Scorpio 1:30 p.m.) Your values, your finances, and your artistic interests play into your life today. With the moon joining Jupiter in your second house, you could be yearning to expand your income. Don't just dream about it. Make it happen. Do research. Network.

Monday, March 28 (Moon in Scorpio) By this afternoon, you're diving into topics that intrigue you and investigating what motivates the people around you. Some of these people may be your siblings or other relatives or an elusive neighbor. Can any of it be possible fodder for a short story or novel?

Tuesday, March 29 (Moon in Scorpio to Sagittarius 6:57 p.m.) Your thoughts may be a bit too subjective and unduly influenced by experiences you've had in the past. Be aware that the tendency exists, and try to be more objective in your dealings with others.

Wednesday, March 30 (Moon in Sagittarius) Treat yourself to a relaxing evening. You've earned it! Do whatever pleases you most; read a book, plan a trip, look for the bigger picture of your own life, or have some friends over. With the moon in Sagittarius, there are many ways to enjoy yourself. First, you have to know what you enjoy!

Thursday, March 31 (Moon in Sagittarius to Capricorn 10:49 p.m.) This moon offers passion, enthusiasm, and optimism. Reserve some quality time for your partner this evening. And if you don't have a partner, get out to be seen.

APRIL 2005

Friday, April 1 (Moon in Capricorn) If you're a writer, now is the time to revise and rewrite whatever you've been working on. By the time Mercury goes direct again on April 12, you should have your project just about where you want it.

Saturday, April 2 (Moon in Capricorn)   With the moon in your fifth house, you find the structure you need for your creative projects. Your kids, if you have any, may need some firmer rules and parameters today. Your pragmatism is accentuated with the moon in a fellow earth sign.

Sunday, April 3 Daylight Saving Time Begins (Moon in Capricorn to Aquarius 2:32 a.m.)   It would behoove you to spend some time today brainstorming with friends or coworkers about what you would like to accomplish this week at home. You're filled with visionary ideas. If no one is around to brainstorm with you, jot your ideas down.

Monday, April 4 (Moon in Aquarius)   Okay, put those cutting-edge ideas to use today. Even if you have to defend them to the higher-ups, your powers of persuasion are strong today. Use them.

Tuesday, April 5 (Moon in Aquarius to Pisces 4:46 a.m.)   An issue that needs your attention surfaces today with a partner—professional or romantic. If you sign any legal contract, while Mercury is still retrograde, be sure you've read all the fine print. Better yet, put off the signing until after April 12 when Mercury turns direct.

Wednesday, April 6 (Moon in Pisces)   Surprise your partner. Plan an intimate dinner somewhere and get a motel room for the night. Your love life could use some spice! Your efforts are sure to be deeply appreciated.

Thursday, April 7 (Moon in Pisces to Aries 7:29 a.m.) There could be a minor problem today concerning jointly held property or property that you would like to buy with a partner. This should wait until after April 12, when there's less chance of miscommunication.

Friday, April 8 (Moon in Aries) You and your new romantic partner spend a sensual evening together. Something that has puzzled you about this person is revealed to be only the tip of the proverbial iceberg. Your interest and intrigue with this individual are completely piqued now.

Saturday, April 9 (Moon in Aries to Taurus 11:50 a.m.) You enjoy the comfort of the Taurus moon. Even if it brings security issues to the forefront of your thoughts, you like the grounding and the pragmatic bent that it brings to your life. You also enjoy the sensuality! In case you haven't done so already, get those tax forms off your desk and into the mail.

Sunday, April 10 (Moon in Taurus) Even though it's a weekend, you may be working at home on publishing, publicity, or promotion ideas. A foreigner comes into the picture and so does a flirtation—either with this individual or someone else.

Monday, April 11 (Moon in Taurus to Gemini 6:55 p.m.) You and your accountant may have a conversation today about your quarterly taxes and some possible tax write-offs for this year. Take notes. By early evening, you're in a more sociable mood and attend an impromptu gathering with professional associates.

Tuesday, April 12 (Moon in Gemini) Your ruler, Mercury, goes direct today. The timing is nice, with the moon in the other sign that Mercury rules. Your communication skills are sharp and you know exactly what to say and when to say it.

Wednesday, April 13 (Moon in Gemini)   A confrontation with authority is possible. It's nothing huge; maybe you get stopped for speeding or called in by the boss. Whatever it is, you talk circles around the other person and head home this evening with a clear conscience.

Thursday, April 14 (Moon in Gemini to Cancer 5:03 a.m.)   The moon joins Saturn in your eleventh house. An issue concerning a promotion or publicity campaign comes to your attention. You may need to make a minor adjustment to pull things off smoothly. A wish or hope that you have is beginning to unfold.

Friday, April 15 (Moon in Cancer)   Tax day. Venus moves into Taurus today, into your fourth house. This is generally a pleasant transit, when you stick close to home and enjoy the peace of your surroundings. Your relationships with family members improve as well. The transit lasts until May 8—make the most of this harmonious time.

Saturday, April 16 (Moon in Cancer to Leo 5:18 p.m.)   Get the family involved in your home-improvement projects. Things will speed along if everyone pitches in. Besides, you should complete a couple of these projects before the moon is firmly entrenched in Leo because tomorrow you won't feel like doing them.

Sunday, April 17 (Moon in Leo)   Do your own thing today. With the moon moving through your twelfth house, you'll want to do that anyway, but in the event that the workaholic side of you is cracking the whip, Virgo, resist.

Monday, April 18 (Moon in Leo)   Work behind the scenes today, but do it with panache and style and an unshakable belief in your abilities. Even if you don't get credit for what you've done, you will know that you did your best.

Tuesday, April 19 (Moon in Leo to Virgo 5:28 a.m.) Today you should take credit for everything you do. The moon is in your sign. If you've been experiencing emotional turmoil lately, this lunar transit should help rectify it or, at the very least, help you deal with it better.

Wednesday, April 20 (Moon in Virgo) You're a whiz at problem-solving today. It's as if your brain is wired for quickness, efficiency, and the ability to hone in on the root of the problem. Use it well, Virgo.

Thursday, April 21 (Moon in Virgo to Libra 3:28 p.m.) There are several ways to put your energy to its best use, and today begin with taking stock of your finances. Check your bank statements, find out how your IRA stocks are doing, and check on your social security records. When you're seeing double, knock off and visit a museum, work on your novel, or find a great art film to see.

Friday, April 22 (Moon in Libra) You may be scrutinizing the finer details of a contract. You're good with details, Virgo; make sure that today your eyes are very sharp. There may be problems with the contract.

Saturday, April 23 (Moon in Libra to Scorpio 10:26 p.m.) It's a good day for community work. Gather up your old towels and blankets, and head to the Humane Society with your kids. Once you've made your donation, visit the animals.

Sunday, April 24 (Moon in Scorpio) A surprise visit from siblings or other relatives is possible. Try to go with the flow if it happens and use the time to heal old wounds. With the moon in Scorpio, you can get to the bottom of the problems.

Monday, April 25 (Moon in Scorpio) You investigate an issue or situation with all the relentlessness of a detective. You call on your extensive network of friends and professional associates, surf the Net, and dig until you've found what you're looking for.

Tuesday, April 26 (Moon in Scorpio to Sagittarius 2:47 a.m.) You awaken feeling restless and anxious, with no apparent reason for either emotion. Blame the moon in Sagittarius. Your earthy Virgo sun isn't fond of the fire moon. Your temper may be short today, particularly at home; try to cool down.

Wednesday, April 27 (Moon in Sagittarius) You may become an armchair traveler today, surfing the Internet for possible vacation destinations. Choose some place you've never been before. The exotic appeals to you, but that may not be true tomorrow, when the moon goes into fellow earth sign Capricorn.

Thursday, April 28 (Moon in Sagittarius to Capricorn 5:33 a.m.) Count yourself lucky. Today the energy is exactly right for working on your own creative projects. It's also a great day to pursue anything pleasurable, whether it's your creative expression, gambling, romance, or sex.

Friday, April 29 (Moon in Capricorn) You're building your creative project today, putting it together piece by piece. You may also be building a closer relationship with your kids. In fact, whatever you do today is a kind of building.

Saturday, April 30 (Moon in Capricorn to Aquarius 7:54 a.m.) Mars goes into Pisces in your seventh house. Buckle your seat belt, Virgo. You're in for a wild ride with partners. If one of them is of the romantic variety, count on your sex life heating up!

MAY 2005

Sunday, May 1 (Moon in Aquarius)   This isn't a comfortable moon for you, Virgo. Today it requires an adjustment in attitude and in the way you approach your coworkers. Try to remain flexible and listen to other people's opinions.

Monday, May 2 (Moon in Aquarius to Pisces 10:43 a.m.)   This water moon is wonderful for imagination and intuition. It forces you to release your left brain's hold on your world so that you can delve into the waters of your unconscious. It also allows you to feel what your partner is feeling and provides a deeper understanding of your relationship.

Tuesday, May 3 (Moon in Pisces)   Your compassion urges you out into the world today to do a favor for someone else. Well, maybe not a favor exactly, but a service, something at which you excel. And in the process of doing so, romance with a stranger is kindled.

Wednesday, May 4 (Moon in Pisces to Aries 2:36 p.m.)   Like the Leo and the Sagittarius moons, this fire moon can give you trouble. It just goes against your earthy nature to feel so . . . well, so incredibly passionate. It's as if your emotions are all over the place, as unpredictable as world politics. Your best venue is to feel whatever you feel today, acknowledge it's part of you, and get on with your life.

Thursday, May 5 (Moon in Aries)   Is it sex that interests you or is it love? Or perhaps it's just the passion

267

of the moment, a smoldering chemistry that demands immediate satisfaction. You need to figure out exactly what you want from the other person and only then will things be clearer.

Friday, May 6 (Moon in Aries to Taurus 8:01 p.m.) It's a crazy day that doesn't settle down until later this evening when the moon moves into your ninth house. You feel the shift in your body, a lessening of tension, and a giving way to increased stability. Enjoy the moment, Virgo.

Saturday, May 7 (Moon in Taurus) Your worldview—your spiritual beliefs, your politics, your higher ideals—seems much clearer to you than it has the last few days. You feel more secure in these beliefs and are ready to defend them if you have to. And guess what? You may have to.

Sunday, May 8 (Moon in Taurus) If you get into a political discussion today, try not to hit the other person over the head with your views. Be willing to listen, to embrace other ideas. It doesn't mean you have to change your opinion, only that you must be willing to listen.

Monday, May 9 (Moon in Taurus to Gemini 3:29 a.m.) Venus moves into Gemini, into your tenth house. Venus, like Jupiter, is the Santa Claus of the zodiac, although allegedly a lesser Santa Claus. At any rate, with Venus transiting your tenth house, you can expect strokes of professional luck through June 2. Make good use of them, Virgo.

Tuesday, May 10 (Moon in Gemini) As the moon joins Venus in your tenth house, your career is definitely the focal point. Strive to cement professional partnerships and to create new ones. Use your network of contacts to gain support for your point of view. And talk, talk, talk. People will listen.

Wednesday, May 11 (Moon in Gemini to Cancer 1:21 p.m.)   Your thoughts turn to the goals that make you feel secure. These goals, however, may not be your goals so much as they are goals passed down from your family. Start looking for the aspirations that are truly yours.

Thursday, May 12 (Moon in Cancer)   Mercury moves into Taurus, into your ninth house. Expect news concerning publishing, promotion, higher education. You could hear news that your novel or another creative project has sold overseas.

Friday, May 13 (Moon in Cancer)   Mom, Dad, home, and apple pie—they just doesn't cut it anymore. Your thoughts turn to a larger picture, how your goals fit into the larger world or vice versa. Why, for instance, is it that in the richest country on the planet, people are starving, homeless, illiterate, jobless, and denied adequate health care? Who's the enemy here?

Saturday, May 14 (Moon in Cancer into Leo 1:18 a.m.)   The moon moves into your twelfth house shortly after midnight. You may have some dreams tonight that seem ridiculous until you look deeper. Once you look, you can't stop looking, Virgo. After all, dreams are the voice of your soul. Figure out the symbolism. It's important.

Sunday, May 15 (Moon in Leo)   Could a romance be happening behind the scenes, out of view of even your family and closest friends? Is it love? Sex? Or is it something more profound? Even you don't know the answer yet.

269

Monday, May 16 (Moon in Leo to Virgo 1:48 p.m.)   By this afternoon, you're just about on top of the world. No more inner voices are haunting you—no more angst, no more inner turmoil. Why can't life always be like this? Well, the good news is that at least the world feels like this sometimes.

Tuesday, May 17 (Moon in Virgo)   Your sex appeal is especially high. Even strangers notice something different about you that sets you apart from other people. Any health complaints you have are directly related to your emotions. If you need surgery, it's best to avoid it during this transit. If you can't avoid it, at least don't have it on your digestive tract, which is ruled by Virgo.

Wednesday, May 18 (Moon in Virgo)   Finish up projects that you've put off at work and at home. You're good at connecting the dots between concepts, but you need to develop a more universal outlook. Once you begin to work in that direction, you'll be able to see the underlying patterns of situations that puzzle you.

Thursday, May 19 (Moon in Virgo to Libra 12:31 a.m.) Neptune, the planet of illusions, turns retrograde today in your sixth house. Until October 26, when it turns direct again, you need to be aware that you may not have the full picture on work-related issues. If you get sick during this time, be sure to get a second opinion. Neptune is a slippery little devil.

Friday, May 20 (Moon in Libra)   You may feel especially possessive today about something that you own or about your belongings in general. It could lead to a conflict with another person. Remember that belongings are merely things to which we attach emotional significance. We can't take them with us when we leave the planet. Is anything you own really worth fighting about?

Saturday, May 21 (Moon in Libra to Scorpio 7:49 a.m.)   This moon is emotionally intense, and that's precisely why you need to get out today and have some fun. It could involve an outing with a sibling or another relative or even with a friend in your neighborhood.

Sunday, May 22 (Moon in Scorpio)   Your sexuality is powerful today and you may want to spend quality time with a partner or lover. The stars favor honest communication and a need to really understand what's going on in your partner's mind—and heart.

Monday, May 23 (Moon in Scorpio to Sagittarius 11:39 a.m.)   As the moon heads into your fourth house, home, family, and your roots become your focus. You may head off in search of your genealogical roots today, surfing the Internet for genealogical sites, or perhaps even driving to another town to check public records.

Tuesday, May 24 (Moon in Sagittarius)   Your mother or a motherlike individual plays into your day's affairs. It may be something as simple as having dinner or going shopping with her—or something as complex as healing an old wound. Whatever it is, just remember that she won't be here forever; so appreciate her while she is.

Wednesday, May 25 (Moon in Sagittarius to Capricorn 1:11 p.m.)   With the moon moving into your fifth house, your focus is on children, creativity, and enjoyment. Do something creative and fun with your kids. If you don't have children of your own, then volunteer to take a friend's children for the day. Use your imagination. Make the outing memorable for all of you.

Thursday, May 26 (Moon in Capricorn)   With the moon in a fellow earth sign, you feel very comfortable today in general and specifically comfortable with your creative project. Whether you're working on a novel, a screenplay, a photography portfolio, or your acting technique, you're building a creative foundation.

Friday, May 27 (Moon in Capricorn to Aquarius 2:10 p.m.)   As the moon moves into your sixth house, your focus is on your daily routine at work and your daily health. Coworkers may not be as willing to embrace your ideas. You may have to defend your plans and argue convincingly. But you're so proficient with details, Virgo, you'll have all your facts lined up before you argue.

Saturday, May 28 (Moon in Aquarius)   Mercury, your ruler, moves into Gemini, a great boost for your already considerable communication abilities. Through June 10, your career will be very much on your mind. Expect news in this area, a lot of activity surrounding your career, and some public speaking. Anything you write during this time will be well-received.

Sunday, May 29 (Moon in Aquarius to Pisces 4:09 p.m.)   When the moon moves into Pisces, it's opposite your sun. You may feel like you're in the middle of a tug-of-war, trying to balance the demands of home and career, work and play, right brain and left. You may feel more emotionally vulnerable. Take it as it comes, Virgo.

Monday, May 30 (Moon in Pisces)   Plan an intimate evening with your partner or spouse. You two need some time to yourselves to exchange thoughts and dreams, goals and hopes. Make sure you're on the same track.

Tuesday, May 31 (Moon in Pisces to Aries 8:08 p.m.)   When the moon moves into fiery Aries, you either let your passions and volatile emotions run wild or temper the impulses with some grounded Virgo energy. The latter is the best course.

Wednesday, June 1 (Moon in Aries)   Your spouse or partner is launching a project in a new direction. You're supportive of the decision, even if you don't understand everything that's involved. Your encouragement is vital to the project's success.

Thursday, June 2 (Moon in Aries)   When it comes to jointly held property and goods, you're short on patience and tolerance today. You want things to be your way. Your partner has other ideas, and this could lead to a disagreement. Put off the issue for another day.

Friday, June 3 (Moon in Aries to Taurus 2:20 a.m.) With the moon in grounded, stable Taurus, you're able to work long and hard at whatever you're trying to accomplish. Venus moves into Cancer today, a nice placement for you. Romance is stirring on the public stage of your life.

Saturday, June 4 (Moon in Taurus)   It's already promising to be a very busy month. But under this lunar influence, you know how to balance stress and work. You take a yoga class, spend time at the gym or get out into nature to recharge your batteries.

Sunday, June 5 (Moon in Taurus to Gemini 10:36 a.m.) Jupiter turns direct today in your second house. This is good news for your finances. From now until October 25, when Jupiter moves into Scorpio, things finally move forward again. Your stocks rise, your pension plan begins to expand, and your investments pay off. A raise or a promotion is also possible.

Monday, June 6 (Moon in Gemini)   Minor professional challenges surface. You may get some resistance from a supervisor who doesn't agree with your strategy.

Just remind the person that it's your gig, and you'll take responsibility for anything that goes wrong.

Tuesday, June 7 (Moon in Gemini to Cancer 8:47 p.m.)   Your nurturing instincts are stirred up this evening, possibly because of something a child says or does. You want to protect the child or another loved one from hurt or pain, but quickly realize that although you can offer support and advice, you can't live this person's life.

Wednesday, June 8 (Moon in Cancer)   Finish up delayed or unfinished projects; fulfill your obligations to others. If you've made promises, keep them. Tomorrow is a high cycle day. Be ready for it!

Thursday, June 9 (Moon in Cancer)   It's a high cycle day. You feel you can tackle just about anything and probably will. Your ideas are backed by intuitive certainty, as well as by facts and statistics. You're well prepared for presenting your case. You can't lose today, Virgo.

Friday, June 10 (Moon in Cancer to Leo 8:40 a.m.) When the moon is in Leo in your twelfth house, it's difficult to withdraw, even if that's what you feel like doing. The Leo moon always wants to shine. But if you can work behind the scenes in some way, doing what you love, it's not such a bad compromise, is it?

Saturday, June 11 (Moon in Leo)   Your thoughts will be on your goals and aspirations, and your energy will be poured into physical activity or into sex.

Sunday, June 12 (Moon in Leo to Virgo 9:23 p.m.)   As the moon goes into your sign tonight, you'll feel sexier, more magnetic. With Mars in your eighth house, you're also going to be in the mood for an intimate evening with your partner.

Monday, June 13 (Moon in Virgo)   Your emotions and your mind pretty much agree on everything today. Even if you feel a bit more emotionally vulnerable than usual, it doesn't keep you from getting things done. If anything, your emotions may propel you to work even faster and more efficiently than you usually do.

Tuesday, June 14 (Moon in Virgo)   Uranus turns retrograde in your seventh house today. Until November 15, when the planet turns direct again, you may be exploring your feelings, thoughts, and beliefs about your professional and personal partnerships. You may experience sudden, unexpected insights into partnership matters.

Wednesday, June 15 (Moon in Virgo to Libra 8:59 a.m.)
With the moon joining Jupiter in your second house, your finances should be booming. If they aren't yet, start laying the groundwork for new projects and new income-producing ideas; expand your network of contacts. Take advantage of the last three months of this transit!

Thursday, June 16 (Moon in Libra)   Visit museums, bookstores, or the theater. Treat yourself to a smorgasbord of the arts, and make sure to take your partner.

Friday, June 17 (Moon in Libra to Scorpio 5:24 p.m.)   Once the moon goes into Scorpio this afternoon, you feel a lot better about things in general. However, your emotions are pretty intense, so be careful that you don't say something that will be difficult to retract, particularly to a sibling or another relative.

Saturday, June 18 (Moon in Scorpio)   Whatever you investigate today—a new piece you find on the Internet, a neighborhood mystery, or just the whereabouts of a missing personal item—you do so with great determination. This moon sign is driven by emotions and intuition.

Sunday, June 19 (Moon in Scorpio to Sagittarius 9:45 p.m.)   You may have to be cooperative with someone at home or a domestic issue requires your cooperation and support. Either way, it's a day when you may have to compromise to settle something to everyone's benefit and satisfaction.

Monday, June 20 (Moon in Sagittarius)   The good news about this moon—at least for you—is that it enables you to see the larger picture in terms of life. Use today to clarify what you would like to accomplish in the next five years and to define where you would like to be professionally, personally, and spiritually.

Tuesday, June 21 (Moon in Sagittarius to Capricorn 10:52 p.m.)   You may want to spend at least part of the day organizing your computer files, catching up on e-mails, and generally tidying up. By the time the moon goes into Capricorn tonight, you'll understand why.

Wednesday, June 22 (Moon in Capricorn)   You're actually in a strong position to tackle your own creative projects. Regardless of what you're doing, you can establish the structure of your project and ground it through careful attention to details.

Thursday, June 23 (Moon in Capricorn to Aquarius 10:37 p.m.)   For most of the day, the moon is in a fellow earth sign, which suits you better than its being in a fire sign or an air sign. You're more ambitious and willing to work as hard and long as it takes to get the job done. Your boss notices. And so does a certain someone. A possible office romance is in the offing.

Friday, June 24 (Moon in Aquarius)   With the moon squarely in your sixth house, that office romance could take off. The individual in question could be idiosyncratic, a rebel who fills you with a sense of adventure.

Saturday, June 25 (Moon in Aquarius to Pisces 11:04 p.m.) For much of today, you're an independent loner, going about your business, lost in your own thoughts. Late tonight, something shifts deep inside of you. Your imagination wakes up and whips you to some faraway place where your creative juices bubble and flow.

Sunday, June 26 (Moon in Pisces) Spend the day with your partner or, if you're single, spend the day with friends who support your ideals. Your compassion compels you to visit someone who's in the hospital or a nursing home.

Monday, June 27 (Moon in Pisces) Mercury goes into dynamic Leo and you're in a high cycle day. What a combination. Leo shouts to be heard and dresses boldly, wishing to be seen. However, since Mercury is in your twelfth house, the accolades may be confined to whatever is going on behind the scenes.

Tuesday, June 28 (Moon in Pisces to Aries 1:52 a.m.) Venus joins Mercury in your twelfth house. This can result in a secret love affair, artistic work done in privacy and seclusion, or in general good fortune related to your personal unconscious.

Wednesday, June 29 (Moon in Aries) With both Mercury and Venus in fire signs and now the moon joining the fire sign lineup, you've got an abundance of physical and sexual energy. You're demonstrative toward your partner, and if you're smart, you'll set aside plenty of time for the two of you to be together.

Thursday, June 30 (Moon in Aries to Taurus 7:46 a.m.) Breathe deeply. The moon moves into Taurus today. You may get news related to a publishing venture in which you're involved. Your spiritual beliefs and your worldview are also involved in today's picture.

Friday, July 1 (Moon in Taurus)   An overseas trip is possible. It could be related to spiritual or political issues. Your personal property and belongings are also high-lighted today.

Saturday, July 2 (Moon in Taurus to Gemini 4:27 p.m.)   By this afternoon, you're in a party mood. You either accept an invitation to a party or you throw a party yourself. Either way, you make new professional contacts. You're gearing up for the Fourth of July, with visitors perhaps arriving from out of town.

Sunday, July 3 (Moon in Gemini)   If you're traveling this weekend, give yourself plenty of time to get there. With the moon in Gemini, a lot of people will take to the highways. Have stuff in the car for the kids to do because the trip may take longer than you think.

Monday, July 4 (Moon in Gemini)   Happy Fourth of July! In addition to having fun today, don't forget to celebrate what the holiday really means: freedom and independence. Although a few domestic issues could sur-face today, just take them in stride.

Tuesday, July 5 (Moon in Gemini to Cancer 3:08 a.m.)
Very early this morning, the moon enters your eleventh house. All sorts of concerns about home and family wash through you. The concerns may not be very specific, at least not to your conscious mind. You have to let your intuition guide you through the labyrinth of your own emotions.

Wednesday, July 6 (Moon in Cancer)   It's a power day. Your focus is on power and money and how the two can be integrated into your professional life. Keep your attention in the moment today, dress for success, believe you're successful, and watch things change!

Thursday, July 7 (Moon in Cancer to Leo 3:11 p.m.)   Now that you've recovered from the July Fourth weekend, you may have some issues from your early childhood creeping into your awareness. These issues may be related to power you have disowned over the years. Work through them, release them, and move on with your life.

Friday, July 8 (Moon in Leo)   It's a high cycle day, a perfect time to launch new ideas and projects, to get your life moving in the direction that you would like it to go. Your self-confidence should be strong today, particularly if you've gained an understanding of childhood issues that may have blocked you somehow in the past.

Saturday, July 9 (Moon in Leo)   Never underestimate the power of your beliefs, Virgo. Today, you have an opportunity not only to discover your deepest beliefs, but to begin changing those that are holding you back from attaining your dreams. Do the inner work—and your experiences will be a faithful reflection.

Sunday, July 10 (Moon in Leo to Virgo 3:57 a.m.) When you wake up today, the moon is in your sign. This is always good news, regardless of what the other planets are doing in your horoscope. It gives you self-confidence and the physical, emotional, and spiritual resources to do just about anything you set your mind to.

Monday, July 11 (Moon in Virgo)   You're usually something of a perfectionist, and when the moon is in your sign, this tendency is enhanced. Just remember that becoming obsessed with perfection can make you lose your way. So don't worry if every "i" isn't dotted.

279

Tuesday, July 12 (Moon in Virgo to Libra 4:09 p.m.)   Your soul is crying out for a change in routine. Go for it. Alter your route to work. Change your style of clothes, your hair style, the music you listen to. Or head out of town and visit someplace you've never been before.

Wednesday, July 13 (Moon in Libra)   Today you discover just what you're really looking for in a relationship. Thank Jupiter in Libra, in your second house, for that. Your concepts of relationships are expanding.

Thursday, July 14 (Moon in Libra)   Your ideas about money are changing and expanding. With both Jupiter and the moon in the second house, you're discovering that money is easier to make than you previously believed and that it can be made in strange ways. It's part of the cycle of your growth.

Friday, July 15 (Moon in Libra to Scorpio 1:51 a.m.)   There are times in your life when your emotions run you over. This could be one of those days. Someone will push your buttons, and unless you're alert, you could blow something way out of proportion. Chill, Virgo.

Saturday, July 16 (Moon in Scorpio)   This is a big transition. Saturn goes into Leo today, into your twelfth house. It marks the beginning of a period that lasts about two and a half years and the end of a cycle of growth. Whatever hasn't worked in the past few years will pass out of your life. You're clearing the way for the new energy that will be ushered in when Saturn moves into your sign.

Sunday, July 17 (Moon in Scorpio to Sagittarius 7:35 a.m.)   Here's another one of those fire sign moons that can drive you nuts if you let it. Use the energy today

o get things done at home or, if you have a home office,
o put things there in order.

Monday, July 18 (Moon in Sagittarius) With the
moon joining Pluto in your fourth house, you may have
control issues today related to your home and domestic
issues. This is sure to drive everyone around crazy—so
ease up, Virgo, or you may have an insurrection on
your hands.

**Tuesday, July 19 (Moon in Sagittarius to Capricorn
9:27 a.m.)** As the moon moves into your fifth house
this morning, you feel a powerful sense of relief. Your
creative energy is flowing, you're in the mood for enjoying yourself, and you're off looking for whatever
brings you pleasure.

Wednesday, July 20 (Moon in Capricorn) You pursue pleasurable activities today. Yes, it's a workday, but
that doesn't mean you have to keep your nose to the
grindstone. Find activities that you enjoy and indulge
yourself.

**Thursday, July 21 (Moon in Capricorn to Aquarius 8:56
a.m.)** Early today, the moon moves into your sixth
house. Your emotions could be squashed or repressed
today as you turn your attention toward your daily work
routine. You're concerned about getting things ac-
complished.

Friday, July 22 (Moon in Aquarius) Mercury turns
retrograde today in Leo and Venus moves into Virgo.
Quite a combination. The Venus transition, which lasts
till August 15, enhances your sex appeal and charisma.
It could spell the beginning of a flirtation or romance
or the culmination of an artistic project. The Mercury
retrograde in your twelfth house drives your conscious
thoughts inward.

Saturday, July 23 (Moon in Aquarius to Pisces 8:13 a.m.)   It's a great weekend to get away with your partner or significant other. Just remember that, with Mercury retrograde, your travel plans could change suddenly. Don't rant and rave about it—look at it as an adventure.

Sunday, July 24 (Moon in Pisces)   If you haven't left town for the weekend, your partner and you may be fixing up your house or apartment. You could be painting, redecorating, and generally beautifying your surroundings. Whatever you do today, it's important that your partner and you do it together.

Monday, July 25 (Moon in Pisces to Aries 9:24 a.m.)   You may investigate some esoteric topics: life after death, mediumship, or reincarnation. Your investigation isn't casual. You're looking for patterns that relate to your own experiences.

Tuesday, July 26 (Moon in Aries)   Your sexuality is racing, and so is your partner's. It could be that your relationship is taken to a whole new level. It's important that you keep your temper in control—minor skirmishes could surface.

Wednesday, July 27 (Moon in Aries to Taurus 1:55 p.m.)   Your attention today turns toward security issues—specifically, what makes you feel the most secure: your belongings, your land, your home, your past? Figure it out today, Virgo.

Thursday, July 28 (Moon in Taurus)   Now that Mars joins the moon in Taurus, your sexuality and sensuality become dominant forces in your psyche. It may be a good idea to get out into nature today to recharge your energy.

Friday, July 29 (Moon in Taurus to Gemini 10:03 p.m.)   News concerning publicity or a promotion. You may get visitors from overseas, hear from friends who live overseas, or plan your own trip overseas.

Saturday, July 30 (Moon in Gemini)   This lunar transit favors your career and professional relationships and the gathering and dispersing of information. Whether you're gathering facts from the Web or from other news sources, you have a goal in mind.

Sunday, July 31 (Moon in Gemini)   As you head into August, Virgo, your ruler is still retrograde, throwing a wrench into travel plans and communication. Saturn has just moved into your twelfth house and Mars is moving through your ninth house. Figure out where you want to be in the future and begin laying down your strategy to achieve your goal.

AUGUST 2005

Monday, August 1 (Moon in Gemini to Cancer 8:53 a.m.)   You experience a tug-of-war today between domestic issues and work. Lunar energy favors putting your house and personal affairs in order before you embark on anything new.

Tuesday, August 2 (Moon in Cancer)   Now that Saturn has left your eleventh house, the moon's presence feels a lot more comfortable. You have a lot of contact with friends and there may be some powerful and positive emotion involved. Express how you feel.

Wednesday, August 3 (Moon in Cancer to Leo 9:10 p.m.)   Your friends support your efforts today and cheer you on. In turn, you support their efforts and may be invited to a social gathering at which the bonds of friendship are confirmed.

Thursday, August 4 (Moon in Leo) You may have problems with your mother or with another nurturing female in your life. It's probably not anything serious; it's linked to an old issue between you that was never resolved. Confront and resolve it.

Friday, August 5 (Moon in Leo) It's a good day to read, go to a movie, or work on creative projects. You benefit from behind-the-scenes work and from deeper thought about yourself and where you're headed.

Saturday, August 6 (Moon to Virgo 9:54 a.m.) With the moon moving into your sign early this morning, you're in a good position to achieve just about anything you want. Your charisma and sex appeal are powerful and your communication abilities are persuasive.

Sunday, August 7 (Moon in Virgo) You're given a problem to solve. You do it with your usual efficiency and penchant for perfection; by the end of the day, the problem is history. It's a high cycle day for you, Virgo. Make good use of it.

Monday, August 8 (Moon in Virgo to Libra 10:09 p.m.) You have the entire day in front of you to call upon your strengths. By tonight, the moon has moved into Libra and your focus shifts. Get moving.

Tuesday, August 9 (Moon in Libra) Relationships and finances are the day's focal points—not necessarily in that order. It could be that a partner and you want to get away for a while, but the expense is holding you back—or it could be that your partner is feeling flush and springs for the bills.

Wednesday, August 10 (Moon in Libra)   You want to buy a quality item for your home or office, but feel it's too expensive. Best to wait until after August 16, when Venus will be in your house of money. The check will have cleared by then.

Thursday, August 11 (Moon in Libra to Scorpio 8:35 a.m.)   The moon joins Jupiter in your third house, expanding and deepening your emotional commitment to your siblings, relatives, and neighborhood. Someone nearby notices you and is immediately interested.

Friday, August 12 (Moon in Scorpio)   You may investigate something today connected to your neighborhood or community. A friend or partner may help you in your investigation. You're looking for the absolute bottom line.

Saturday, August 13 (Moon in Scorpio to Sagittarius 3:48 p.m.)   As the moon moves into your fourth house this afternoon, you head out for a place you've never been before. You do it in the spirit of all explorers—just to see what's there.

Sunday, August 14 (Moon in Sagittarius)   You're seeking the larger picture of your home life and the foundation of who you are. You're not sure what this larger picture contains, but you know that you need to find it or define it before you can move fully forward in your life.

Monday, August 15 (Moon in Sagittarius to Capricorn 7:14 p.m.)   Your ruler, Mercury, turns direct today in Leo. As it continues its forward movement through your twelfth house, people comment on how different you seem.

Tuesday, August 16 (Moon in Capricorn)   Venus moves into Libra, your second house. This is usually welcome news financially. Over the next three weeks, you may get a raise, a check could arrive, or a bank error is in your favor. Venus here can also spell good luck for artistic projects.

Wednesday, August 17 (Moon in Capricorn to Aquarius 7:39 p.m.) You may have to compromise about a work issue. Your cooperation is needed on a team effort. Even if you resist the compromise, all works out to your benefit.

Thursday, August 18 (Moon in Aquarius) Take your cutting-edge ideas and implement them at work. Not only do you attract the attention of a supervisor, but you're noticed by a person who has had an eye on you.

Friday, August 19 (Moon in Aquarius to Pisces 6:53 p.m.) Your romantic interest and you deepen your relationship and commitment to each other today. Neither of you is expecting to do so. The bond simply unfolds from a natural order of events.

Saturday, August 20 (Moon in Pisces) Be sure to read over any contracts with great care. Even though Mercury is no longer retrograde—so the chances of contractual errors are less—you may have missed something during your first reading.

Sunday, August 21 (Moon in Pisces to Aries 7:02 p.m.) Jointly held finances and property are the focus. Perhaps your partner and you are considering the purchase of a piece of property. Be sure that you agree on the terms.

Monday, August 22 (Moon in Aries) Calm down; strive for patience. Even if calm and patience seem impossible today, you'll get farther exhibiting those qualities than you will by exhibiting their opposite.

Tuesday, August 23 (Moon in Aries to Taurus 9:58 p.m.)   Finance and power are your focuses today. You may feel particularly stubborn about an opinion or an idea that you've put forth. Don't be afraid to defend your stance.

Wednesday, August 24 (Moon in Taurus)   Fulfill your obligations, finish projects, and honor promises to others. You're freeing up energy that you'll need tomorrow. You may get news concerning publishing.

Thursday, August 25 (Moon in Taurus)   Your personal belongings may play a part in today's affairs—specifically, your possessiveness about certain things that you own. But because the Taurus moon is an earth sign, just as Virgo is, you're able to reach a satisfying solution.

Friday, August 26 (Moon in Taurus to Gemini 4:43 a.m.)   You're in a party mood as the week winds down. In fact, you either attend or have one this evening. Be sure to hobnob with your professional peers and anyone else connected to your career.

Saturday, August 27 (Moon in Gemini)   Expect news concerning your career or professional relationships. You desperately need a change of scenery. Why not get out and enjoy what's left of the summer? New experiences will boost your spirits.

Sunday, August 28 (Moon in Gemini to Cancer 2:57 p.m.)   As the moon moves into Cancer, your nurturing instincts are triggered. It could concern an animal, a child, or even your mother. Give your support and love freely.

Monday, August 29 (Moon in Cancer)   Expect news concerning a workshop or seminar that you're attending or even teaching. There could be some minor changes in the schedule.

Tuesday, August 30 (Moon in Cancer)   It's a good day to get your finger on the public pulse. Your intuition is strong today; so follow your inner guidance.

Wednesday, August 31 (Moon in Cancer to Leo 3:15 a.m.)   With the moon entering your twelfth house at the end of the month, you may be inclined toward secrecy. That's okay as long as you're aware of your motives for secrecy.   ˎ

SEPTEMBER 2005

Thursday, September 1 (Moon in Leo)   Whatever you do behind the scenes proves beneficial. It's a private sort of day when you may want to experiment with alternative systems like aromatherapy, acupuncture, or reconnective healing. It's not that you're sick; you're merely curious.

Friday, September 2 (Moon in Leo to Virgo 3:57 p.m.)   Pluto turns direct in your fourth house. This planet's effects are always profound, permanent, and subtle. By now, you should have some idea how Pluto's transit through Sagittarius is affecting you.

Saturday, September 3 (Moon in Virgo)   The moon is in your sign again, always a welcome reprieve for you in the lunar scheme of things. Your emotions and your intellect work hand in hand, and you're able to cruise through any challenges you may encounter.

Sunday, September 4 (Moon in Virgo)   With Mercury joining the moon in your sign, you are able to communicate as clearly about your feelings as you can about your thoughts. Expect news related to writing, communication, and travel. The Mercury transit lasts through September 18.

Monday, September 5 (Moon in Virgo to Libra 3:53 a.m.) Your artistic abilities are raging. Honor them, express them, and don't be afraid to take creative risks. Try to find people of like mind.

Tuesday, September 6 (Moon in Libra) The lunar energies favor relationships. You may be striving to find balance in one or more of your relationships. What you need to ask yourself is what you're trying to balance.

Wednesday, September 7 (Moon in Libra to Scorpio 2:11 p.m.) You work better as part of a partnership or team. You have a strong intuitive sense about the people with whom you're working. Trust that sense. It won't steer you wrong.

Thursday, September 8 (Moon in Scorpio) Your emotions are a strong force in your life. They can be so powerful that, if directed with intent and desire, they can enable you to change elements holding you back.

Friday, September 9 (Moon in Scorpio to Sagittarius 10:04 p.m.) Opportunities come wrapped in strange packages. Before you seize them, it's best to organize your own thoughts and goals in terms of the larger picture of whatever you're trying to accomplish.

Saturday, September 10 (Moon in Sagittarius) A new romance may be in the offing today and it could be with someone you already know. But what are you looking for: a flirtation or something bigger?

Sunday, September 11 (Moon in Sagittarius) Venus moves into your third house today. Venus transits are usually pleasant. This one triggers your social life and makes you realize how beautiful your everyday world is. Not too bad for a Sunday!

Monday, September 12 (Moon in Sagittarius to Capricorn 2:57 a.m.)   With Venus in your third house until October 7, you're not in a frame of mind to tackle heavy issues. You are simply in the mood for fun, light romance, and the appreciation of beauty.

Tuesday, September 13 (Moon in Capricorn)   With Venus in your court and the moon in your fifth house of creativity, your creative energy should be flowing without impediment. The Capricorn moon urges you to put in the time to nurture your own creativity in an organized way.

Wednesday, September 14 (Moon in Capricorn to Aquarius 5:03 a.m.)   Your mind is quick and your insight is visionary. Be careful how you apply this at work because there are people around you who prefer the status quo.

Thursday, September 15 (Moon in Aquarius)   An office flirtation is possible with someone whose ideas may be radical in some way. You enjoy this person's eccentricities—no matter how radical.

Friday, September 16 (Moon in Aquarius to Pisces 5:25 a.m.)   Partnerships assume importance. It may be that you need to pay closer attention to what's transpiring in a business partnership. Are your interests being compromised somehow?

Saturday, September 17 (Moon in Pisces)   Your partner and you should ease up on your usual weekend routines. Get out together and do something new. Make time to listen to each other. Watch out for extravagant spending.

Sunday, September 18 (Moon in Pisces to Aries 5:43 a.m.) Romance is in the air. You're excitable and impatient. Your best bet is to channel your energy into something physical.

Monday, September 19 (Moon in Aries) It would be a good idea to control your impulses. Persevere to get things done, build a creative base for yourself and your projects; try to keep your energies from being scattered.

Tuesday, September 20 (Moon in Aries to Taurus 7:48 a.m.) Mercury moves into Libra, into your second house. Your conscious thoughts are more balanced, particularly when it comes to finances. With the moon moving into security-conscious Taurus, listen to your inner promptings about money.

Wednesday, September 21 (Moon in Taurus) Avoid confusion and conflicts, if at all possible. Even though others may delay making or living up to commitments, don't worry. Gather information related to publicity, promotion and education, but don't make a decision until tomorrow.

Thursday, September 22 (Moon in Taurus to Gemini 1:07 p.m.) Justice and communication are the day's keynotes. With the moon moving into your tenth house, it's important to avoid self-deception and to express your desires and thoughts.

Friday, September 23 (Moon in Gemini) Finish what you start. Since the moon is still in your tenth house, it's important to strive for universal appeal in whatever you do or take on. Look beyond the immediate toward your long-range professional goals.

Saturday, September 24 (Moon in Gemini to Cancer 10:11 p.m.) With the moon moving into your eleventh house tonight, strive for creative independence. Don't deal with people who have closed minds. You need the support of friends and people who share your views.

Sunday, September 25 (Moon in Cancer)   Diplomacy is called for in a domestic situation. Be kind and understanding; don't show your resentment or irritation. Your role should be one of cooperative sensitivity.

Monday, September 26 (Moon in Cancer)   Nurture yourself with the same care that you use to nurture others. You're filled with charm and wit, but remain flexible and open to any opportunities that come your way. Your mother plays a part in today's affairs.

Tuesday, September 27 (Moon in Cancer to Leo 10:03 a.m.)   Your warmth and passion take over. People are attracted to you for this very reason. Even though you may hope to shine in a more public way, today it's important to remain behind the scenes.

Wednesday, September 28 (Moon in Leo)   A possible move or relocation for today. Any obstacles that you encounter will be overcome with ease. Your dreams are especially vivid—strive to remember them and then write them down.

Thursday, September 29 (Moon in Leo to Virgo 10:45 p.m.)   It's a day to create harmony and to improve your surroundings in some way. Given your penchant for perfection, Virgo, this should be fun for you. An adjustment in your domestic situation is possible.

Friday, September 30 (Moon in Virgo)   It's great to end a month with the moon in your sign. It provides you with self-confidence and allows you to get through the day with ease. On some level, you journey into the unknown and enjoy the mystery!

Saturday, October 1 (Moon in Virgo)   Today people in your personal world meet your ideal expectations. Even so, your cooperation may be required in a domestic situation, with someone needing your support or advice. Mars turns retrograde today in your ninth house. There could be delays with promotions, publicity, or long-distance travel.

Sunday, October 2 (Moon in Virgo to Libra 10:25 a.m.)   You may prefer being with a special someone today. It's also likely that you'll discuss your financial plans or hopes with another person. The Libra moon is always about relationships, and when it's in your second house, your focus is finances and your personal values.

Monday, October 3 (Moon in Libra)   Expect an e-mail or a call concerning investment opportunities from a friend. Don't make a decision today. Wait until the moon has moved into your own sign again.

Tuesday, October 4 (Moon in Libra to Scorpio 8:04 p.m.)   Get to the office before your coworkers do. You've got a lot of work to plow through and promises to fulfill. Once you get through all this, you'll be able to allow yourself looser rein tomorrow.

Wednesday, October 5 (Moon in Scorpio)   Variety truly is the spice of life. With the moon joining Venus in your third house, a flirtation or romance is possible with someone from your neighborhood or community. It promises to be emotionally intense.

Thursday, October 6 (Moon in Scorpio)   When the moon is in this sign, your sexuality often takes center stage. You may be somewhat secretive about a romance;

your insight into your lover's motives and psyche will provide you will a lot of information.

Friday, October 7 (Moon in Scorpio to Sagittarius 3:28 a.m.)   Venus moves into Sagittarius, in your fourth house. This placement favors peace and harmony at home. If you're married or committed, your sex life and romance in general heats up. If you're single, then use the next 28 days to get out and be seen. A new romance is likely.

Saturday, October 8 (Moon in Sagittarius)   With Mercury moving into your Scorpio, your conscious mind takes on a decidedly investigative and mystical bent. You may find yourself delving into esoteric topics, looking for the absolute bottom line.

Sunday, October 9 (Moon in Sagittarius to Capricorn 8:44 a.m.)   Take creative risks today. You need a change of perspective, a new point of view, and the Capricorn moon in your fifth house helps you find it.

Monday, October 10 (Moon in Capricorn)   Your kids play a major role in your affairs today. If you don't have children, other people's children are key. With the moon in the fifth house, your enjoyment is of prime importance.

Tuesday, October 11 (Moon in Capricorn to Aquarius 12:05 p.m.)   The moon moves into your sixth house. This places the day's emphasis squarely on daily work routines and your daily health. Take care of dental and medical obligations. Your emotional balance is key to successful negotiations.

Wednesday, October 12 (Moon in Aquarius)   You're drawn to cutting-edge technology and future trends. Your coworkers may not be ready for your visionary ideas; make sure to couch these ideas in practical, easily understandable ways.

Thursday, October 13 (Moon in Aquarius to Pisces 2:06 p.m.)   It's time to visualize the future—of your relationship with your partner, of your career goals, and of your professional partnerships. With the moon in intuitive Pisces, you're able to access very deep levels of your own being and use what you find to galvanize higher forces in your life.

Friday, October 14 (Moon in Pisces)   Today favors romance: new romance, existing romance, romances that are yet to come. Sounds odd, doesn't it? But there's a psychic element to this moon sign that knows no boundaries of time or space. You have the ability today to be your own prophet.

Saturday, October 15 (Moon in Pisces to Aries 3:40 p.m.)   By this afternoon, you're not feeling very psychic. You're feeling impatient, sexual, deeply restless. Don't bother with home-improvement projects or the domestic routine. Get out and about. Go someplace new. Indulge the fire that rages in your blood.

Sunday, October 16 (Moon in Aries)   When you wake up, promise yourself that you will do everything differently. Try something new and exotic for breakfast. Surf new Web sites. Go to a flea market, a carnival, or a palm reader. Since you can't resist the fire of the Aries moon, surrender to it.

Monday, October 17 (Moon in Aries to Taurus 6:05 p.m.)   Today you find something in a book that intrigues you so deeply you pursue its lead to other books. It concerns something in the distant past, perhaps a historical event. Keep notes. This may provide fodder for creative work in the future.

Tuesday, October 18 (Moon in Taurus) A sudden trip is possible—or plans for a trip—relating to education, law, or publishing.

Wednesday, October 19 (Moon in Taurus to Gemini 10:45 p.m.) As the days now turn toward autumn, you're in a more sociable mood. Professional contacts are highlighted and so are professional goals.

Thursday, October 20 (Moon in Gemini) You've got the gift of gab, Virgo. Don't use it frivolously. Channel it into persuading others that your ideas and methods are sound and far-reaching.

Friday, October 21 (Moon in Gemini) A flirtation or romance with a supervisor or an older person is possible. Be careful about mixing business with pleasure. It could backfire. Collect your facts first.

Saturday, October 22 (Moon in Gemini to Cancer 6:42 a.m.) With Venus still in your fourth house, you grasp the larger picture of your love life and aren't so sure that you like what you see. Well, if you don't like it, take steps to change it now. Your point of power, Virgo, always lies in the present.

Sunday, October 23 (Moon in Cancer) The moon is now forming a harmonious angle to your sun that facilitates an ease between your emotions and your ego, your ego and your intuition, your head and your heart. Nurture your dreams and then reach for the future.

Monday, October 24 (Moon in Cancer to Leo 5:49 p.m.) For part of today, you could be feeling nostalgic for the good ol' days, whatever you perceive them to be. You may feel a deep connection to your past, your heritage, the collective of your family. Put it into perspective and move forward.

Tuesday, October 25 (Moon in Leo)   Jupiter moves into Scorpio today, into your third house, where it will be for about a year. This transit will expand your experiences with siblings, other relatives, and your neighborhood and community. It will also expand your communication abilities and the ways in which you delve into whatever interests you.

Wednesday, October 26 (Moon in Leo)   Neptune turns direct today in your sixth house. This will be a subtle shift of energy, but over the next few weeks and months, you may notice that things at work aren't quite as fuzzy and confusing.

Thursday, October 27 (Moon in Leo to Virgo 6:29 a.m.) With the moon in your sign, make decisions that you've put off. Your charisma is strong and your communication abilities persuasive.

Friday, October 28 (Moon in Virgo)   Romance flourishes. You and your partner deepen your commitment to each other. Is it marriage you want, Virgo? You may have to decide.

Saturday, October 29 (Moon in Virgo to Libra 6:15 p.m.)   Music plays into your affairs today. You may get an invitation to a ballet or an opera. Collect your facts. Knowledge is essential to your success.

Sunday, October 30—Daylight Saving Time Ends (Moon in Libra)   You're drawn to real estate, perhaps property that would make a sound investment. Unexpected money arrives—a royalty check or repayment on a loan. In speculative matters, stick to number 8.

Monday, October 31 (Moon in Libra)   Happy Halloween! It's a good day to plan a long trip. Then clear up odds and ends at work and rush home to find a costume so that you can trick or treat with your kids this evening.

NOVEMBER 2005

Tuesday, November 1 (Moon in Libra to Scorpio 2:29 a.m.)   Your spirituality and intuition are highlighted today. It's important that you see things as they are, rather than as you wish they would be.

Wednesday, November 2 (Moon in Scorpio)   There's a chance that today you'll be recognized in some way for the work you are doing. This could be related to your community or neighborhood involvement.

Thursday, November 3 (Moon in Scorpio to Sagittarius 8:55 a.m.)   Be selfless today. You are collecting the pieces of the larger picture related to your home life, and you're going to fit that vision with the larger picture for your career.

Friday, November 4 (Moon in Sagittarius)   You may travel on short notice today. Usually, you don't like last-minute trips, but this one really appeals to your sense of adventure. Go with the flow, Virgo!

Saturday, November 5 (Moon in Sagittarius to Capricorn 1:17 p.m.)   As Venus moves into Capricorn, your creative drive accelerates. You suddenly know how to structure whatever you've been working on, and you are delighted when the structure works correctly.

Sunday, November 6 (Moon in Capricorn)   Expect news related to your creative life or to your children. Or you may receive an invitation for an impromptu party. Whatever happens, this is a day to enjoy yourself.

Monday, November 7 (Moon in Capricorn to Aquarius 4:31 p.m.) You may be examining budgets today related to your daily work routine. Don't allow your energies to become scattered. Persevere. Missing papers or objects are located.

Tuesday, November 8 (Moon in Aquarius) You feel emotionally independent and somewhat rebellious. Best to take that rebellion out of the office and pour it into some other area of your life.

Wednesday, November 9 (Moon in Aquarius to Pisces 7:23 p.m.) Try not to smother or crowd your mate or significant other, who may need some space. Even though you may feel emotionally vulnerable and threatened, step back.

Thursday, November 10 (Moon in Pisces) If anyone is working against you in either your personal or professional environment, it's likely you already know who that person is. With a bit of effort and compassion, you can win this individual to your side.

Friday, November 11 (Moon in Pisces to Aries 10:23 p.m.) It's a perfect time for a romantic weekend getaway. The getaway doesn't have to be distant or exotic, just private. Make it so, Virgo!

Saturday, November 12 (Moon in Aries) Your passion and sexuality are exceptionally powerful today, much too powerful to resist. So surrender to them. What you discover about yourself and your partner may surprise you.

Sunday, November 13 (Moon in Aries) Creative people play a role in your affairs. Get out and meet new people, have new experiences, and do something you've never done before. Express your opinions dynamically.

Monday, November 14 (Moon in Aries to Taurus 2:04 a.m.)   Mercury, your ruler, turns retrograde today in Sagittarius, in your fourth house. This could result in delays related to your home, finances, and travel. The possibility of miscommunication is also higher. It lasts until November 26.

Tuesday, November 15 (Moon in Taurus)   Uranus turns direct today in Pisces, in your seventh house. The insights you have gained about partnerships since Uranus went retrograde in mid-June can be applied in your life. You may still experience sudden and unexpected beginnings in partnerships, but your intuition will give you forewarning.

Wednesday, November 16 (Moon in Taurus to Gemini 7:11 a.m.)   Your career is highlighted with the moon in Gemini. The focus is on your professional partnerships and networks and possible news related to this area. Get your professional life in order.

Thursday, November 17 (Moon in Gemini)   Today you overcome obstacles with relative ease. You need to take risks and express your thoughts and opinions. Approach today with an unconventional mindset. Look at everything as an opportunity to grow and learn.

Friday, November 18 (Moon in Gemini to Cancer 2:43 p.m.)   This lunar position is about nurturing. You may visit a family member or relative who is ill. Emotional outbursts are likely that make unfair demands on your time and energy.

Saturday, November 19 (Moon in Cancer)   Try to avoid conflicts and confrontation and maintain your emotional balance. If any secrets are entrusted to you, keep them to yourself. You and a close friend may commiserate this evening.

Sunday, November 20 (Moon in Cancer)   It's a day to kick back and stay close to home. Nurture yourself and your loved ones and do something together as a group that creates memories for your kids.

Monday, November 21 (Moon in Cancer to Leo 1:10 a.m.)   As the moon joins Saturn in your twelfth house, you may be mulling over past failures. Get out of that frame of mind immediately! Focus on your many successes.

Tuesday, November 22 (Moon in Leo)   Saturn turns retrograde in your twelfth house. Sometimes, this period can result in a heaviness of heart that really isn't justified. You may feel guilty about things that have happened in the past. You may feel depressed. Strive to remain positive. Visualize yourself wrapped in a cocoon of blue light, protected, happy.

Wednesday, November 23 (Moon in Leo to Virgo 1:42 p.m.)   Once the moon moves into your sign, much of the heaviness you felt yesterday dissipates. Your sex appeal is high, your mood more buoyant. Take advantage of this overall healthy feeling by starting an exercise routine.

Thursday, November 24 (Moon in Virgo)   Your spirituality is highlighted. Foster generosity, play your hunches, and find unity in small groups. Your popularity is on the rise. Happy Thanksgiving!

Friday, November 25 (Moon in Virgo)   You may be tidying up today, getting things done around the house that you've put off. Once you finish, you and your Thanksgiving guests get out and about to see the sights. Today should go very smoothly with family and relatives.

301

Saturday, November 26 (Moon in Virgo to Libra 1:58 a.m.)   Mercury is still retrograde in your fourth house. Don't be surprised if news that you need is delayed or misconstrued in some way. If you're planning a short trip, check your travel schedule. There could be some delays.

Sunday, November 27 (Moon in Libra)   You may visit some antique stores or even garage sales in search of small treasures today. You're looking for something to spiff up your house. If you're really ambitious, you may start painting your rooms in soft pastels.

Monday, November 28 (Moon in Libra to Scorpio 11:33 a.m.)   The moon joins Jupiter in your third house, deepening your intuition and insight into the hidden forces in your life. Use this time to record your thoughts and feelings in a journal.

Tuesday, November 29 (Moon in Scorpio)   Your emotions and your thoughts work together flawlessly today, one bolstering the other. An e-mail from a sibling or another relative confirms something that you previously suspected.

Wednesday, November 30 (Moon in Scorpio to Sagittarius 5:33 p.m.)   The moon joins retrograde Mercury in your fourth house. You may feel emotionally vulnerable and volatile today, so be sure that you think before you speak. Remain calm and centered.

DECEMBER 2005

Thursday, December 1 (Moon in Sagittarius)   You head into the final month of the year with a lot going for you. This is a high cycle power day when your opportunities for recognition are especially strong. It's also a nice day for romance and love.

Friday, December 2 (Moon in Sagittarius to Capricorn 8:43 p.m.)   In terms of your creativity, disregard any preconceived notions you may have about how things work. Trust your inner resources and intuition. You're up to the challenge, Virgo!

Saturday, December 3 (Moon in Capricorn)   Mercury turns direct today—good news for Geminis and Virgos. This should facilitate your creative efforts and smooth out your life in general.

Sunday, December 4 (Moon in Capricorn to Aquarius 10:37 p.m.)   You may be somewhat regimental with your children today. If you're imposing rules just to impose them, think twice. You could have outright rebellion on your hands.

Monday, December 5 (Moon in Aquarius)   Are your coworkers ready for your visionary ideas? That depends. If you can rally support before you present the ideas to your boss, things will work out in your favor.

Tuesday, December 6 (Moon in Aquarius)   Your organizational skills come in handy today. You're somehow able to arrange your domestic schedules and your professional schedules so there isn't a conflict. It's a good day to revise, rewrite, rethink.

Wednesday, December 7 (Moon in Aquarius to Pisces 12:45 a.m.)   Take a break today. And take it with a romantic partner. You really do need a change in your routine. A move or relocation is possible.

Thursday, December 8 (Moon in Pisces)   Your partner needs your support now. It's time to set aside your own concerns and express your support and understanding. It strengthens your relationship.

Friday, December 9 (Moon in Pisces to Aries 4:03 a.m.) Mars turns direct tomorrow. Your physical energy hums right along, perfectly aligned with your higher mind and ideals. With the moon in Aries, which is ruled by Mars, you may be in for a passionate and very sexual day.

Saturday, December 10 (Moon in Aries) If your patience is short, strive to step back and detach. People will test you today for no particular reason—it's just how the energy is running.

Sunday, December 11 (Moon in Aries to Taurus 8:47 a.m.) The moon joins Mars in your ninth house. This stimulates your sexual drive and your passion for learning and for travel. Romance with a foreigner is possible.

Monday, December 12 (Moon in Taurus) You're off to a fresh start this morning. You feel comfortable with the earthy Taurus moon and are able to express your opinions persuasively and decisively. Wear red today!

Tuesday, December 13 (Moon in Taurus to Gemini 3:00 p.m.) You could find yourself counseling others today, perhaps professional peers or associates. Your cooperation is required in a personal matter. Be diplomatic.

Wednesday, December 14 (Moon in Gemini) As the holidays near, social activities are highlighted. Dinners, speaking engagements, even short trips are likely. Spread your good news.

Thursday, December 15 (Moon in Gemini to Cancer 11:01 p.m.) As Venus moves into your sixth house, your daily work routine unfolds with great ease and smoothness. A pay raise, promotion, or award is possible. Nurture yourself.

Friday, December 16 (Moon in Cancer)   Last-minute holiday shopping claims your weekend. You've got gifts to buy for your loved ones and you don't want to buy just the same old things. Poke around in unusual shops. Surf the Internet.

Saturday, December 17 (Moon in Cancer)   Now it comes down to a big holiday question: at whose house will you celebrate this year? You probably prefer to stay home, but you may have to compromise.

Sunday, December 18 (Moon in Cancer to Leo 9:18 a.m.)   Self-deception is a possibility. It may concern old issues that originated in your childhood. Let the issues surface. Confront them. Resolve them.

Monday, December 19 (Moon in Leo)   You shine behind the scenes and work behind the scenes to beautify an area. You may be decorating your house or your office. You may be visiting a relative who is confined to an institution. Go with the energy. Don't resist.

Tuesday, December 20 (Moon in Leo to Virgo 9:39 p.m.)   Even though the moon doesn't enter your sign until later this evening, you sense its approach throughout the day. Your energy and vitality increase by the hour. You knock off work early and head out to finish up your holiday shopping.

Wednesday, December 21 (Moon in Virgo)   Don't follow others today. If the new love of your life is eccentric but kind, why should you be concerned about what others think? The only opinion that matters here is yours—and that of the new person in your life.

Thursday, December 22 (Moon in Virgo)   A discussion about marriage is possible. If you're already married or committed, there's talk about the relationship and the direction in which it's going. Overall, things work very well today.

Friday, December 23 (Moon .in Virgo to Libra 10:27 a.m.)   Around the holidays, personal values are often called into question or challenged somehow. Someone close to you may not understand just how deeply the development of your artistic abilities matters to you.

Saturday, December 24 (Moon in Libra)   Oops. Venus turns retrograde in your second house. Relationships may go slightly out of whack for a while or you look inward to assess your true values.

Sunday, December 25 (Moon in Libra to Scorpio 9:04 p.m.)   Merry Christmas! You have plenty of freedom in thought and action. Surrounded by people you love, your day—and theirs—unfolds with great emotion.

Monday, December 26 (Moon in Scorpio)   Here's the intense moon again, right smack in your third house. During the holidays, you have more contact with siblings and other relatives; these encounters may bring up intense childhood issues.

Tuesday, December 27 (Moon in Scorpio)   You have a mystery to solve. With your usual grace and attention to detail, you get to the bottom of it by the end of the day. Your dreams are vivid and provide you with information about your present—and your future.

Wednesday, December 28 (Moon in Scorpio to Sagittarius 3:45 a.m.)   It's odd about these fire sign moons. On the one hand, you feel invigorated, but on the other, you may feel tense, challenged. At any rate, you use the energy to find the larger picture of your personal life.

Thursday, December 29 (Moon in Sagittarius) As the year begins to wind down, your goals are winding up and assuming greater clarity. Don't start anything new until early next year. Fulfill this year's obligations first.

Friday, December 30 (Moon in Sagittarius to Capricorn 6:36 a.m.) This is a great moon for the end of the year. You're able to ground whatever you do today and to make your plans practical and useful to others.

Saturday, December 31 (Moon in Capricorn) As you move into the new year, only Venus is retrograde. Your life is pushing forward, your goals and dreams clear in your mind, and your intuition is as strong as it has ever been. Tonight make a list of your goals for the next year. Then promise yourself you will make them happen.

HAPPY NEW YEAR!

ABOUT THE AUTHOR

Born on August 5, 1926, in Philadelphia, Sydney Omarr was the only person ever given full-time duty in the U.S. Army as an astrologer. He also is regarded as the most erudite astrologer of our time and the best known, through his syndicated column (300 newspapers) and his radio and television programs (he was Merv Griffin's "resident astrologer"). Omarr has been called the most "knowledgeable astrologer since Evangeline Adams." His forecasts of Nixon's downfall, the end of World War II in mid-August of 1945, the assassination of John F. Kennedy, Roosevelt's election to the fourth term and his death in office . . . these and many others are on the record and quoted enough to be considered "legendary."

ABOUT THE SERIES

This is one of a series of twelve Sydney Omarr®
Day-by-Day Astrological Guides
for the signs of 2005.

The Ultimate Guide to Love, Sex,
and Romance

SYDNEY OMARR'S® ASTROLOGY, LOVE, SEX, AND YOU

Whether your goal is a sexy seduction, finding your
soulmate, or spicing up a current relationship, this
all-in-one volume will guide you every step of the
way—with a little help from the stars.

Includes:

• An in-depth description of each sign for men and women

• Compatibilty forecasts

• A fantastic section on romantic dinners for two, featuring
a complete kitchen-tested menu for each sign

• Myths and symbols associated with each sign

• An introduction to each sign's shadow

• Ratings on which signs are the most passionate

• and much more

206932

Available wherever books are sold, or
to order call: 1-800-788-6262

S456/Omarr